Published by CelebrityPress™, Orlando, FL
A division of The Celebrity Branding Agency®

Celebrity Branding® is a registered trademark
Printed in the United States of America.

ISBN: 9780985364359
LCCN: 2012937427

This publication is designed to provide accurate and authoritative information with regard to the subject matter covered. It is sold with the understanding that the publisher is not engaged in rendering legal, accounting, or other professional advice. If legal advice or other expert assistance is required, the services of a competent professional should be sought. The opinions expressed by the authors in this book are not endorsed by CelebrityPress™ and are the sole responsibility of the author rendering the opinion.

Most CelebrityPress™ titles are available at special quantity discounts for bulk purchases for sales promotions, premiums, fundraising, and educational use. Special versions or book excerpts can also be created to fit specific needs.

For more information, please write:

CelebrityPress™
520 N. Orlando Ave, #2
Winter Park, FL 32789

or call 1.877.261.4930

Visit us online at www.CelebrityPressPublishing.com

Contents

CHAPTER 1

The Results Fitness Mission: To Change The Way Fitness is Done

By Alwyn & Rachel Cosgrove

As we grow as a company, it has become more and more important to define the Results Fitness mission. At this point we have 350 members of Results Fitness and over 100 trainers in our mastermind group, many of whom you'll hear from in this book, who are running businesses based on the Results Fitness model and are a part of our mission to change the way fitness is done. We are so proud of each and every one of them and excited that we could create a book including all of the knowledge that our mastermind group has in one place, to really make an impact and change the way fitness is done around the world.

Whether you read this book and get new ideas about how to train yourself, or you find one of the authors has their business nearby where you live, and you can go in and experience first-hand how we, as a group, are changing the way fitness is done, or you are a trainer who wants to learn from some of the best minds in the industry, the authors in this book will not disappoint.

As we are setting out on our mission to change the way fitness is done, we are consistent in living the core values that we as a company and as a team have defined – to communicate who we are and what we are all about. I wanted to take the opportunity of including a chapter in this Results Fitness book to explain what Results Fitness is all about. Below are the 11 core values we live by every single day at Results Fitness:

1. Bring your best
2. Be professional
3. Be honest and transparent
4. Communicate clearly with mutual understanding.
5. Have only good days and great days
6. Be "WE" Not "ME"
7. Constantly learn, always improve
8. Have fun and a sense of humor
9. Strive for profitability
10. Exceed expectations
11. Keep leading

These core values are not something we as a team (when I say "team" I am referring to our employees, our mastermind members who you'll hear from in this book, and anyone who has joined our mission and supports us in changing the way fitness is done) "put on" when we come to work each day and then take off as soon as we leave. These core values are who we are and how we live everyday whether we are at work or not. Anyone who is part of our team exemplifies and lives by all of these core values. Our 11 core values are reflected in how we think, how we act, and how we communicate in a huge way in our culture.

A brief description of each of the 11 core values is below and how they are reflected in our day-to-day operations to change the way fitness is done, so you can get to know what we stand for and that what you are about to read in this book has been filtered through these core values. Every author in this book is considered a part of Team Results Fitness and a part of our mission to change the way fitness is done.

(1). BRING YOUR BEST

To **bring your best** you must be passionate and determined about what you do. You must love what you do. These are the things that fuel and drive our company forward. Qualities that we value: Passion, determination and perseverance.

Everyday we ask ourselves - Did I bring my best today? Any action no matter how big or how small; whether it be answering the phone, training a client, writing a program, answering an email, making a shake… ask - Am I doing my absolute best?

We are inspired because we believe completely in what we are doing and where we are going. We don't take "no" or "that'll never work" for an answer because if we did, Results Fitness could never drive the change needed so badly in the fitness business. We also don't accept "going through the motions." We also don't use words like "try" or "but" or "sorta" or "kinda" in our language.

To **bring your best** means that you come to work every day ready to be the best part of everyone's day. You dress for success and come ready to share what we have with our clients and work together with the team to create an amazing experience for anyone who connects with our company that day. Passion and determination are contagious; truly enjoying what you do is contagious. When you bring your best every day, you inspire others to do exactly the same.

To **bring your best** is also something we do as a company in every decision we make - we never get involved in something or implement something that we will not do everything we can to be the absolute best at it. We are the best at personal training, semi-private training, group fitness, our shakes, our customer service, our business coaching and in every aspect of our gym. As a company we never do anything with half-effort, we always bring 100% and take every aspect of what we do to its maximum potential.

Bringing your best is also something we ask of our clients. With each workout, we want them to get the most out of the time and effort they put in. If we ask them to do push ups, it doesn't matter how many they can do as long as they give it everything they have and bring their best.

This is also why as a company we are closed on Sundays, to have one full day of rest to allow all of us as a team to reboot and to be able to bring our best into the week.

We expect nothing but the best from ourselves, our co-workers, our clients, the company, our mastermind coaching members. Everyday we bring it!

(2). BE PROFESSIONAL

Be professional is an extremely important value that we have as a company that sets us apart from others in our industry. We portray this in the way we dress, the way we act, the way we talk and how we treat our customers, each other and anyone who comes in contact with our company. More than once we have been complemented that we are "so professional" in what we do. Since this is rare in our industry it is even more important that we ALWAYS exemplify this value.

This professionalism is the key to building trust and the strong relationships we have built. This includes building trust with our members, but also with magazine editors, book editors, seminar hosts and anyone who wants to use our company in a professional setting or situation. Anyone who meets us, walks away thinking - Wow! What professionals!

Tying this value into #1 **Bring your best**, because we bring our best in everything we do we automatically dress and act as professionals.

With our broader goal as a company, to change the way fitness is done. One of the aspects we are passionate about changing is the way fitness professionals are seen by the general population. We want to change the image to one that is respected and seen as a professional as much as a doctor, a lawyer, a dentist or any of the other professionals in a person's life. We are just as important and can make a huge impact on people's lives. They won't trust us until they see us as professionals. We must lead by example and dress, act and treat others in a professional manner. Every author in this book is a true professional and exemplifies this core value.

(3). BE HONEST AND TRANSPARENT

Every relationship we have as a company, with each other, with the members and anyone who works with us is honest and transparent. We as a company never sell anything we don't use ourselves, we never train anybody with a program we haven't tried out ourselves - we practice what we preach and believe in what we do.

We will never sell a product or a service to make money if we don't feel it works. To us, that would go against our values of having integrity. We also practice what we preach as a team. If you do not take advantage of the gym, the knowledge and the benefits of the exercise and nutrition recommendations we preach on a consistent basis, you will not be a good fit for our team. You cannot sell what we do with integrity and honesty if you don't use and believe in it. Working out in the gym and living the lifestyle that we teach our clients to live is required to be a part of this team in order to stay in alignment with this core value.

This again builds trust with our members, and with other professionals including magazine editors, seminar hosts and anyone who comes in contact with our company. This also builds trust among each other. We are who we say we are.

This is a complement we always get from our Results Fitness University attendees - "I can't believe how open, honest and transparent they were."

We never want anyone who meets us or who works with us to feel like we are hiding something from them. We want to be ourselves and let them get to know us, who we really are.

(4). COMMUNICATE CLEARLY WITH MUTUAL UNDERSTANDING

As our company has grown to now include 20 employees working on our team, along with the over 100 mastermind coaching members spreading our mission around the world, communication has become one of the most important priorities to us as a company. This will ensure we clearly understand each other, our expectations and what we need from each other, to continue moving forward to change the way fitness is done. The key to this core value is mutual understanding, which most importantly, includes listening.

The best way we have found to keep lines of communication open is to have regularly scheduled meetings – where everyone is encouraged to share, ask questions and **Be Honest and Transparent.** In addition, we make ourselves very available to our members, our mastermind coaching members and always set aside time to help each other.

One rule we have always lived by is that – *We have two ears and one mouth for a reason*, and as a company we do our best to listen twice as much as we talk, taking in what those around us need, whether they are a client, a co-worker or a mastermind coaching member. Listening to each other is how we communicate best.

(5). HAVE ONLY GOOD DAYS AND GREAT DAYS

Life is too short to have a "bad day." Being diagnosed with cancer, going through fighting for your life, we have a whole new perspective on "having a bad day." We are very aware every day of how amazing life is and that we are all on this planet for a reason, to serve a purpose. Everyday is a gift and you should never take a single one for granted. You never know who is going to walk through our door that day that you can turn their day around and change their life. No matter what you have going on there is nothing better than that.

We stole this core value from Lance Armstrong who said: "I take nothing for granted now. I only have good days and great days."

We all count on each other to show up everyday as professionals **bringing our best**. It is refreshing to know that whatever you have going on outside the doors of the gym you can come in and escape from it. We do not tolerate negativity because none of us can function at our best in an environment of negativity. We don't tolerate it from our team and we also don't tolerate it from our clients. If we have one negative client they can bring the energy down in the entire gym costing us all of the other member's happiness - it isn't worth it.

As a company we have always had the policy that if someone is being negative every time they come in and really affecting their environment, we will be honest and transparent with them and explain that we work hard to create a very positive environment. We have asked clients to leave, offered to cancel memberships and refunded members because it is not worth it to us to have someone coming in everyday who is not having a good day or a great day.

When someone asks you, "How are you?" The only answer you should ever respond with is a positive one. "Fantastic, Brilliant, Amazing, Fabulous, Excellent, Great!" Just by answering with a positive response you have already made your day and their day better. As a team we never respond to this question by saying - "OK" or "Alright." These types of answers are unacceptable. – We only have good days and great days! And if you aren't having a great day, then fake it until you feel it or take the day off and reboot.

Our company as a whole and everyone on our team approaches everyday with a positive attitude and a smile working with passion for what they do.

(6). BE WE, NOT ME

Working together to create an atmosphere where everyone on our team has a chance to contribute and achieve success. When you have a united team of people all working together with a common vision anything is possible. We all count on each other every single day to **bring our best**. You can accomplish so much more as a team than you can ever accomplish on your own. By surrounding yourself with positive people who are professionals, bringing their best everyday you can do powerful things.

Be We, Not Me includes open communication and respect for each other, while learning from each other encouraging interdependent thinking as we strive for excellence. Trust, faith and belief among team members are extremely valuable to our success as a company. Every one of us knows we can trust each other to do our part and contribute 100% to being the best part of our member's day everyday. Leaning on our core values and the systems we have in place together we know the path we need to take to accomplish our bigger goals as a team.

We also encourage a team environment with our clients offering semi-private and group training. We believe a team is powerful not only in our business but in our client results. Creating the camaraderie, support and accountability a team environment provides is part of our culture and environment with everything we do.

Working in alignment with our core values we can overcome any obstacle we come up against as a team and set new standards for this industry as a whole.

(7). CONSTANTLY LEARN, ALWAYS IMPROVE

A huge part of our success at Results Fitness is our ongoing restlessness to never sit still - constantly learning, improving and staying ahead. As a company, we not only do not fear change, but we embrace it enthusiastically and, perhaps even more importantly, encourage and drive it. This includes reading books, going to seminars and conferences, asking questions, learning from other people and businesses and challenging each other to step out of our comfort zones and grow as individuals. We are constantly innovating and as a team everyone has to keep up.

As a team we have to all continue to grow as individuals, learning new skills and striving for more. If one of us does not live according to this core value, they will hold the rest of the team back. As each of us pushes to learn and grow we encourage and inspire each other to learn and grow. We encourage each and every person on our team and in our mastermind group to look for opportunities to learn to improve and change the way fitness is done. Every one on the team has individual goals in addition to our goals as a team. We encourage vision boards, goal setting and keeping focused on moving forward.

We encourage reading at least 10 minutes a day and attending at least 1-2 seminars a year for professional development – in addition to attending as many of the weekly staff training and educational opportunities we offer at the gym.

Others can try to copy what we are doing and recreate what we have, but by living by this core value they will never be able to evolve as fast as we can as long as embracing constant change is part of our culture.

(8). HAVE FUN AND A SENSE OF HUMOR

If you are not having fun, it is not worth doing. Do not continue doing anything in life that you are not having fun doing. Life is too short.

Bringing fun and humor into the work place does not mean we have to give up being professional. There is a balance between these two that can actually keep professionalism from being too stale, and fun and humor from getting out of hand. It is actually very important that these two co-exist to keep each other in balance.

Bringing fun and humor in lets us be personable and lets our clients get to know us. To be the best part of our member's day we have to be able to make them smile and laugh. Telling a joke or saying something to make a client smile is something we strive to do on a daily basis.

We also know how to relax and are not your typical gym rats who never splurge or enjoy a drink. Our clients can relate to us because we understand how important it is to have flexibility when it comes to your nutrition and lifestyle. We know how to have a good time and relax while still maintaining our professionalism.

(9). STRIVE FOR PROFITABILITY

Part of running a successful, sustainable business long term is maintaining a profit and practicing the power of investing in order to get a return. We strive as a business to pay competitive salaries to our employees, offering benefits and a rewarding work environment while reinvesting in the surroundings of our business to always keep everything up-to-date, clean and working properly.

As a team, every decision we make must be in the best interest for the profitability of the company. This includes coming up with new ideas to add to the "funnel" to keep revenue flowing in, striving to hit our daily goal as a team, and looking for ways to plug any leaks that may be draining our revenue.

As a team, we maintain what we call an "abundance mindset." Even in tough times in the economy, we as a team do not let ourselves get into a scarcity mindset but instead look for opportunities to become even more – and seek answers and new solutions. We never use language such as, "can't afford" or "we'll never hit our goal" or anything that can pull us away from the direction we want to head as a team, which is to be a profitable, successful company.

As a company, we have an open book policy where we are **completely honest and transparent** about all of our numbers and where the money we make as a team is being spent and how much is coming in. There are no secrets.

The more profit the business makes, the more the entire team makes and the more we can reinvest in the gym to continue to constantly improve and innovate.

In addition, the concept of INVESTING is a common theme that we translate to our members and our mastermind coaching members. When our members set aside time to work out they will get better results if they invest in a coach and join a gym like Results Fitness. Their time will be used more effectively. We are always looking for ways to deliver above and beyond the time and money our clients invest to join our gym, making sure the results, the experience and what we add to their lives far outweighs the investment. In fact, we have had clients give up cable TV before giving up their gym membership with us because they realize what a valuable investment it is, and that it is a necessity that reaps rewards over and over, adding quality to their lives. So in this way we strive for our client's to also make a "profit" by investing in our membership, by providing them with value far beyond the money they invest with us.

(10). EXCEED EXPECTATIONS

Our primary job is to attract, satisfy and maintain the loyalty of our clients and mastermind coaching members in order to reach our mission of changing the way fitness is done, but we don't just want to be average at our job - we want to be above average. In our industry it is not hard to exceed expectations when it comes to customer service. The standard in the fitness industry is unfortunately so poor that we have a huge opportunity to go above and beyond anything our members expect.

To us, it is the little things that exceed our customer's expectations and make their day, turning them into customers for life. These little things include the notes and cards we send out to them right from the start of our relationship, knowing their name and about their personal life and caring about them.

As a company we are always looking for new ways to WOW our customers and give them an experience they didn't expect. We want them to have the kind of experience with us that they want to tell other people about it. We use words such as "Absolutely!" and "I can do that for you!" and "Is there anything else I can help you with?"

(11). KEEP LEADING

Spring boarding off of #7 – **Constantly Learning, Always Improving** is our ability to keep leading. As a company we will not sit still, continuing to run ahead of everyone else in our industry – being leaders. As long as we are constantly pushing our limits to reinvent, innovate and **bring our best,** we will continue to be leaders in this industry.

Every single person on this team (our employees and our mastermind coaching members who you are about to hear from) is a leader. Whether they are a leader to our members, a leader to our newest team member, to a co-worker or to a fellow mastermind-coaching member. Everyone in our company leads by example and has a positive mental attitude at all times living by the above core values.

A few important leadership qualities we look for are:

(a) a strong belief in what you do

(b) having a positive attitude

(c) having courage to make decisions

(d) being prepared, and

(e) working together as a team

Also, as a leader we practice what we preach. We cannot, with integrity, sell our services if every single one of us on the team does not believe and take advantage of what we offer.

To learn more about Results Fitness, go to: www.results-fitness.com or www.resultsfitnessuniversity.com.

Reference: This chapter has been influenced and inspired by the Zappos Core Values Document by Tony Hsieh.

About Alwyn

Born in Scotland and initially exposed to fitness training through an intense competitive sport martial arts background, Alwyn Cosgrove began reading and studying any training-related material he could get his hands on. This led Alwyn to formal academic studies in Sports Performance at West Lothian College and then progressed on to receiving an honors degree in Sports Science from Chester College, the University of Liverpool.

During his career as a fitness coach, Alwyn began with assisting in martial arts lessons in 1986 and teaching fitness classes in 1989. He has studied under all of the top fitness professionals and coaches in the world and has worked with a wide variety of clientele, from general population clientele to several top-level athletes, World Champions and professionals in a multitude of sports.

A sought after 'expert' for several of the country's leading publications including being a regular contributor to Men's Health magazine, Alwyn has co-authored four books in the "New Rules of Lifting" series and currently spends his time training clients, training his staff at Results Fitness, speaking on the lecture circuit and coaching fitness trainers worldwide in their businesses.

For the past decade, with his wife Rachel, Alwyn runs Results Fitness in Santa Clarita, California- which has been three times named one of America's Top Gyms by Men's Health Magazine, a gym which specializes in programs for real-world busy people, and prides itself on "changing the way fitness is done – period!"

About Rachel

Rachel Cosgrove is the best selling author of The Female Body Breakthrough (published by Rodale November 2009), and is a fitness professional who specializes in getting women of all ages into the best shape of their lives.

She owns and operates Results Fitness with her husband in southern California. She has a BS in Exercise Physiology and earned her CSCS from the National Strength and Conditioning Association. She has competed in fitness competitions, is an Ironman triathlete and has set a powerlifting record. She has her own column in Women's Health Magazine and has also been featured in More Magazine, Real Simple, Muscle and Fitness Hers, Shape Magazine, Fitness Magazine, Men's Health, Men's Fitness and Oxygen. She has also had TV appearances on Fox, ABC and WGN. She is on a mission to help as many women make a breakthrough as she can.

For more information on Rachel visit: www.rachelcosgrove.com.

And for more information on her book and belonging to her community of Fit Females go to: www.thefemalebodybreakthrough.com.

CHAPTER 2

Mind Matters: The 10 Mental Keys to Finally Achieve and Keep The Body You Always Wanted

By Rob and Shannon Yontz

*This chapter is dedicated to our daughter, Carley,
who personifies these qualities
and shows us daily what a true champion is.*

A Native American boy asked his grandfather, "What do you think about the world today?"

The grandfather replied, "I feel like two wolves are fighting...one with hate and fear, the other with love and acceptance."

"But Grandfather," asked the boy, "which one will win?"

The grandfather answered, "The one I feed."

Right about now you're probably wondering if you opened the wrong book. After all, this is supposed to be a book about getting fitness and health results, and what does a story about a Native American boy and his grandfather talking about wolves have to do with getting and keeping the body you've always wanted?

Actually, quite a bit. In fact, it's most likely the one ingredient you have been lacking.

Clearly the story isn't about wolves – it's about mindset, or attitude. The grandfather uses the wolves as a metaphor for elements that are inside all of us, both the negative (hate and fear) and the positive (love and acceptance). When we "feed" our negative mindset by focusing on it, the negative will win. Conversely, by choosing to feed the positive – by focusing on love and acceptance – the positive will triumph.

Believe it or not, fitness works the same way.

When you feed your positive mindset – when you build up that part of you and make it as strong as it can possibly be – it gives you exactly what you need to achieve your fitness goals, or really *any* goals that you might have in life. It's the missing piece that so many people forget when they embark on a fitness journey…and what they don't realize is, it's the most important piece of all.

FINDING OUR TRUE NORTH

Helping people find that missing piece – discovering the results-oriented mindset they need to not only reach their fitness goals, but remain in shape for life – is what we do in our business, True North Fitness and Health. To accomplish this, our work isn't just focused on the body. We strengthen our clients' mindset as well, giving them the inner strength they need to accomplish incredible things in all aspects of their life.

Admittedly, our systems are a bit unconventional - even revolutionary. Some of this is likely due to the fact that fitness is a second career for both of us. Rob was in the Navy and then a reliability engineer, and Shannon worked as a food and catering services director for several major hotels, then was on the travel staff team for a meeting-planning company.

But that all changed shortly after we met. Because neither of us was truly and deeply satisfied with what we were doing, we decided to pursue our passions in life and defined our values and our goals. We decided to start a fitness and health-based business, beginning with opening a Stretch 'N Grow franchise location, which was (and is) a great youth fitness company. It was a perfect fit for us, and an excellent opportunity to help kids discover how great it feels to be strong and healthy – as well as take care of their bodies. We felt it was the best way to begin to achieve our ultimate goal of coaching healthy lifestyles to families.

Then a wonderful thing happened. A lot of the moms and teachers wanted to get fit in the fun and positive way their kids were, and they asked if we would create a program for them. So we launched Adventure Boot Camp for Women. Soon afterwards, we had many more people who wanted to train with us outside of the camp - including our Boot Camp members' families and friends. So we opened our studio, where we now help a wide variety of clients transform their bodies, their mindsets, and their lives.

It's actually a really natural place for us to be and there is a real synergy between our backgrounds. Rob has a science and sports background. Now at 50 years of age, he has to fight to maintain his athletic base. And Shannon knows firsthand what it's like to lose weight and keep it off. After growing up overweight, she made the decision to transform her body at 28, and has grown more and more in love with fitness ever since.

That's when Shannon really began to explore the mindset aspect of weight loss. When she decided to get fit once and for all, she found that it wasn't just about changing her body, it was about figuring out what mindset was causing her to keep the weight on. By changing that mindset, she would make sure her weight loss would be permanent - because if you've ever "lost" weight before, chances are you already know that the biggest challenge with fitness isn't getting there...it's staying there.

WHY WE STAY FAT

Currently, over 70% of the American population is either overweight or obese. This means being overweight has become the new "normal" in our society. However, this doesn't mean that we, as a society, have given up that elusive dream of losing weight and looking great. Need proof? Go to your computer and log onto Amazon.com. Don't worry...we'll wait. Okay, now look up "diet and weight loss books." The last time we checked, there were 31,924 books on this subject.

Yes, you read that right. If you read a book a week, it would take you *over 600 years* to read them all.

But despite this plethora of "information" on "weight loss," we remain knowledge-starved when it comes to finding a solution that actually works. By some estimates, more than 80% of people who lose weight through diet and/or exercise regain that weight, plus some, within 2 years. A recent UCLA study of 31 long term diets found that 2/3 of the dieters they followed regained all weight they lost (plus some) in 4 to 5 years.

Why does this happen? What is it that's preventing people from getting off the weight roller coaster once and for all?

The answer goes back to the story of the Native American boy and his grandfather. It's all about your mindset.

IT IS ALL IN YOUR HEAD!

When people make the decision to get in shape, usually they start with exercise...then they go to nutrition. And with both, most people don't just struggle; they fail - because their mindset was never addressed to prepare them for long-term success.

For most overweight people, it is their mindset that is the real dilemma – and if you don't deal with that, at some point it will get in the way of lasting weight loss. Most diet and exercise books and programs miss this point entirely.

We all know that there are winners and losers in the world – but what we might not realize is that we control whether we're a winner or loser. It is simply a choice; winners look at a problem and see the opportunities it presents. Losers just see...the problem, and then make excuses. We coach our clients to spend their energy looking through problems for solutions, rather than spending their energy complaining about them. We encourage them to use what we call a "champion mindset" – to fight for their health, for their bodies, for their future. A champion always expects to win, and enjoys a good challenge.

When you engage a champion mindset, you have a bigger reason to defend your health. It means you accept ownership for your condition – whether you want to get rid of 10 pounds or 100 pounds, at that moment you draw your line in the sand, you stop making excuses, and you find solutions. Intellectually, you already know much of what you need to do. A champion mindset provides you with the conviction, strength and dedication you need to see it through and get it done.

Over the years, we've learned that a champion mindset is not a normal state for most of us. You might not realize it, but most people naturally approach situations from a negative perspective. For example, in the game of golf, imagine you need to hit the ball over a water hazard to get to the green, where the hole is. Most people immediately think..."Don't hit the water, don't hit the water," and guess what happens? They hit the water because that is what they are thinking about. Instead, you need to focus on the green...on the goal...on what you want…so you put your thoughts and energy into getting it.

In our case, we're very specific about focusing our words into a positive context when we talk to our clients. We avoid saying, "don't bend your knees" if they need to keep their legs straight because when we say, "don't bend your knees,"…well, if you've been paying attention, you probably know what happens.

Ultimately, achieving long term and permanent success is all about finding solutions and taking action, consistently. When Shannon made her commitment to weight loss, she realized that it was all about her – not anyone else. And once she cultivated her champion mindset and became solution focused, she was able to successfully achieve her solution permanently. When you reconfigure your mindset instead of just "trying on" some diet or exercise program, you have a far greater chance of success.

THE 10 KEYS TO MOLDING A CHAMPION MINDSET

Through our experience running True North Fitness, we've identified 10 Keys to Molding a Champion Mindset that have helped both ourselves and our clients push forward through difficult times to achieve and maintain their goals. We'd like to share them in the hope that they will help you find your way to the best fitness outcome possible.

Key #1: Lifestyle fitness is long-term, a marathon.
Imagine someone who thought they only had to clean their house *once* for the remainder of the time they lived there. Now, imagine walking through the door of the place a few years later - it would probably look like an episode of the cable show, "Hoarders!" For as long as you want your health, you must continue to re-earn it.

Key #2: You must have goals - and you must put them "on the record."
Without goals you will lack direction and follow-through. You must set goals and, just as importantly, write them down, prioritize them, review them regularly, and measure your progress toward them. Goals should be qualitative as well as quantitative - a quantitative goal would be to have 3 workouts a week or lose 3% body fat, a qualitative goal would be that you want to climb the stairs without getting winded or to feel

better in your jeans.

Key #3: Recognize success - and utilize healthy rewards.
When you achieve a significant goal, celebrate! Enjoy the accomplishment and celebrate with something *healthy* that reinforces your next goal. For example, get a new workout outfit or get a new bathing suit that shows off your new rockin' body.

Key #4: Enhance your Environmental Positivity.
Your mind grows what you feed it much like a garden grows what you seed it with. So plant and cultivate roses, flowers and vegetables. Make it a practice to begin each day with a positive phrase, quote, or story. And make sure to eradicate any negative "weeds" throughout the day that attempt to infest your mental garden.

Key #5: There IS Support in Numbers.
The National Weight Loss Registry has documented that one of the 3 top success keys to long-term weight change is a regular and positive support group. Surround yourself with people who are positive, active, fit, and are like what you want to be like. You will be more successful in this crowd.

Key #6: Know how to handle "flat tires."
When you're driving somewhere and you get a flat, you don't jump out and slash the other tires, do you? Heck no! You handle it and drive on. The reality is that we all encounter crises from time to time that can threaten our goals. Be ready for them in advance; have a plan for how you're going to resolve these surprises and 'keep on keepin' on.'

Key #7: Stand out from the crowd.
More than 70% of the population is fat or unhealthy for a reason. Understand that by choosing fitness and health, you will actually be in the minority. So, when your friends make those common lifestyle choices that are a detriment to their fitness and want you to do the same, be strong in your conviction and make the correct choices to achieve your healthy lifestyle.

Key #8: Cultivate your "champion mindset."
You are playing in a hard-fought basketball game, there has been several lead changes. There is a one-point difference with two seconds left in the game. You have the ball and you're at the top of the key. What

do you do? If you said, "Shoot," as most people do, you're not thinking with a champion mindset. *A champion thinks, "keep dribbling and run out the clock" because they know they are in the lead!*

When you have a champion mindset in place, the only outcome you can see is winning. Every move you make is solution-based towards achieving your goal. That kind of champion mindset will help you frame your fitness challenges in a positive pro-active way that will spur you forward.

Key #9: It's more than just exercise and diet!
Your whole lifestyle has to be focused on staying in the best overall health you can achieve. That means dealing with all the lifestyle co-factors that need to be addressed; drinking enough water, getting enough sleep, rest and recovery time after a workout, mitigating stress, and quiet time to put your mind at ease and relax.

Key #10: Review and renew.
Ongoing maintenance is vital to see where you are and what you've done. Every three months, you should sit down, reexamine your goals and, when necessary, re-set them to make sure you're headed in the right direction. You might need help from a coach to make sure you're being objective in your assessments and optimizing your actions - we both have personal coaches ourselves for just that reason.

The opening anecdote we began this chapter with concerned a Native American boy and his grandfather discussing which "wolf" would win control of us - the wolf of hate and fear, or the wolf of love and acceptance. Well, when you tap into the right mindset, you also begin to starve the wolf that will wear you down and stop you from enjoying an awesome life. You also provide an example for the rest of the world to emulate.

Your attitude creates your thoughts,

Your thoughts create your words,

Your words create your actions,

Your actions create your habits.

Your habits create your character.

And your character determines your destiny.

America doesn't have to be 70% overweight. We can all make the change – and make this country a healthy and vibrant place.

ABOUT SHANNON and ROB

Shannon and Rob Yontz co-own and operate True North Fitness & Health located in Ventura, California. Established in 2003, using their hunger for academics and application of physical sciences, Shannon and Rob rapidly ascended to being recognized by their colleagues as regional and national experts in their fields of fitness nutrition, youth fitness, large group training and customized semi-private personal training. Together they have earned more than 30 certifications in the Fitness field of study.

Nine years later, they have successfully worked with more than three thousand clients, of all kinds - adult athletes, junior Olympic athletes, crazy busy moms/dads; doctors, nurses, attorneys, stay-at-home moms, accountants, grandmas and granddads, students, firemen, law enforcement, military; people with metabolic disease, total hip replacements, total knee replacements, scoliosis and others with multitudes of other functional inefficiencies and chronic or acute physical ailments - to help them realize a life where they feel better and have the health and body of their dreams. Their clients have achieved life quality improvements of fat elimination, improved strength and flexibility, improved cardio-respiratory performance, and refocused mindset, to live a renewed and refreshed higher quality of life.

Today, Shannon and Rob continue to expand their reach to impact more lives by building their team at True North Fitness & Health, as well as to help educate and develop fellow fitness professionals in their businesses and applications – through their affiliate groups with the international Adventure Boot Camp professionals group and the Results Fitness University Platinum Mastermind Members Group.

Shannon and Rob are frequently sought after health and fitness experts for local and regional radio show interviews and newspaper articles, and they have been published in Women's Health magazine as well as having three (3) healthy meal recipes published in the international Adventure Boot Camp Recipe Cook Book – which can be purchased through our web site.

Contact Information:
website: www.TrueNorthFitness.com
e-mail: Info@True-North-Fitness.com

CHAPTER 3

The Whole Approach: Sinner & Saint - Unlikely Partners with Extraordinary Results

By Travis Barnes & Mat Dewing

Everyone wants results. Who wakes up in the morning and says, "I think I'll go through the motions today and just pretend I want a better life." Nobody I know! Well maybe one or two people, if you know what I mean, but generally we align ourselves the best we can with people, products, and concepts that can get us where we want to go.

That's what we're all about! We love seeing our own lives change. More thrilling for us, is helping others truly change their lives! I'm Travis Barnes. I was born in the little town of Sayre, PA and I started pursuing a bodybuilding dream at the age of 12. I moved to Las Vegas at the age of 18 and took my first big fitness job at the Gold's Gym. From there on, it was the fast life and too much crazy living that led me to a point from which most don't recover, but to go too much further into that would be another book altogether. Not long ago, I returned home to Sayre, PA to meet Mat Dewing, who I now proudly call my friend and business partner. Mat is a man of faith and integrity, a father of seven and business man who had built himself from one PT clinic to twelve PT clinics and three gyms. Mat, a PT himself, had a thriving PT business when we met. He had built it on extraordinary results, but he had failing gyms. We

(Mat and I) are, to say the least, surprising friends and business partners given my colorful past and his high moral standards. I am grateful for his grace that allowed us to become partners, help so many people and now help you.

Mat and I are part of the Results vision to change how fitness is done. We have helped many people using our 'secret recipe' for fitness success and now we don't have three failing gyms. We have five successful coaching centers with a reputation that, just like the ProCare Physical Therapy clinics, is built on extraordinary results.

The truth that we know about fitness is that we need a new stimulus to get a new result, and the truth we know about physical therapy is that we have to correct, not reinforce, dysfunction to make for a healthier person. We put these ideas into a program that gets people results faster than anything on the planet! Insanity is doing what you have always done and expecting a new result. We design programs and get our clients to do things they have never done so they can get extraordinary results.

You have probably heard that something was going to get you extraordinary results before, only to be let down. What happens when we choose a product, process, or idea that claims to deliver everything we are looking for? "You'll get skinny fast with this pill." "You'll get rich with this business system." We all buy based on that enticing emotion, but we move on to validate with facts. In other words, if we trust the salesman, then we take him/her at their word initially, because we don't really know how to achieve the result without their help! If we knew, we would do it without them, right? Here is the good news if you agree with me so far, we are not selling you anything, but only telling you how others are experiencing the results you are seeking.

My point is that for maximum success in changing any, and all, areas of your life, trust someone else that is experiencing the kind of result you are looking for and learn from them! At ProCare Physical Fitness we know that our results speak for themselves. In truth, this chapter could be our before and after photos of our clients, and those pictures as they say would be worth a thousand words, but that would leave you asking, "How did they do it?" What is their secret?

In order to understand our secrets, you must first understand fuel efficiency. In our "green world," fuel efficiency is a hot topic in the auto-mobile and transportation industry. How does this concept of auto fuel efficiency translate to our bodies? At our best, there's an inverse relationship of fuel efficiency as it relates to food (our fuel) and energy (our body). Let's talk about that. The muscles in our bodies are much like engines. Our engines burn gas and our muscles burn calories. In comparison, our bodies are much more efficient than engines. To illustrate the difference let's take my Chevy truck that goes 17 miles on a gallon of gas. Not great by today's efficiency standards but, how far would my body go if I could drink gasoline? A gallon of gasoline has 31,000 calories. A 200 pound person will burn an average of 120 calories walking a mile, so I could walk 258 miles on a gallon of gas. In comparison to my truck that is 241 miles farther.

What is my point? Stop eating food and start drinking gas? No! My point is that you don't want your body to be as efficient as it is! Fat is stored energy. A calorie is a unit of energy. So is there a way to make your body as inefficient as a gas-guzzling monster truck? That is exactly what we do. Here are our five secrets that will tell you how we keep the engine (muscles) burning a lot of fuel!

Secret #1 - Take the path of most resistance: Our first secret to the amazing results that we achieve for people such as yourself is how we discover what you are inefficient at and use it in your favor. One of the best ways to discover inefficiencies is to go through the Functional Movement Screen with a fitness trainer. The Functional Movement Screen tests your mobility and stability within the seven basic movement patterns. Based on your lower scores we are then able to design you a program that will challenge your body in ways that not only improve how you move, but also burn the highest amount of calories due to the body's inefficiency. To further discover the energy pathways that are inefficient in your body, we then make sure you are seen by one of our physical therapists for a movement analysis. The physical therapist then adds their suggestions to the program, allowing us to create maximum metabolic disturbance. A maximum metabolic disturbance is accomplished because our programming does not allow you to use established energy pathways. Established energy pathways are one of the things that make your body really fuel efficient. Let's take for example walking. Many people walk to try and lose weight. However, there are few things your body is as efficient at as walking. You have walked since you were a child. You walked your way into weight gain. Remember, insanity is doing what you have always done and expecting a different result. So why do people walk to lose weight? I have NO idea. What's my point? When you do new things the energy pathways are not established, therefore your body has to work harder to do that new thing than it would to do something at which you are already practiced.

Secret #2 - Build the engine: Build muscle with strength training. This is one of the components of our program design and arguably one of the most important for any fat loss client. Your muscles burn calories even while you sit reading this book so the more muscle the better. Women, I know that you don't want to be big and bulky, and I promise that is not what I am talking about. But since we lose muscle as we age, we should all be doing some kind of resistance training to reverse the signs of ageing, and keep our metabolism from going down the drain. So what methods do we use to help you build muscle? Our routines are whole body, periodized, and most importantly, they are probably the last things you would ever think of to do on your own. We are very "outside the box." How do we get outside the box? See Secret Number 1.

Secret #3 - Keep the engine revved: Our third secret is that we create EPOC in your body. The need for oxygen to replenish ATP and remove lactic acid is referred to as EPOC (Excess Post Exercise Oxygen Consumption). The idea is that the more oxygen our body demands, the more calories we burn. So how, within the muscle, do we deplete ATP and create lactic acid to be removed? One way is with the resistance training we discussed. Another way would be with anaerobic and aerobic interval training that we write into our clients' workouts and ask them to do when they are not working with us. ATP is energy used by your muscles and lactic acid accumulates proportionally to the level of intense exercise. Bottom line - the greater the intensity of the exercise, the greater the ATP spent, the greater the lactic acid accumulated, and the greater the EPOC. We recognize that we can't be with our client's 24 hours a day, seven days a week. In fact, we see many of our clients for only 2 hours a week. So, what we do for them during that time is accelerate their metabolism by creating EPOC that lasts until we see them again. While they are away from us, they are burning calories at a higher rate than usual.

Secret #4 - Use the fuel that makes the engine burn best: To stop at number three would be wrong because "you can't out-train a bad diet." This means that the fuel we put in our tank is important. So beyond our physical therapy, and beyond our fitness, is our nutrition. For too many of us, nutrition is "beyond" in our thinking because we are naturally more motivated to exercise than concern ourselves with healthy nutrition. Wise nutritional choices should be our foundation! I would argue that nutrition is more important to our health than exercise, and I'm an exercise expert! So what do we advocate? How do we help people with their diet? First of all, we individualize each nutritional program because we have learned that dieting is not "one size fits all." Dieting is as much a progression as working out. I could tell you my diet and maybe you would try it; or you could try the latest fad diet because you heard how well it works, but these ideas are hard to stick to. We will meet your diet where it is, and set new goals each week that take your nutrition, just like your fitness, to where it needs to be, one step at a time.

Here are nutrition truths that we know work:

- Eating when you first wake up. This is starting your engine.

- Eating every few hours. This keeps the engine working.

- Eliminating processed snacks. Eliminate the stuff that stops the fat metabolism. (That stops the engine.)

- Eating whole foods. You know that it's true "natural is best" (use the best fuel.)

- Not drinking your calories. Water is best and it helps with weight loss. What we don't need is the empty calories that come from drinking. This would be like poor fuel clogging up the engine.

- Having a high protein diet. Yes, it is true: protein has a higher thermogenic effect than carbohydrates!

These are things that work, but if our diet is currently drastically different than this, then changing it all at once will result in failure, more often than not. Besides, we don't need to change it all to see results. We need to change the one thing we can commit 100% to changing. Once we have conquered that, we need to change the next thing.

So you see our results that we will achieve for you are achieved by allowing you to examine the evidence and then choose what you can do first. If you have any special conditions such as diabetes, we will recommend you consult with your doctor in helping you make the next smart choice in your diet. The bottom line is that we stop the yo-yo diet by taking it one manageable step at a time, which results in weight loss week after week, rather than allowing you to go from one extreme to another, and suffer through weight loss only to gain weight the next week. Regarding good nutrition choices, ask yourself "What is the one thing I can commit to 100%?" …And then do that one thing consistently until you are ready to do the next thing.

Secret # 5 - Stay on the road: There is still one stone unturned, that if we did not talk about it, then this chapter could not be called 'The Whole Approach.' You have heard about our program design (the path to a calorie-burning journey), our muscle building (how to build your engine up), our metabolic acceleration (how we get your engine idling at higher rpms), and our nutrition (how we use fuel that helps our engines burn the most gas). However, maybe you have had a good workout before and a good diet, yet something still stopped you from achieving your goals. That is the psychology of training, and at ProCare Physical we ask the tough questions to get in your head and find out what has stopped you in the past from achieving your fitness goals, and how we are going to make this time different. In other words, how are we going to stay on the road? There is a saying, "When the student is ready, a teacher will arrive." In our business it is, "When the client is ready, a coach will arrive." It is our job to get you to open your mind. Why do you want what you want? Why is it absolutely important you get it? What will it do for you to achieve this? What are you willing to give up in order to get it? If you are not willing to give it up, then is it really as important as you say? When we can finally narrow it down to the absolute must, and make it a true priority, then, and only then, can we achieve your fitness success.

In conclusion, let's put it all together. Our first secret is to utilize superior programming that helps you achieve your goals faster than anything on the planet. If you want to get there fast then you must take the fastest route. One of the primary components of your program will be resistance training and this is our second secret because it won't be just any form of resistance training but the one your body needs the most, because you are the most inefficient at it. This is the form of training we will use to increase the size of your engine and turn your body into a gas-guzzling monster truck. Our third secret is to accelerate your metabolism so you are burning more calories – even when you are not with us. This is also done through our programming with what we design for your workouts, and with what we ask you to do afterwards. Think of it as keeping the engine revved. Our fourth secret is how we help you with nutrition; getting you to understand that diet is not temporary but permanent. For permanent change to take place we have to go one step at a time with you, making changes following proven nutritional guidelines. Your engine needs the right fuel to keep running at its best. Last, but not least, the fifth secret is the psychology of your fitness success, which includes anticipating roadblocks and how you will overcome them. Most of all, we help you find the motivation from within to carry you through. The first four secrets will only work if we keep the car on the road.

Remember, the journey of a thousand miles begins with the first step. If it's a long journey, you may as well take the first step; otherwise you will be no closer next time you look. I hope this chapter helped you discover that the journey of a thousand miles is sometimes faster with the right approach, in this case the whole approach.

About Travis

Travis Barnes is known as "Max Metabolic" for the maximum metabolic disturbance that he creates in his clients with the workouts he writes. He is a bestselling author and fitness guru.

Travis' success is built on achieving extraordinary results for people where other trainers failed. He is the C.O.O. of ProCare Physical Fitness, which now includes four personal coaching centers. As C.O.O., Travis has the job of developing coaches to a level of excellence that will help them give every client the breakthrough they are looking for. Travis partners with every coach at ProCare to oversee the development and administration of each client's program. Travis is an ACE certified trainer with a certification in sports nutrition as well. Travis has over 20 years invested in fitness. He has worked in all areas of fitness working as a Coach, Program Director, Manager, SPIN instructor, Swiss Ball instructor, group instructor, program designer and now C.O.O.

Travis states "My biggest reward is never the pay. I live to help people achieve fitness success. Fitness is my life." Travis, Mat and ProCare can be found online at: www.procarephysicalfitness.com.

About Mat

Mat Dewing is the owner, and CEO/President of ProCare Physical, which is an amalgamation of two companies: ProCare Physical Therapy, and ProCare Physical Fitness & Performance. Mat received his Masters degree in physical therapy from Ithaca College in 1995. He is a licensed Physical Therapist and licensed Certified Athletic Trainer in Pennsylvania. His passion lies in coaching individuals into life-changing personal success.

Mat excels in applying the art and science of coaching to various arenas, including life coaching, especially in the area of leadership and managerial excellence, rehabilitation, fitness training, athletic performance, and injury prevention. While coaching others is Mat's passion, he has varied interests and pursuits, which include the operation of his real estate companies, Healthy Properties, Inc. and Dewings Management, LLC, and filling the CEO function of a national consulting company called PT Compliance Group, LLC, which helps owners of physical therapy companies take their personal integrity and infuse it practically throughout their organization.

People trust Mat quickly because he doesn't judge them, and he finds it natural to see things from their perspective. Mat is a highly responsible person, and totally transparent. He is married to his high school sweetheart, Janice, and together they home school their seven rambunctious children on a small country farm in Bradford County, Pennsylvania.

Mat thrives on the notion that many people in life rely on him, and he is intensely loyal, cultivating many life-long friendships.

CHAPTER 4

Metabolic Skills Training: Turning Strength Training into Skills Training for Mountain Bike Riders

By James Wilson

I admit it - I bought my first new mountain bike to commute to work, not realizing that it could do far more than simply get me around town. I only lived a couple of miles from the office where I worked at in downtown Santa Barbara, CA and I had been thinking about getting a bike. When I heard an ad on the radio saying that a local bike shop had a mountain bike on sale, I figured it was fate telling me to go check it out.

One day I got bored and decided to pedal my bike up a fire road to check out the view and then charge back down - little did I know that an innocent ride up and down a dirt road would shape the rest of my life. I was instantly hooked on the unique challenges presented by navigating a bike on dirt and rocks and my training immediately started to take on a new direction.

I was no longer concerned about how much weight I lifted in the gym or "bodybuilding" to get bigger arms and pecs, I just wanted to be able to ride my bike faster, longer and with more confidence on the trail. Despite having lifted weights since I was 13 years old, and running track in high school, I quickly realized that what I had been doing was not optimally preparing me for my new passion. At the time I was a new strength coach and worked for a major personal training certification organization, and so I used the vast resources at my disposal to look for training strategies that would help me accomplish my new goals.

However, I quickly discovered that there were no good training systems for the unique demands of mountain biking. Everything I found was either telling me to train like a road cyclist (who needed massive cardio but low levels of strength and skill), or to train like a bodybuilder (who simply cares about pumping up his muscles, not riding faster). I knew from my experience as an athlete and a strength coach that there was far more to improving my power, endurance and skills than what I was finding, and so I started to experiment with my own training strategies.

Because I did not come from a cycling background, I was not con-strained by previous ideas on how to best train a rider, so I blended ideas and tools from non-traditional sources like strength and conditioning training and martial arts. After a few years of experimenting on myself and some clients, I realized that I had created something that was truly unique in how it approached improving a rider's fitness. I also knew that other mountain bikers would benefit from as it well; and so I created MTB Strength Training Systems to help spread the word.

THE BIRTH OF METABOLIC SKILLS TRAINING

While I had always known that the right exercises could help improve your technical skills, I had one experience that took my understanding to a new level. I was attending a skills clinic when I noticed that several riders were struggling with the most basic skill on the bike – body posi-tion. After watching the instructor try unsuccessfully to get one of them into better position, I realized that they needed to get off the bike and learn to perform the movement without the added stress of balancing and moving.

It then dawned on me that instead of simply looking at strength and conditioning as a way to improve fitness, I could strategically choose exercises that helped refine and strengthen the fundamental movement patterns behind the technical skills riders needed on the trail. This would effectively turn "strength training" into "skills training" and led me to see my training programs in a whole new way.

Metabolic Skills Training is the term I gave to the art of using strength training exercises to improve your technical skills on the bike. By understanding how each exercise relates to the skills you need on the trail, you can ensure that you are getting maximum transfer from the gym to the trail. In addition, the right exercises done correctly will help you more easily learn and apply technical skills on your bike.

When you move with more efficiency and power, then you will find that everything you do on your bike comes more naturally, resulting in more of the elusive "flow" that so many riders hear about but rarely get to experience. As a mountain biker you cannot just pound out mindless reps and hope that it will help you on the trail - you must understand the movement lessons behind the exercises. Most exercises in your training program should be chosen because they represent a way to work on a fundamental movement skill that supports a technical skill that you need on the trail.

THE FIVE BASIC TECHNICAL SKILLS AND TOP FIVE MOUNTAIN BIKE EXERCISES

Everything you do on your bike can be broken down into a combination of Five Basic Technical Skills. In my experience, training riders at the highest levels of mountain biking, there is also a list of Top Five Mountain Bike Exercises that need to be included in your program to help refine and strengthen the movement patterns behind those skills.

Here is a description of the Five Basic Technical Skills with the corresponding Top Five exercises that help improve the movement pattern behind the skill:

Technical Skill #1:
BODY POSITION - This is your ability to achieve a balanced position where you can most effectively control your bike. The two main factors are how well your center of gravity (your hips) lines up with your bike's center of gravity (somewhere near the bottom bracket) for balance and how much weight you can keep on your front end to steer effectively and maintain control.

Most riders lack the ability to hinge at their hips while keeping their spine long and straight, and so they end up making a compromise between the two. They end up either having their hips back far enough so they don't get tossed over the handlebars, but lack pinpoint steering control or having enough weight on their front tire to steer, so end up getting tossed over the handlebars a lot.

When you can keep your hips back while maintaining a long spine and hinging at the hips instead of the lower back, you can achieve both things simultaneously - balance and control. Knowing how to achieve this most basic of all technical skills will not only improve your riding immeasurably by itself, but will also allow you to more effectively apply all the higher level skills listed below.

Top 5 Exercise #1:

DEADLIFT - This exercise represents the most essential skill that you need on the bike - to move from the hips and be able to achieve a good "hip hinge." A hip hinge is your ability to drive your hips back behind your heels while letting your chest come down towards the ground. Most riders cannot get down into this position and have very little strength in it. Mastering the deadlift and being able to lift 1.5 to 2 times your body-weight will mean that you can more easily achieve and maintain good body position on the bike.

Technical Skill #2:

SEATED PEDALING - This is your ability to get yourself into a strong position while sitting down that doesn't place excessive strain on your low back, shoulder and neck while being able to power your pedal stroke with your hips as much as possible. Contrary to popular advice, you don't want to "pull up" or "spin circles" to power your pedal stroke - several studies have shown that driving your lead leg foot hard into the pedals is the best way to go and this comes from the hips, not the quads and hip flexors.

Top 5 Exercise #2:

SINGLE LEG DEADLIFT - Like any good deadlift, a single leg deadlift should find you in a good hip hinge position at the bottom and maintaining optimal core and upper body position while driving out of the bottom. This means that your torso maintains its "lean" at the bottom and the initial move is not the torso driving into an upright position. This requires core strength and hip drive one leg at a time, which is exactly what we do to power-seated pedaling efforts. When you can do ½ your bodyweight for five clean reps on each leg you'll be able to power seated pedaling efforts much more effectively.

Technical Skill #3:

STANDING PEDALING - This is your ability to stand up and lay down massive amounts of power to the pedals. This requires more core and hip strength and a different body position/ posture than seated pedaling, which means that your body looks at the two types of pedaling completely differently. The fitness you build from seated pedaling simply does not translate well over to standing pedaling, which is why a lot of riders find standing pedaling to be "hard" when they simply need to work on and strengthen the movement patterns behind this different type of pedaling skill.

Top 5 Exercise #3:

SINGLE LEG SQUAT - Standing pedaling requires a more upright position, which results in the hips moving forward towards the handlebars in order to get stacked up under the shoulders and allow for more hip-drive into the pedals. When you are seated, you are pushing the pedals in front of you - when standing you want to be driving the pedals down and behind you. A single leg squat will teach you how to stack your torso and drive down into the ground/pedals, meaning that when you can lift ¼ of your bodyweight for five clean reps, you'll be able to easily stand and deliver power to the pedals.

Technical Skill #4:

CORNERING - This is your ability to lean your body and your bike in harmony around turns. The least effective way to turn your bike is by turning the handlebars - the rider wants to lean over and counter-steer with the handlebars. This complex skill stems from being able to lean laterally from the hips and counterbalance the lean of the bike (which results in the bike's center of gravity falling inside the turn) with your hips by pushing them outside the turn. You have to let your upper body lean inside to keep just enough weight on the handlebars to keep the front wheel biting and your weight distributed between the front and back end of the bike.

Top 5 Exercise #4:

WINDMILL - The windmill does two things for us - it gets us into a split-stance position and it reinforces the lateral lean of the torso needed to corner your bike. It is a unique and challenging exercise that requires a lot of hip mobility and core strength to execute properly. When you can do 35-55 pounds for five clean reps on each side you'll find your ability to confidently lean into a corner in order to maintain speed through it.

Technical Skill #5:

MANUALING/BUNNY HOPPING/JUMPING - This is your ability to drive powerfully from the hips in order to bring the front end of your bike up. It stems from keeping that all-important relationship between the bike and your center of gravity. You want to drive the bike in front of you by extending your legs and hips while keeping the arms relatively relaxed.

You need to avoid pulling the front end up with arms (which results in bent elbows) or by simply leaning back forcefully with the lower back. This results in the bike center of gravity changing without your center of gravity compensating. You have to remain balanced in order to manual, bunny hop or pop off a lip, and the ability to drive from the hips and the arm is the key.

Top 5 Exercise #5:

SWING - The swing is as close as you can come to a hard trail ride without throwing your leg over a bike. It ingrains body position, teaches you how to absorb impacts with your hips and builds massive forearm strength and endurance. However, the most important lesson you learn from it is how to keep the arms relaxed and drive the hips forward. It is a forward-backward projection of energy which makes it a unique way to learn how to drive the bike forward, which means that when you can do 50 reps with a 16 kg (women) or 24 kg (men) kettlebell, you'll be able to more confidently loft your bike into the air.

You will notice that I included some pictures to show the basic form for each exercise, however I strongly encourage you to visit my blog at: www.bikejames.com to find video demos of these exercises as well. In them I break down each exercise, explaining where you should feel it and how to fix common mistakes.

For too long, mountain bikers have been treated as an afterthought in the cycling world. Riding technically-demanding trails requires a unique blend of skills and fitness like few sports in the world. As such, it requires it own training system and a unique perspective on the best tools and strategies to use. Metabolic Skills Training is a fresh look at what it really takes to help you ride faster, longer and with more confidence on the trail.

About James

James Wilson is the owner and head strength coach for MTB Strength Training Systems, the world leader in creating training programs that help you ride faster, longer and with more confidence on the trail. As the strength and conditioning coach for 3 National Championships and several World Cup Teams and riders, his programs have been proven at the highest levels. As a regular contributor to Decline Magazine, DeclineMagazine.com and Pinkbike.com, James has helped thousands of riders just like you improve their speed, endurance and skills on the trail.

His innovative workouts and training programs have been featured in Mountain Bike Magazine, Mastering Mountain Bike Skills 2, VitalMTB.com, LeeLikesBike.com, NSMB.com and Singletracks.com. To learn more about how MTB Strength Training Systems can help you enjoy riding more, visit: www.bikejames.com and be sure to sign up for the free "Trail Rider Fundamentals Video Mini-Course."

Contact Information: www.BikeJames.com

CHAPTER 5

Before You Can Move Forward, You Must First Look Back To Your Childhood

By Robert Kelly

"Bobby, go outside and play and I don't want to see you until LUNCH!" My mother would beckon as I ran out the door. Lunch would come, a quick peanut butter and jelly sandwich and out again I scamper, followed by, "Play nice with your friends and I don't want to see you until dinner!" This is an accurate example of my years ranging from 8-15 when days were spent playing hide and go seek, climbing trees, and every single sport that used a ball or a stick.

Think back to your youth. How did you spend it? No matter what your current age, if you think about it, you probably had at least a few years when you were active outside simply playing or at least you were involved in a sport a few days per week. You had fun playing for sure and if you were learning how to play a sport or activity, you developed skills like hand eye coordination, rhythm and body movement that are crucial to who you are today.

Now take a moment and look at your current day- Do you take time out for fun? Do you participate in an activity or workout a few days a week? Too often at Results Only, our gym in Phoenix AZ, when people first walk into the facility, they have forgotten the basics of a healthy lifestyle. Sure it is great to have a flat toned stomach or sexy legs and who wouldn't kill for sleek arms and a body to die for! The questions you should ask are...

- "What is the REAL point of living a life that is active and vibrant?"
- "Why do you absolutely need to guarantee yourself time, **every day,** for movement and fun?"

The answer is simple but too often overlooked. Sure, movement makes your body a well-oiled, functioning machine. You know every time you set aside time for exercise you are fighting off medical challenges like, heart disease, diabetes, and numerous other maladies that creep in when you become sedentary. Activity, especially when done with others, always brings out the best in people. And while developing a killer body is arguably a great benefit of exercising, the real reason you need to make time every day is overall happiness. I told you it was simple.

Back to our story. When you were a child, you probably woke up early so you could get a jump start on your fun and didn't you constantly beg for your elders to play with you or allow you to go and play with other children? Of course you did. You were a "kid." It was your job and sole desire in life to run around, be as active as possible, smile often, and... BE HAPPY.

Now, as an adult, think about the inherent difficulties thrown in front of you each and every day posing a threat to your happiness. Deadlines, traffic, pollution, and politics are just a few stressful things everyone deals with daily. Maybe you are a parent and your days are full of carpools, laundry, PTA and countless other activities too numerous to mention that stifle all chances of taking a few minutes just for yourself.

Time for a 'Reality Check': It is your responsibility to yourself and to the people around you to guarantee time every day for movement. Movement = Fun. Fun = Happiness. Who doesn't want to be around cheerful vibrant people? Everyone does. You instantly become a better spouse or parent. You transform into an integral part of your work environment. By being an overall easier person to be around, each and every day, you become a driving force of energy. When anyone comes in contact with positive energy, it brings the whole environment to a higher level. People work better, people feel better and lives are changed.

Children are bundles of energy. They never stop moving, asking questions, constantly learning and then when they finally run out of steam, they crash hard and sleep. The question you should ask is, when was the last time you ran all day, so busy but happy the whole time, and then when the time came for you to wrap it up, you fell asleep knowing three things; you just had an amazing day, you can't wait until tomorrow and you will sleep through the night like a baby? If you don't answer yes to these questions every single day then it is time for you to take a good hard introspective look at your lifestyle.

By picking up this book you have already taken steps towards looking and feeling your best and you are acknowledging a pivotal fact about your life - something is not right. We shout from the mountaintops to every single client that walks into Results Only… "If your way was working, you wouldn't need to be here today." You know deep inside there are things in your life you want to change and beginning today, you are ready to make those changes. Change is inevitable and the key to happiness and permanent lifestyle change is commitment.

The culture at our gym, and many of the other gyms you will read about in this book, is what sets us apart from all other facilities within 100 miles. Sure we have an educated staff that is upbeat and personable but many gyms can make that claim. The gym is clutter free and clean but that shouldn't be unique. What makes us different is that we support every single client to commit to themselves and ensure they are happy to be in our facility as soon as they walk in the door. As you arrive, there is a sign that greets you before you walk through the door,

"Whatever is going on in your day, leave it outside! Commit to yourself for the next 60 minutes!"

People have walked through the door smiling; even screaming 'Thank You,' because they know for the next hour it is all about them. It is all about happiness. It is all about commitment. Occasionally, someone walks in the door in tears because their day has been rough and no one in their life has cared about them at all. A simple hug or a pat on the back states they are in a safe place where we will focus on nothing but them. It is a culture that, beginning today, you must find too and if it isn't easily accessible, start to build it yourself.

When you run a facility in Phoenix, Arizona there are unique challenges to contend with at different points of the year. When it is 115 degrees outside we know it is tough to get motivated to sweat. IT IS HOT! So all year long, we divide exercise and making time for "you," down into four simple steps-

1. Every night before you go to bed pack your gym bag with workout clothes, sneakers and everything you need to get your workout in tomorrow.

2. Every night make an itemized list of the things you need to do tomorrow – prioritizing the list from most important to least important. Make sure you get the most important thing done first.

3. When you wake up the next morning, figure out exactly when you will make time for a class, your personal trainer, or to be active outside for 30-45 minutes.

4. Finally, **SHOW UP.** Don't let any excuses get in your way. No matter what. If your day gets away from you, this is as important as anything else. Probably more important.

That's it. The rest is up to us. We make sure we develop the right conditions for your success. You walk in and get changed into your clothes. All you have to do is lace up your sneakers and leave the rest to the professionals. After saying hello to your other likeminded and committed friends, you grab a clean towel, fill your water bottle and head to one of our staff to get you started. The trainer presents you with an easy to follow routine. That doesn't mean it is an easy program. You don't want easy. If it was easy, everyone would do it. You are special. It simply means you won't be challenged by the difficult practice of figuring out your exercises and the science behind the protocols of your personalized routine. You can focus on challenging your body to push itself to the limit.

The music is cranking and always creates a high-energy ambiance. You recognize everyone around you wants what you have - **A desire to be healthy, look your best, feel amazing and be happy**. You know spending this time on yourself brings you joy amidst the sweat, fatigue and movement. Working hard doesn't tire you out or deplete you, but rather you feel invigorated and energized. You tackle every repetition as if it is going to bring you the strength to accomplish anything you set your mind to today.

Out of the corner of your eye you see people you know feeling the exact same exuberance as you feel right now and you are surrounded in an environment of greatness. And then, just when you have taken your body farther than you ever thought possible, you see another smiling face who says, "You did an amazing job today. I bet you feel good."

Need a little more convincing? This is how important one client made working out for him. He was a very high profile lawyer. He worked 80 hours a week. It was high stress and cut throat. Many of his contemporaries would kill for his job and do anything to take him down a rung so they could climb higher up the corporate ladder. He knew that leaving in the middle of the day to get 45 minutes of a butt kicking workout done would make him feel better, clear his mind, and make him more productive. He understood working at his highest potential would help earn the firm more money and that leaving for lunch and making himself better, would help the whole team. However he worried that co-workers would dismiss it as "personal" time and his partners would look down on it.

The compromise? His secretary scheduled every Monday, Wednesday, and Friday, 12:30-1:45pm for his "Psychiatrist". No one in the office would ever second guess a guy who needed a "Psychiatrist". Who wants a co-worker losing it from stress and being overworked coming in and going postal on everyone. If anyone asked where he was the secretary would simply answer, "He is at his Dr.'s appointment." Enough said. No reason to second guess because he was taking care of himself. All we did was change the method of therapy. Right?

Maybe you don't live in Phoenix AZ, so making it into our culture every week is not possible for you. Please know that if you are ever in the area, simply look us up at: www.resultsonly.com, click on the schedule, bring your book by and we will invite you to experience an hour at Results Only. It is something everyone should experience at least once in their lifetime. We will sign it too.

Throughout this book, you will read about cutting-edge exercise protocols from trainers at the top of their field. You will learn how to shed body fat, perform better and develop a lifestyle that is unique for you with guidance from the pros that do it every day. If you follow their advice, you will create a body you can live in for decades to come.

BUT NONE OF IT WILL WORK IF YOU DON'T SHOW UP

As you continue to read, think back to the days of being a 'kid'. The days when everything was simpler, and your only responsibilities were to have fun and enjoy life. Reintroduce yourself to that person, the next time you look in the mirror. Children have a unique ability to read people. They gravitate to positive, trustworthy, happy individuals and shy away from mysterious, complex, and burdensome people.

The only way all of the information in this book will be complete is if you develop a culture for yourself that is upbeat, positive and fulfilling. Starting today, you need to think like a child. Sure you need to be a responsible and fulfill your duties as an honest member of society. But you need to enjoy life and you must surround yourself with likeminded people who share the same dreams, hopes and goals as you do. Then and only then you will see and feel what it's like to BE HAPPY.

About Bobby

Bobby Kelly is a 20+ year veteran of the fitness industry. As a highly sought after strength, speed, & conditioning coach, personal trainer, motivational speaker and consultant, Bobby takes his role as catalyst coach very seriously. His goal is to ignite a change in people's perspective on life, health and wellness within minutes of stepping on a stage or meeting one-on-one.

Bobby owns and directs Results Only, a cutting-edge performance center focusing on teaching clients simple and effective ways to reach their full potential in all walks of life. He has created numerous DVD programs and products including his latest book and exercise and nutrition program, The Solution. Bobby has a unique ability for pulling out a higher level of passion, commitment, focus, and development from his clients and audiences. It has been said that working with Bobby is like "riding an extremely fast-paced and spiraling roller coaster, holding onto the seat of your pants the whole time, only to get off ready to climb right back on again."

Bobby connects and empowers people through fitness and health, engaging each participant to strive to be the best and transform their life. His goal-setting techniques as well as ability to deliver energy and enthusiasm are arguably his best attributes as a coach.

Bobby graduated from the University of Maryland with a Bachelor of Science degree and is a Certified Personal Trainer. Bobby has been interviewed, featured, and utilized as an expert advisor on CNN, Fox News, ABC, NBC, and CBS as well as local affiliate stations in numerous markets. He has been interviewed or featured as an expert in *The New York Times, Wall Street Journal, Washington Post, Arizona Republic, GolfWorld, GolfOnline, The Washingtonian,* and *Prevention Magazine* to name just a few. He has had the luxury to train and work with people from all walks of life including **elite athletes, CEO's of Fortune 500 Companies, members of the Department of Commerce,** and **the President of the United States.** Results Only and Bobby have been named Fitness Facility and Trainer of the Year in Phoenix multiple times.

CHAPTER 6

Why Did The Pilot Check To See If There Was A Wing Attached To My Plane?

By Mike Wunsch

So it wouldn't fall off during my flight. He was just following the simplest of protocols to ensure success of an extremely complicated task. The overwhelming majority of people who come into Results Fitness are looking for fat loss, and this is their complicated task. The vast majority of these people have tried several different times to lose fat. They have tried several different methods and measures to attempt this goal. They have tried the quick starvation fix, the TV miracle program, the 4-minute a day three times a week workout, the 90-minute every day workout, and just about any other method of fat loss. They seldom reach their goals, and in some rare chance they do, as soon as (insert trick diet here) is done, they rebound and are in worse condition than when they started. After these fads are experienced, the person is now a smaller, fatter, weaker, more tired version of themselves. By the time a client has come to Results Fitness, they've tried it all, and are tired of the way they still feel. They are unhappy with their bodies and the way their bodies make their minds feel. This is the critical aspect –their bodies make their minds feel terrible. Their bodies will not give their minds permission to be happy.

We all have set goals. Take a quick second and picture yourself after you reach your goal. How would your day go? Take another second and experience the happiness that you deserve – feel the sense of pleasure that comes with it. This is what we all seek after all: happiness. The reason we choose to exercise and eat right is to make ourselves happier. The middle result – smaller dress size, lower body fat, a healthier body, a stronger body, the ability to be active in our golden years are merely the mediums for happiness. All of these things make us happier. So, as we all come from different places and times, each goal met is merely "permission" to be happy. This is why setting short term goals, followed by medium term goals and finally a long term goal, will allow us "permission" to be happy several times a day, every day and not just when this distant goal becomes a reality. Therefore, the short-term goals are just as important as the medium and long-term goals. As each goal has a different time frame, each goal allows a different amount of happiness. As short-term goals allow us to be happy daily, medium-term goals allow us less frequent bouts of happiness, but each success is enjoyed more, and lastly, the long-term goals allow us the zenith of happiness.

There are two keys to this process. One is to conduct "Reverse Engineering" or simply working backwards. This was applied during military conflicts and it describes what soldiers did in combat when they found an enemy foreign object. They did not know what it was or what it did. The first thing they did was to take it apart. In this fashion, a complex unit that is incomprehensible begins to make sense. What was once a complex unknown unit became pieces of recognizable parts likes gears, screws, pins etc. We do not yet know what the entire unit does, but because we have broken the unit down to recognizable parts, we may begin to understand its function. After they broke down the unit into recognizable parts, they were able to reconstruct the item and even more important – make improvements on it. The other key is to follow a Standard Operating Procedure (SOP).

A SOP is merely a checklist one goes through before any procedure. The two very common SOP's are the ones airline pilots and surgeons use. Before a pilot takes off, he or she follows a standardized SOP. Even the most simple, mundane item such as making sure the wings are attached is a crucial step in the process. Obviously very difficult items are on the checklist such as atmospheric conditions that must be checked off the list as well. The most experienced pilots all the way down to pilots making their maiden flight must fill out the SOP checklist every flight, every time. Surgeons have their SOP's as well. The surgeon must pre and post op fill out their own SOP. Again, the most intricate details such as structural anatomy down to the most simple of items such as making sure the surgical tool count is the same before and after the surgery must be checked off the list. These tasks and checklists sound simple, and they are. They are exceedingly simple done step-by-step, in order to avoid the critical mistakes that can easily fall through the cracks. It is these simple tasks that can hinder our goals the most. It is never the "big thing," but typically the smaller simple tasks that hurt us.

So we can use this model and apply it to our daily lives. We set our perfect day in our minds and visualize how we feel. We imagine we have met our long-term goal. What would be different? What is the first thing we would notice when we woke up that day that would make us know we have "made it"? What would we have done to get there? What did we do yesterday? What were we doing two weeks ago? What would we have done three months prior to that, to get there? What was done one year before that? If we can reverse engineer our goals, what was once an unknown, insurmountable task now becomes something very familiar and very easy to overcome, and very easy to reconstruct.

We have set up a Standard Operating Procedure (SOP) for goal setting. This SOP goal setting process allows small daily successes that keep us moving forward. These small successes allow us to be happy daily and keep pushing us towards the medium-term goals. These medium-term goals are the ones that REALLY keep us going by giving us some tangible feedback about our progress. The medium term goals really re-kindle the fire and give us the boost we need to keep momentum going to our long-term goals. The SOP dictates then that we begin with the long-term goal that may be in the distant future and work back to what our next meal will be or our next training session. The great thing about a SOP is that it is individual for every person when it comes to goals. One simply inserts the items on the "checklist" to be crossed off the to-do list.

HERE IS A TYPICAL STANDARD OPERATING PROCEDURE (SOP) FOR A GOAL OF 30 LBS OF FAT LOSS:

- **Long-term goal:** 30 lbs fat loss and four dress sizes.
- **Medium-term goals:** Periodization scheme and nutritional plans approved.

- **Medium-term goals:** Complete monthly workout phases.
- **Medium-term goals:** Complete monthly nutritional guidelines.
- **Short-term goals:** Weekly workout schedule set.
- **Short-term goals**: Weekly nutritional guidelines set, grocery store shopping, menu planning.
- **Short-term goals:** Daily workout met.
- **Short-term goals:** Daily meals met.
- **Short-term goals:** Getting up every 15 minutes to stretch and re-set your body from our daily work regimen.
- **Short-term goals:** Eating every 3-4 hours.

As one can see, there is a goal set that is out of reach and currently impossible – losing 30 pounds. On the other end of the spectrum, there are goals that anyone can succeed at, at any time: getting up every 15 minutes to stretch. The ability to continually meet and succeed at even the most simple of goals is extremely important for the human psyche. We as people need continuous feedback and affirmation that what we are doing is working. We do not want to wait until we reach a distant goal for affirmation; we want immediate feedback to know what we are doing is working. The key to this type of goal setting is making sure the simplest of goals met are the next pieces to the puzzle we are trying to solve. The smallest of pieces will make the larger pieces come together, and these larger pieces will eventually make the largest of pieces fit like a glove. An important factor in this is to make certain these goals are related to each other. We have to make sure the smallest of goals will make the medium goals easier to reach, and thus the medium goals will make the largest of goals a reality.

Here are the rules (SOP) to abide by when setting your goals. Notice that these guidelines are set to short-term goals that are by themselves very simple to attain. These will have a synergistic effect on each other. The wonderful part about this is that each simple goal met will help every other goal on the SOP list. Each simple goal met will help build momentum towards the next goal. These procedures give us several opportunities throughout the day to succeed and feel happy.

RESULTS FITNESS NUTRITIONAL
STANDARD OPERATING PROCEDURE:

- Eat within 15 minutes of waking up.

- Eat every 3-4 hours.

- Have a quality protein at each meal.

- Drink half your weight in ounces of water. (150 pound person should drink 75 oz of water.)

- Reduce processed starches.

- Always have a high protein workout shake. (At least 20 grams of protein.)

- Take a multivitamin and fish oil.

- Have a fruit and/or vegetable at each meal.

- Keep a food journal.

- Plan on splurging 10% of the time.

There are very solid reasons for each of these items on the SOP list, and we'll discuss why each one works:

This immediately fires up our metabolism and gets our body to awaken and start the calorie burning furnace that is our body.

This gives us a steady amount of energy throughout the day, along with a steady amount of vitamins and minerals necessary to keep out bodies healthy. It also helps keep our bodies from the roller coaster ups-and-downs of blood sugar regulation.

Quality protein at each meal gives our bodies the building blocks to repair the daily damage that occurs during exercise. It gives our body the tools it needs to keep our muscle tissue healthy. This is critical for long-term fat loss because it makes it easier for our body to have an elevated metabolic rate, or the amount of calories we burn throughout the day.

Simply put, if we have enough water in our bodies, our kidneys can function properly as a filter for the by-products of what occurs during fat loss.

If we reduce processed starches, and instead utilize high-fiber carbohydrates such as fruits and vegetables, we have another tool in our belts to keep us off of the blood sugar roller coaster...

It is a must to have a workout shake – either immediately before, during, or immediately after exercise. This is crucial to support fat loss. After exercise, our bodies are primed and ready to be refueled. This is a very small window of opportunity for success here.

Multivitamins are like insurance policies. They plug any gaps that we may have nutritionally speaking. The fish oils are a must as well. There are several studies showing the positive effects that fish oils have on fat loss. If we have enough high-quality fish oils, our bodies are primed to burn fat.

Fruits and veggies at each meal allow us to have a bounty of fiber, minerals and vitamins, and allows us to keep our blood sugar levels at a nice medium level, avoiding the roller coaster of highs and lows of blood sugar. This helps us stay in an even fat-burning zone.

Keeping a food journal allows us and our coaches to see where we are hitting and where we are missing in our diet. We can see what we are putting into our bodies, and this allows us to be more aware of our nutrition.

No one is perfect! Not one of us can stay 100% on any regimen, or lifestyle. If we plan on splurging, we can enjoy ourselves a bit more and not be unhappy when we have a non-compliant meal. Therefore, instead of being upset at our imperfections, we can plan to have them, enjoy them and move on.

We now have a solid, results-proven SOP that if followed will yield tremendous results. So to review: set your long-term goal, work backward to medium-term goals that will help the long term goal, and set daily short-term goals that allow us to fulfill the medium-term goals. Follow the SOP we have set up for you and you are on your way to being granted permission to be happy!

About Mike

Mike Wunsch is the Director of Program Design and Training, for Results Fitness – voted one of Men's Health Top Ten Gyms for several years in a row. He is responsible for getting everyday people into the best shape of their lives in the shortest, safest and most fun time possible. The happiness that Team Results Fitness makes possible and exceptional customer service, set it apart in the industry.

Mike has worked with several top-name companies such as Nike, Microsoft, MSN, and publications such as *Men's Health, Women's Health, Shape, Men's Fitness*, and *Experience Life* magazine. He also is a presenter for the National Strength and Conditioning Association, and Perform Better.

Results Fitness also has several products ranging from exercise DVD's to Mentoring Fitness Professionals on how to run a profitable gym.

For contact info: www.resultsfitnessuniversity.com
Tel: 661-799-7900

CHAPTER 7

THE TOP 3 MYTHS OF NUTRITION: WHY MOST DIETS DON'T WORK (AND WHAT DOES!)

By Josef Brandenburg

As an award-winning fitness trainer, I make it my mandate to give you "The Body You Want." I know how important it is for my clients to achieve that end goal - because, for years and years, that was all I wanted to achieve for myself. And for those years and years, that mission seemed more impossible than anything Tom Cruise ever attempted in one of his action movies.

Frankly, I got into fitness out of desperation. I'm not ashamed to admit that I grew up as a fat kid. My low point was probably when I was around nine years old and my parents sent me to a summer sports camp at Georgetown University. All the kids were playing a game of baseball...well, okay, it wasn't even baseball, we were using tennis rackets at the plate because most of us didn't have the hand-eye coordination to use a real bat.

Anyway, I came up to hit and as I stood there waiting for the pitch, the kids on the field began to sing the old rock song, "Wild Thing." Only they changed the words to "Blubber Thing." Not real creative, but it did the job on my psyche. Nor did it come as a big surprise - a doctor had already told me a year earlier that I had to lose weight and I was only eight.

As I grew older, I did everything I was supposed to do in order to shed the extra pounds and get the body *I* wanted. That meant I kept trying to eat less and less, while exercising more and more - the standard school of thought to this day. At one point I was doing twelve to fourteen hours of aerobics a week, and eating 1,200 calories per day or less. And yeah, I lost weight (and was dizzy and miserable), but then I ended up putting it all right back on twice as fast as I took it off.

That's why writing this chapter is so important to me - and hopefully to you as well. After being a yo-yo dieter for twelve years, relying only on the prevailing myths of society about exercise and diet to guide me, I finally realized there had to be another way.

There was. And it all starts with what you eat.

COMBATING CONVENTIONAL WISDOM

There was no one more motivated than me to lose weight - I did everything I could to make it happen. And yet, it didn't.

Now, traditional thinking would have you believe that resulted from being too lazy or some kind of out-of-control glutton. Nothing could have been further from the truth. The truth is you can have the strongest, most directed mindset in the world - but if that mindset is pointed in the wrong direction, it doesn't matter. Yes, I was doing two hours or more of aerobics a day - but *I was still getting fatter.* Alwyn Cosgrove, the man whose name is on the front of this book, was one of the first people to point out that aerobic training never did work or never could work as a tool for fat loss.

That's why I began my quest for *something that did work.* Again, I had spent over a decade trying to lose weight and keep it off. And I slowly realized the vicious cycle that was created by eating less and exercising more. The first attempt works pretty well - but the weight eventually comes back on. On the second attempt, it takes a lot longer to lose the weight, but the weight comes back on a lot faster. That pattern continues to worsen - it gets harder and harder to lose weight and easier and easier to pack those pounds back on as you try it all over again.

So there I was, still waking up at 5 am, doing the first half of my workout, going to work, and then, at night, finishing my workout until 11 p.m - and getting up the next morning to see that I still had man-boobs.

Because I was trying to eat as little as possible, I felt dizzy and weak from hunger a lot of the time. Frankly, it wasn't working at all in any aspect of my life.

I finally gave myself permission to listen to people outside the mainstream and study things that had different ideas. I had heard these kinds of ideas before, but I had always dismissed them - because I had my officially-sanctioned education stuck in my head. (I think I got 'stupider' studying nutrition in college.) Now, I opened the doors to other advice - and mustered up the courage to try it.

I had already tried cutting out all red meat from my diet, then becoming a vegetarian and then, finally, a vegan, all with bad (very bad!) results. Now I went the other way; I started eating meat. Lots of it, along with vegetables and healthy fat foods. Instead of counting calories, I now focused on the quality of the foods I was eating.

And it worked.

As a matter of fact, it worked quite well. I could finally think clearly and I wasn't lethargic and depressed. I *cut down* on my exercise time - by 75%! I had time to have a life - and actually date. And I didn't have to worry about what my body would look like if I ended up taking my clothes off.

That was about ten years ago. At my worst, I was around 240 lbs with an over-40 inch waist - with a height of 5'10" - while I was working out and not eating much. With my new approach, I lost about forty pounds, even though I put on about twenty-five pounds of muscle - leaving me with a sixty to seventy pound body composition improvement.

So why did all that suddenly work - when exercising like a maniac and eating like a bird didn't? There were actually a lot of firm scientific principles behind my new diet, that I'd like to share with you now - by exploring the Top Three Myths we are routinely fed (pun intended) about food by society at large.

MYTH #1: LOW CALORIE DIETS WORK

In 2003, *The Journal of the American Medical Association* published a study on the effectiveness of the Weight Watchers program - they followed participants over two years. The result? They discovered that the average person following the Weight Watchers guidelines only lost on average *six pounds*. Yes, only six pounds over two years - not what you'd call a real happy outcome.

That's because the low calorie approach just doesn't work. Another myth behind this one is that humans possess some kind of "thrifty gene" that causes us to hoard fat so our bodies can access it when food is unavailable - which is why we supposedly have to starve ourselves to prevent this internal hoarding. James Neel, a professor of Human Genetics, is the man who first coined the term "thrifty gene". He spent 20+ years looking for his "thrifty gene" with no success, and concluded that the new obesity and diabetes epidemic was the result of "specifically the use of highly-refined carbohydrate."

There are three scientific reasons why the low calorie approach isn't effective:

- **Reason #1: 50 to 75 percent of the weight you lose with a low calorie diet is *not* fat.** If you lose twenty pounds, *at least half of that* isn't the type of body weight you wanted to lose - it's actually lean body mass. And the less lean body mass you have, the easier it is to put on fat later.

- **Reason #2: Low calorie diets simply make you too hungry - and if you can't keep the diet up, you can't keep the weight off.** The fact is that hunger is not a lifestyle. And sooner or later, that hunger will cause you to break the diet.

- **Reason #3: Low calorie diets disrupt all your internal regulators that determine how much fat your body has.** You have a biological urge to eat - and a low calorie diet causes your body to make you as hungry as possible as it quite reasonably thinks it's not getting enough food. This is true of 98% of the population - and your body will fight you all the way until it wins.

MYTH #2: A CALORIE IS A CALORIE IS A CALORIE

Any diet book you read says when you eat fewer calories, you lose weight. Unfortunately, all calories were not created equal.

Ancel Keys was a 'big shot' nutrition scientist who developed the K-Rations for soldiers in World War II. During that war, he wanted to understand more about the physical effects of starvation so the U.S.

could properly treat the victims of widespread famine in Europe be-cause of the ongoing conflict. He gathered together 36 men who were conscientious objectors to the war for a study that was called the Min-nesota Starvation Experiment.

For the first twelve weeks of this study, these 36 men were very well fed and happy. The next 12 weeks, however, were the exact opposite. The men were fed only 1,560 calories a day (the technical term for that is a "semi-starvation diet") and mostly the kind of food that war survivors would have access to - foods such as macaroni, potatoes, rutabagas and turnips, basically a high carb grain diet (which the USDA today would look very favorably on, by the way).

The result? Most of the subjects experienced periods of severe emotion-al distress and depression. One man actually cut off three of the fingers of one hand with an axe. The group's sex drive was drastically reduced and the volunteers also showed signs of social withdrawal. They had trouble concentrating and making sound judgments. And they were ex-tremely preoccupied with food, not surprisingly.

Of course, nowadays, a doctor can put you on an 800 calorie liquid diet - and they won't call it a semi-starvation diet.

After the men were once again well fed, they regained the weight they lost and then some. Their body composition also included *more fat*. Sound familiar?

Now, let's look at a different study made by Dr. John Yudkin, a British professor who ran an obesity clinic in England. He gave his patients some simple advice - eat meat, eggs and green vegetables, and *don't* drink beer or ingest sugar or bread products, but eat as much as you like.

This diet proved very successful for most of the people he treated. As he did not put a limit on their caloric intake, he was now asking them to keep track of how much they were eating because he was curious about what they were taking in. Check out the results: Voluntarily, spontane-ously, and with no sense of deprivation, he found they were eating 10 calories less a day than the Keys group's semi-starvation diet!

So it does matter what you eat - and if you eat the right things, your in-ternal regulators will work correctly and you will know when you have actually eaten enough. And you will know it *without* having to count calories. On the other hand, eating refined carbs makes you hungry even when you really *aren't* that hungry. (Bad calories make you hungry.)

That's because both sugar and high fructose corn syrup contain fructose[1], which is what really fools the brain - fructose simply *does not register as food*. If you drink a big bottle of Pepsi or Coke, your body doesn't see that as food - the sugar screws up your internal record-keeping. That's why they're called "empty calories" - except the problem is those so-called empty calories fill up your body with fat.

Would you believe that sugar is actually more addictive that cocaine? In one study, rats were able to choose between having cocaine or sweet water put into them intravenously.

94% of the rats chose the sweet water.

MYTH #3: YOUR FAT CELLS ARE PASSIVE TRASH CANS

This myth ties in to what we just talked about in Myth #2 - what causes fat to build up in the body. Most people believe that, when you eat too much, fat cells just fill up with the excess. When you have the will power to stop eating too much, they'll just empty out, just as you would empty out a full trash can.

The "trash can" theory violates basic 4th grade science. Since that was a long time ago, here is the recap of basic cell biology (this will be simple, don't worry!):

The most important part of a cell is its membrane – the part that separates the inside from the outside. If you don't have an inside and an outside, then life is impossible. To be alive, you need food. And just like us, when cells take food in, they put waste out.

Food must come in from the outside – through the membrane - and waste must go out – through the membrane. If the cell runs out of fuel (food), it dies. If the cell has to eat its own waste, it dies. So keeping that straight – what goes in and what goes out – is fundamental to life. That is called "regulation".

All cells everywhere, in *every* creature are *regulated*. This is basic and uncontested scientific fact.

---

1 Actually agave nectar is *the* least healthy sweetener of them all. It has more fructose than the highest high fructose corn syrup. Fructose is the fattening part of sugar/sweeteners.

Your entire blood system should have no more than the equivalent of a teaspoonful of sugar. If you're diabetic, it's a teaspoon and a quarter. In other words, the difference between being diabetic and non-diabetic is a quarter of a teaspoon of sugar in all of the blood running through your body. That's a very small difference between healthy and unhealthy - and it illustrates just how strictly your body regulates itself. Human fat cells are just like all cells – tightly regulated.

What screws up this regulation is grains and sugar. When you replace those with meat, eggs, healthy fats, veggies and some fruits (berries in particular), you'll find yourself functioning better on all fronts. Even your memory will improve.

The above three myths emphasize how wrong most of the thinking is about weight loss in American today. My experiences with my clients back up what the best research tells us - calorie counting simply doesn't work. People hate to do it, and, when they do try it, they usually don't do it very accurately. I also don't think it's necessary. When you eat the right things, your body can take it from there.

If you're interested in pursuing this path, start by eliminating the worst things first - bread and sugar, especially liquid sugar (soda and most fruit juices). Let your body tell you what portions to eat. Unless you're a competitive bodybuilder or similar type of athlete, three meals a day are fine - you don't have to eat six small meals a day as many dieticians advise. It's just counterproductive.

Obviously, I can only cover so much in this chapter, so I suggest you do your own research, email me at: info@thebodyyouwant.com or visit my website at: www.thebodyyouwant.com .

There is another, more effective way to have the body you want, besides conducting your own personal Starvation Experiment.

And, believe me, it's a better way.

About Josef

Josef Brandenburg is founder of The Body You Want Fitness Solutions in Washington, DC – it's the place you to get the body you want in the time you actually have, and have a good time doing it.

Josef first got interested in health, fitness and nutrition when his physician told him he was "too fat for your own good" at age 9. That, and being made fun of at summer camp sparked a drive to learn everything he possibly could about looking better without his shirt off, so that he could go to the beach without feeling ashamed of his body.

Eventually someone asked Josef for help with their workouts, and that first request has turned into a calling, a 15-year career, and the opening of The Body You Want Fitness Solutions.

Josef is the co-author of *The Body you Want, The Client Success Manual*, and several other books. Josef was also the fitness expert for the PCOS challenge reality TV series, and has been featured in The Washington Post, on ABC, WUSA 9, and in newspapers coast to coast. He's also received certifications through ACE, NASM, FMS, CHECK, and the NCEP.

To learn more about what Josef and his team can do for you, and how you can "try before you buy" visit: www.TheBodyYouWant.com or call 202-316-1457.

www.TheBodyYouWant.com

CHAPTER 8

PRESS RESET – ACHIEVING FAMILY FAT LOSS

By Dianne Sykes Scope, MS, NSCA

Listen to your favorite song. It draws you in and captivates your soul. Collectively it's powerful music but break it down and each instrument carries a specific rhythm. Those beats are critical, and when they blend produce something amazing. Your body is similar. It follows physiological rhythms to create the symphony of life. These days we have lost our groove so to speak. American families find themselves trying to cram their physiology into their busy schedules. We tend to ignore the rhythms of sleeping, eating and physical activity the most. They take a back seat to life's other demands. This is not a successful strategy for survival, long-term health and fat loss. So we are going to literally press reset with your whole family. By the end of this section, you will have reset your family schedule so that it follows your physiology – NOT the other way around.

Do you excel at work? Do you live for your kids? Are you over-delivering in just about every aspect of your life? If so, I can relate. As a kid I competed on a community gymnastics team. It was a great testing ground for developing the skill of perfection, only to realize after 30 years that this was a delusional ideal. It was an impossible expectation, but as a business owner, parent and healthcare practitioner it drives me in just about every aspect of my life…except fitness and nutrition. Sound familiar? So you are a great parent, a reliable friend and exemplary employee but you are out of shape. I recently found myself in that very situation.

Having always been an athlete, it was easy to stay fit until I had my first child. What a humbling experience it was to find myself flabby and out of shape! For you guys who think you cannot relate, my ex-pro athlete husband, Rawle, gained more weight during pregnancy than I did, and kept it on longer. We share an entirely different reality now. With an amazing baby girl in our world, our lives were not our own. She always comes first. The freedom to exercise when and where we wanted to was not possible. I knew it was time to apply the system I've been teaching clients for over 15 years to my own life. When our daughter turned one, I had melted the additional 40 pounds I gained and am now ten pounds thinner than when I became pregnant. Rawle is also in competitive shape and his beloved 6-pack abdominals have resurfaced.

Our team has helped thousands of families. We've analyzed a variety of schedules and coached folks to reset their time and put health first. We've seen the collective waistlines of families shrink together and will share three powerful strategies to get you started.

What is your reality? Your life is intensely busy: work, kids, and carpool. These all drain the endocrine system. When your body is mentally stressed, you secrete hormones responsible for fight or flight. When your body senses danger, it prepares to flee or stick around and battle it out. Both require intense physical effort. However most of us experience stress in a way that does not cause physical output. Think for a moment about driving. Is it stressful to you? Let's say someone cut you off. Chances are your physiology triggered a stress response. Your heart rate and blood pressure rise. You release sugar into the bloodstream preparing for the '*danger.*' You have a very volatile internal environment with no active outlet. Multiply this experience by several hundred hours a year and you face serious health issues including fat and weight gain.

You've followed diets before. You have tried exercise programs and although some of them might have been great in theory, none of them are workable in practice because they NEVER consider the schedule of a busy family until NOW! The key to it all is FOLLOWING your physiology.

STRATEGY #1 – OPTIMIZE BREAKFAST TIME

After compiling years of research and experience coaching families, a pattern has emerged. Families seem to have the most stress on weekday mornings. Now that you have some insight about how the body responds to stress, you can use it to your family fat-burning advantage! Turn your chaotic morning into serious caloric expenditure. Don't sit down from the minute you rise until the second you commute to work. With this multi-tasking habit at work, you optimize fat burning while preparing your family for the day ahead. Additionally, you are creating a direct outlet for your stress response! Every calorie counts and they add up over time. Park further away from your office or school. Run instead of walk to get to and from activities (it's a great calorie burner and time saver). Try the traffic light squeeze. Each time you get stuck at a red light, pull your belly button in and press it against your spine. Hold until the light turns green.

**Reset Alert – Challenge each family member to optimize their time by seeing how quickly they can perform their responsibilities (showering, making the bed, and getting dressed) and get themselves to the table for their morning meal. Make it a fun competition and time everyone! Get those metabolic engines going by drinking a tall glass of water in addition to a morning dose of Vitamin C.

STRATEGY #2 – POWER PRIORITIZE

You're extremely busy. As a member of an over-scheduled family, it's easy to be bombarded with tasks. Your physiology HAS to come first and your family's body fat depends on it. Here is a helpful analogy. Every morning, no matter how busy you are you brush your teeth, right? Of course! And when it's late at night and you long to hit that pillow it would not occur to you to skip the ritualistic tooth polish? No way. Why? It's a habit! However if you stop to think about it you understand the importance of oral hygiene. If you don't brush your teeth they rot. You never skip brushing your teeth because you are too busy or too tired. This is the excuse for not exercising…and guess what? Your body will literally rot!

Carve 4-6 hours a week out of your schedule for exercise and nutrition. You might laugh but this is doable. Consider this - the average adult watches 5 hours of television per night and kids accumulate 29-33 hours weekly! Funny that we all think that this does not pertain to us but take a cold hard look at your family life. Facing the brutal truth means getting out in front of your fat loss! You can find 4-6 hours in a week. So what will you do with this non-refundable time? Power prioritizing means looking at what will have the greatest impact on your fat loss with the least amount of time spent. Now that's a strategy we can all use and it involves a ranking system of 1 to 5 with 5 having the heaviest impact on fat loss. Nutritional planning easily ranks a 5, having the most powerful impact on family fat loss success and only takes about an hour of solid planning time per week. Super high impact at high speed makes this priority *numero uno*.

Our essential nutrition behavior checklist:

- Eat every 2-4 hours.
- Eat grass fed lean protein and veggies with every meal.
- Reserve complex carbohydrates for after exercise.
- Enjoy healthy fats found in nuts, fish and coconut oil.
- Get creative with your palate and challenge your family to try one new spice per week (that's 52 exciting ways to scintillate your taste buds).
- Remove all refined sugar and say *Adios* to family fat!

There is no cookie cutter fat loss solution. If there were, then those countless diet books you've collected over the years would have worked! For a complete family nutrition plan, along with meal plans, convenient grocery lists and customized strategies to ensure your family success go to: www.achievefitnessny.com.

**Reset Alert – Nutri-meter:
Get a whiteboard and create a chart that the whole family can see. Draw three buckets. Based on the recommended macronutrient percentages (for more information on a customized family plan visit: www.achievefitnessny.com) each bucket should represent lean protein, complex carbohydrates and healthy fats. Using magnets to represent the nutrients in your consumed meals, fill each bucket accordingly. Use one side of the board for veggies and accumulate magnets for each serving. This is interactive and fun for the whole family. It harnesses the habit of reading food labels and creates a reward system to keep everyone motivated.

Next on our power priority list is metabolic resistance training. It packs a lethal fat-singeing punch. It has the strength of a 5 and takes between 2 to 2 1/2 hours per week. It's a powerful priority but what is MRT? This is strength training designed specifically to increase metabolic demand. Due to it's intensity your body continues to burn calories to bring all the systems back to their resting state long after the activity has ended. It creates lean mass and makes you toned and fit. For more information on a customized exercise prescription for your whole family, visit our website: www.achievefitnessny.com. Next we prescribe high intensity interval training with an impact of 4 and an implementation speed of about 60-120 minutes a week. Keep long slow cardio last. As implied in the name, results are slow and the duration is long.

Two examples of interval training that the family can do together:

Day 1 – Yard Sprints = get out in the backyard and SPRINT as fast as you can from one end of the yard to the other and jog back. Repeat 10x (compete as a family).

Day 2 – Stair Challenge = Climb a flight of (carpeted) stairs 15x and SLOWLY walk down as rest in between each set and hold on to the banister.

With respect to rest it almost seems counterintuitive to power prioritize it, however, this is one of the most neglected activities. Although the impact here is a 5, we can't deny the fact that the time investment of restoration is considerably lengthy as compared to the other priorities. It is during rest that we repair and replenish our bodies. Periods of rest are what turn your body into the fat burning machine it was meant to be. The cellular repair that takes place during rest promotes the production of anti-aging and fat-burning chemicals.

**Reset Alert – Always work backwards when it comes to sleep. If you have to be up at 6 am and require 7 hours of sleep then what time should you go to bed? Answer - 11pm. No excuses for you or your children. This one reset will have a profound effect on your fat loss, overall health, productivity, and quality of life.

STRATEGY #3 – CATEGORIZING YOUR DAY TYPE

We have created day mapping so that you can identify your changing schedule, carpool days from hell, lazy family fun days, working-late days, sick days, and vacation days. Track this for a month. How many of each day do you experience? We suggest day mapping in the following way. Get a calendar and mark each day as one of the above day types. Then tally up how many of each day type you've had. You can now map your schedule around your physiology and reset yourself and your family for fat loss.

As an example, let's look at one of our clients. Her name is Stacey and she sells real estate, has three children and cares for an ailing parent. She performed the day mapping exercise and had 16 carpool days from hell, 1 lazy family day, 8 work-late days, 3 sick days and a 3-day weekend vacation. We can clearly see her pattern in order to press reset. Pressing reset means that you deduct 4-6 hours from your week first, and then plan your schedule with the remaining time. Make the conscious decision to build your time around the life sustaining rhythms of physical activity, planned nutrition and rest. The change to a healthier lifestyle is in the midst. Shift towards creating opportunities to work with your body. Use the Power Prioritizing technique and create your reset formula:

1. Carve out 1 uninterrupted hour per week for nutrition planning.

2. Plug 12 strength-training days into your schedule for the month.

3. Fill your week with 2-3 high intensity interval sessions.

4. Include 4 relaxation days in your family's monthly plan.

Combine this with your day mapping. Let's get back to Stacey's example and what we coached her through:

- Saturdays were designated as relaxing family days (these made great nutritional cheat days which are an essential part of family fat loss success; for more on strategic cheat meals, visit: http://www.achievefitnessny.com).

- On Sunday, Stacey found it very realistic to wake up early and spend an hour in her quiet kitchen planning the family's nutrition for the week. She also set a family date every Sunday at 4pm for a strength training session.

- Mondays, Wednesdays and Thursdays were typically carpool days so we used interval family activity on these days. These 20-minute fat blasts were ideal for busy days.

- Tuesdays and Fridays were mostly working-late days for either Stacey or her spouse and were used for strength training since the kids did not have as many activities.

- We used sick days to reflect on meal planning, identifying missed opportunities and adjusting for overall success at the end of the month (could also be an additional interval training session – depending on the sickness situation).

- Vacation days were ideal for restoration and were reserved for some overfeeding. Walking/hiking were a part of long weekends and on longer trips sticking to strength and interval training was easier without the time crunch from work and school.

**Reset Alert* – *With the stress of work, activities and in Stacey's case, caring for a sick parent, it is crucial to schedule relaxation days in order to reduce stress. Remember that stress causes fat-storing hormones to be released in the system.*

This is about pressing reset. Evaluate your priorities and ask yourself – How important is it to you to have a fit family? If this goal is truly what you want, then we have given you some solid tools to shape your behavior and reset the button on your physiology. Whether you have six kids or one baby, an ailing parent or a special needs child. If you are a single parent or keep a strictly kosher household it can be done. Don't fall victim to your own self-limiting beliefs. Decide what's important and get your habits on track to match your family fat loss goals. 'Too busy' and 'too tired' are too dangerous to your family's health!

About Dianne

Dianne Sykes Scope MS NSCA is the CEO and head exercise physiologist for Achieve Fitness. She has 15 years of personal training and exercise physiology experience and is certified by the National Strength and Conditioning Association. She has eight years of health club management experience. Dianne received a Bachelor of Science in Sport Management from the University of Massachusetts and continued on to earn a Master's Degree in Exercise Physiology from Adelphi University. Her dedication to fitness exceeded academia, as she was a Division I Track & Field athlete and Atlantic 10 Conference champion at UMass in the 400m hurdles.

Dianne was appointed to the New York State Directorship for the National Strength and Conditioning Association in 2004 and was published in the American College of Sports Medicine's journal for scientific research on personal training effectiveness in May of 2007. She is a nationally renowned speaker on topics in the field of family fat loss for disease prevention, and is dedicated to enhancing the family practices of health professionals throughout the country. Dianne has gained a depth of field experience working with families over the years and is considered a leading expert in family fat loss.

Dianne is a master educator for Equinox Health Clubs and Soul Cycle where she regularly contributes, creates and teaches curriculum. She works directly with personal trainers and instructors on the foundations of exercise physiology.

She has been featured in *Shape Magazine* and *Parent Guide News*.

Whether she is coaching families, training clients, teaching professionals or writing articles, it is her focused mission to create healthier lives for parents and their children. Dianne's fervor for family fat loss infiltrates every family coaching visit, personal training session, and presentation and looks enthusiastically to a fitter future for American families.

For more information on her services or to set up a family fat loss plan,

Please call 516-568-7507 or email: dscope@achievefitnessny.com.

CHAPTER 9

It's Small Steps, NOT Massive Change to Success

By Derek Decater

Decater, you're FAT!

I heard that phrase a couple of times my freshman year of college. It may sound harsh, but as coach liked to say, he was "motivated by the truth" — and the truth was I was a little on the chunky side. I just thought I was big-boned.

At the time it was just another day at practice, but looking back that was the beginning of this whole journey.

Over the course of the next four years, my dreams of playing professional baseball slowly started to shift. Each year, after each surgery, I dove deeper into the field of physiology, physical therapy, sports performance and nutrition. I found myself studying physiology and biomechanics in the locker room when I should have been out on the field working on my swing. Problem was it hurt to swing and throw, which just made me study more. Ultimately, I earned my degree in physiology, became a certified strength coach and have been learning ever since.

Years later, I had developed all the skill and knowledge to start fixing my body. I had a good grasp on injury mechanics and fat loss, my two personal weaknesses. I looked at the big picture and determined what needed to change for me to reach my goals.

The foundation was there it was just a matter of doing it! So I did and went from 220 and fat to 180 at 5% body fat. There was no magic to it. No secret diet. No secret program. It was just consistent work.

LESSONS FROM COACH

I learned a lot from coach, yes, that I was fat, but also life lessons that ring true outside of the baseball field. One that always stood out was to, "Execute the process." Without knowing it, I had actually listened. Not so amazingly, the results came...weird!

Fast forward a few years...

I'm now training athletes and the general population full-time. I was writing some legit programs and designing some awesome nutrition plans. The only problem was my clients weren't getting the results they should have been!

Around this time, I am getting fed up with non-compliant clients and decided I wanted to try something new, something that at the time I thought would be more challenging. I took a position at a physical therapy clinic working with post-rehab patients. I had always thought about going to PT school, so I thought this would be a good fit.

It's a good thing I did because physical therapy is slow! Too slow, and just like at the gym, patients just flat out weren't doing their exercises that we knew would keep them healthy. Thinking that it was the clientele that was the problem and my own desire to have clients that were actually motivated, I left the clinic and opened Decater Performance.

Like everyone who opens a business, I thought this was going to explode! I mean seriously...check out these programs I'm designing right? I know this works...I did it!

Here's what the business plan looked like back then: –

- Give clients a great workout
- Include injury prevention strategies within the great workout
- Give them meal plans
- Give them corrective exercises
- Give them flexibility, mobility, stability and a lot of other "-ibilities"

- Give them the template for success.
- They get great results
- I get more clients
- Everyone loves me
- I'm famous
- Hollywood makes a movie about the greatest fitness program in the world staring Ryan Reynolds as Derek Decater

Still waiting on that movie.

Nowhere in that business plan did reality enter my mind. The reality was clients were still not getting the results they wanted. Enter some serious internal reflection, more studying, more mentorship programs and more program design.

IF THEY CAN'T DO IT, HOW CAN I GET YOU TO?

At the time, I was also training some college and professional athletes and noticed something. Even they had bad workouts. How does someone being paid to be in-shape have bad workouts and be inconsistent with their nutrition? Finally I started to piece things together. I looked at what I had been doing the last few years. I looked at what guys like John Barardi and Alwyn Cosgrove were doing and a light bulb went on.

If professional athletes aren't 100% compliant, how could I ever expect a mother of three, with a job, soccer practice, homework to be supervised and meals to be made, do it?

The light bulb was this. I was giving everyone the wrong plan! I was giving them what I knew would get results but I wasn't giving them the tools they needed to execute. We used to joke about it in college when asked what the plan was against a tough team. "Score more runs than them."

That's what I had been doing. I taught them that we needed to score more runs (duh), but I never taught them how to bunt, how to move runners, how to play defense, how to pitch, how to steal or most importantly, how to think.

Everything had to change and it had to change now. (I was still waiting on the movie deal.)

MEET APRIL

April is a 50-year old woman who recently lost 45 pounds, got off all of her medication, had to buy all new clothes, gained tons of self-confidence and has loads of energy. April had been fighting an uphill battle her whole life. Statistically her chance and your chance of rapid and sustained weight loss in a self-guided program are small. It's a step above nil, nothing, nada.

So what was the secret to her success? Going to boot camp, lifting weights, going to spin class, going to yoga classes and eating like a champ. Easy, right? Exercise more and eat less. OK, that's not the secret because that's what I and thousands of trainers and coaches all over the country tell their clients to do. The secret is that I didn't tell April to do any of this, at least not initially.

April is no different to any of you. She is no different than the hundreds of clients I've had before her. She came to me with vague goals, no plan, no nutritional education and no exercise experience.

In her own words, she said, "When we started, my goal was just to try and lose a little bit of weight. I didn't really know what my expectations were, because at that point I didn't understand how lifting weights and building muscle led to weight loss. That was foreign to me."

She was shy and quiet and used the lightest weight possible. It's funny for me to think about this now as I'm writing this, because April is not the same person anymore. She comes to class and jokes around, she grabs the heavy stuff and she flat out gets after it!

So what got her where she is today? Executing the process. Executing her new habits. The habits we systematically developed and implemented into her life that would set the foundation from which the true "plan" could be achieved. For her, it was about "slowly getting rid of old behavior patterns and learning how to eat in a healthy way."

The "plan" was to increase exercise and improve nutrition, just as the "plan" to win a baseball game is to score more than the other team. The habits were the steps needed to execute the plan.

HABIT BY HABIT

Each piece of the plan has smaller pieces and habits within it. Exercise and nutrition each had specific habits that needed to be built into the program. Throughout the program, all the habits were small and achievable.

The first was to get up an hour early three days a week and come to boot camp. Once that was easy we started to add to April's fitness tool box. From the exercise side of the fat loss equation we progressed from the ground up. Teaching movement and technique was essential before moving on.

Each core exercise was broken down into its pieces and learned. Eventually each piece came together to form the whole. Through this process exercise technique was engrained and the foundation was cemented. Only after her technique and knowledge of the movements became second nature, could we progress to truly training.

Before moving on, this brings up another important key to April's success and your success. Your goal is not to exercise; your goal is to train. Exercise is mindless movement. Training is purposeful. We trained with a goal in mind: to build technique so that future training could, one, not be side-tracked by injury and two, to have a foundation from which we could add to.

Too often, I see people skipping steps in their exercise programs. They are not giving the foundation enough attention and being impatient to get to the big money exercises. In the end strength gains, muscle gains and fat loss potential is limited by your lack of a technical foundation. This makes continued progress difficult and stalls most casual "exercisers" progress. Try to build a skyscraper on the foundation of a house. You'll make progress, always flirting with disaster, until the inevitable happens and everything crumbles to the ground.

OK, back to April and her transformation. Eventually through this process of habit acquisition April become much more versed in her exercise skills. Yes, they are skills.

What started as three days a week of boot camp evolved – first a spin class…then another spin class…then a strength program at the gym - which we looked at as an entirely new habit and as such started with a basic program, again going through the same process of building habits at the gym. Note that going to the gym was a habit in and of itself. What she did at the gym were all entirely new habits so we took it slow.

The gym program progressed and what started out very basic is now much more complicated. April went to a yoga class. She liked it so we added it. Nutritionally the process was the same. Start with this, add that, then add this and so on. Next thing you know she's eating healthy without even having to think about it and it all becomes much more manageable.

Today the process has come full circle for April – "For the first few months, I was afraid to eat out in a restaurant. But over time I realized that I have control over what I order and can eat out and make healthy food choices and not feel like, Oh my God I'm going to gain weight this weekend because I went out to dinner. So it's really been a lifestyle change – not being on a diet. I have really changed the way I eat for life, and I feel so much better and have so much more energy now. That has a positive affect on everything else in my life."

Had I gone to April from day one and said, "Ok, you want to lose 40 pounds, get off medication and increase energy levels. After looking at your goals and going over our assessments, I've developed a plan that will be guaranteed to get you those results. All you need to do is go to three 5:30 am boot camps a week, two spin classes and do this program at the gym 2-3 nights a week. At the gym I want you doing X, Y and Z in a circuit format with 70% of your 1-rep max. Oh, and here's a meal plan you need to follow. I've designed it so that you will be getting around 25% carbs, 40% protein and 35% fat. Each meal has been broken down into grams to make things easier for you. You'll need to revamp your kitchen by removing all the "bad" stuff and adding in all the "good" foods I've outlined here. Yes, I know you've never heard of Quinoa, and you don't have time to eat 4-5 meals a day, but if you want results this is what you have to do."

Can you imagine going from not exercising or eating healthy to trying to add all this to your already busy life? Hell no! Yet that's exactly what many do…I know I did.

THE SECRET IS NOT NUTRITION AND IT'S NOT EXERCISE

If weight loss was as simple as nutrition and exercise, we wouldn't be where we're at as a society today. There is more information on the subject than ever before. You can see it on reality TV, you can find it on magazine racks and you can search for it online. Yet we are as 'out of shape' as we have ever been, and it's not because we don't know what needs to be done, it's because we don't know HOW to get it done.

How to get it done is what April learned and it's what I teach our members. No matter what your goal is, you need to learn 'how to execute the plan' before you can actually execute the plan.

This simplistic approach is what makes the difference.

MY CHALLENGE TO YOU

Keep it simple. Start with a goal, put a timeframe on it, ask yourself how important this goal is and how achieving this goal will change your life. Now... learn how to swing the bat before you jump into the game.

A few ideas to help get you started.

- Find a group, a class, a boot camp or a training partner. Commit to driving there, that's it, that's the habit. Let the group make the decisions about the workout for you. (Obviously do your research here. Find an experienced, trained, competent partner and/ or trainer.)

- Wake up 20 min early. Don't even worry about making breakfast yet. Just get up. Next week you can think about breakfast. I've been in this situation. I used to not get up (still sometimes won't) early because the thought of getting out of bed AND making breakfast was too much. It was two new things I had to deal with. One habit at a time.

- Eat slower. This is just plain physiology. It takes time for your brain to signal you are full so give it that time.

- Focus on learning one new exercise, not the entire fitness magazine glossary.

- Foam-roll for a few minutes each day and build on it.

- Add a protein to each meal. Then starting eating it first. This little gem plus eating slower will seriously help in controlling food intake.

- Swing a Kettlebell for five minutes a couple times a week. Add to it next week.

These are all just a few of many great ideas…a few small goals to get the ball rolling in the right direction. Any one of these would be a great start. Then, like April, you pick another and add it.

Over time, like in life, you build and learn what works for you and what doesn't. Which brings me back to coach, "If something you're doing isn't working, you'd better try something else." (Definitely paraphrased right there.)

So if you've been trying to change everything all at once and it hasn't worked, maybe it's time to change one thing at a time.

Best of luck! I'd love to hear how it goes for you.

About Derek

Derek Decater is the owner of Decater Performance just outside of Seattle, Washington. Known for his comprehensive approach to adult fat loss bootcamps and his expertise in training baseball players, Derek is a performance coach sought after in the Greater Seattle area.

Derek earned his bachelor's degree in physiology from the University of Arizona's School of Medicine while also playing for the Wildcat Baseball Program. Derek went on to earn his CSCS from the National Strength and Conditioning Association and began training soon after graduation. After taking a position as Wellness Director at a local physical therapy clinic, Derek made the decision to take what he learned in the physical therapy field and start applying it to performance training.

Derek's science-driven fat loss bootcamps are quickly becoming the model for those in the industry. Having combined his expertise in Russian kettlebell training, TRX training, injury prevention and corrective exercise, nutrition, metabolic training and strength training, Derek's bootcamps have consistently produced results all while staying in-line with his most core belief, *that training should not only be about fat loss but about improving health and function.* Always mindful that not all exercises are right for all people at all times, Derek's bootcamps are always adapting, from member to member, from class to class, so that everyone walks away feeling better, looking better and most importantly – educated on exercise and nutrition.

Athletes at all levels have gravitated towards Derek's approach to performance training. Derek has proven that strength, power and performance can all be achieved while maintaining an emphasis on total body function and injury prevention. His athletes not only gain strength and power, but also reduce their risk of injury.

Whether coming to Derek for fat loss or athletics, clients soon see the difference between working out and training.

You can find-out more about Derek and Decater Performance at:
www.DecaterPerformance.com
Or at his blog: www.DerekDecater.com

CHAPTER 10

Role of Conditioning: Specific Stages of Fitness Development

By Gary Steffensen,
Peak Results Fitness

INTRODUCTION

You've finally decided to get into the gym to lose fat and get fit. Good for you! Your general wellbeing, across all five dimensions of health – physical, emotional, social, cognitive and spiritual – can dramatically improve by maintaining a basic level of fitness. New research has also shown than fitness helps combat aging, helping the body "recycle" itself by constantly renewing and rebuilding cells.

But maybe you're feeling a little anxious. Mentally and physically, you're not sure what to expect. Will I be sore? Will it hurt? Can I keep up my regular routine and activities as I begin a new fitness program? You might be uncertain about whether a particular fitness facility and coach can meet your needs.

These are all good questions!

After twenty-five years experience as an elite ski coach, I can tell you that the most challenging part of any program for elite athletes is to develop a sound mental and physical foundation. With preparation, top-notch athletes are able perform to the highest level in practice and competition. Without preparation and a good mental attitude, they can't perform up to par and become injury-prone.

These same stages of fitness and skill development also apply to you, as you make your quest for fitness and make the choice to adopt a new, healthy lifestyle.

Whether you're already very fit, or are starting from square one, you can benefit from working with a good trainer in a good fitness facility, or starting a well-considered program at home.

Be confident; you can make great strides toward becoming fit, even if you don't feel you're destined to become a world-class athlete!

STAGES OF FITNESS DEVELOPMENT

1. Discomfort stage
When you begin an exercise program you'll undergo many levels of transformation. Initially, you may feel tired. You'll likely have "delayed onset muscle soreness" (DOMS.) You must learn techniques for and the importance of recovery. Fitness may seem like a far off dream.

A good fitness coach and a plan for staying motivated will help get you through these hard times!

2. Physical stage
Once you're past the initial discomfort stage, you'll begin to experience the fruits of your labor. Improvements become obvious: you have more energy and your clothes fit better. Maybe your cholesterol, your blood sugar, or your blood pressure drops.

Your exercise regime is now an integral part of your everyday activity. You start to look forward to the results. Maybe fitness is within your grasp after all!

3. Psychological stage
In this stage, your brain takes over. You exercise religiously regardless of the circumstances. You work out not only for the physical benefits, but also for the psychological effects.

Whether you want to achieve overall fitness (health-related fitness) or you're training for a specific sport (sport-related fitness), you'll benefit at this stage. Health-related fitness means you maintain your body's systems at a level that allows you to perform your daily activities without excess fatigue, illness or stress. Sport-related fitness ensures you can successfully complete the specialized movements required by a particular physical activity, like skiing, running or swimming.

From now on, I predict you will crave fitness and physical activity, and it will become an intrinsic part of your everyday life.

NUTRITION

Establishing and maintaining a healthful diet is crucial to your overall success on any fitness program. The right foods help regulate blood sugar, balance hormones, and maximize energy, all of which promote optimal fat burning and muscle development.

The proper balance of the basic macronutrients – carbohydrates, proteins and fats – is often debated. The truth? The correct mix depends on you and your individual biochemical needs. Eat the right amount of food at the right times.

When I worked as a ski coach, I would tell my athletes, "A proper diet can't make an average athlete elite, but a poor diet can make an elite athlete average."

How often and how much should I eat?
A combination of four to six meals and snacks daily is right for nearly everyone. Think of fueling a fire – your metabolism – and you'll understand why consuming small, frequent meals is the best way to eat.

Eat more to burn more
Our society wants us to believe that low-calorie diets always lead to weight loss. But those super-low calorie diets (1000-1200 calories daily) can actually backfire: your body actually goes into "efficiency mode", conserving fat because it perceives that you are starving!

Post-exercise recovery
Want to avoid a post-workout crash? Pay special attention to refueling your body after exercise with a high-quality protein shake with micro-nutrient-dense carbohydrates. You've earned your carbohydrates! Eating the right food at this stage means you're accelerating your fat loss and rebuilding your glycogen stores lost as you exercise.

Research a high-quality, organic protein powder that works for you. Whey-based protein should come from grass-fed beef, and soy should be derived from non-genetically modified soy plants. Mix protein powder with real fruit or look for a high-nutrient fruit pureé. Experiment until you find a combination you like.

Hydrate!

Water promotes fat loss and helps the body function properly. Drink half your body weight in ounces every day; if you weigh 145 lbs, drink 72 ounces of water every day, or about nine eight-ounce glasses of water daily.

MAKING TIME TO WORK OUT

In today's world, finding time to work out is a big challenge. You **must** make your workouts a priority: no one else is going to make this happen for you! Just as you apply the 80/20 rule to the rest of your life, apply it to your workouts. Focus eighty percent of your time and energy on the twenty percent of the activities that matter most. "Work smarter, not harder" means also working on the things that matter most!

A key to this concept is making sure the facility you've chosen has the right environment. Are they focused on your wellbeing? Are the workout programs designed based on scientific concepts? Are the workouts challenging? As you become more fit, does the intensity of exercise become more difficult? Workouts should generally not last more then sixty minutes. The approach should be fresh, energetic and positive!

Of course, every day is different. You'll naturally have some fluctuations in your abilities to perform in the gym, but **the trend of your overall fitness will be upward.**

Frequency of exercise

Plan to exercise two to four times per week, with appropriate passive and active rest days between sessions at the gym. Your workout should change every four to six weeks. This is really important: your body gets used to the same old workout. If you've been doing the same thing for years, your body has adapted and your workout is no longer effective. If you want to boost your metabolism, increase strength, decrease your injury rate and improve your functional movement, you must change your routine.

While the specific exercises change every four weeks, the best workout all follow this formula:

- SMR (self myofacial release) with foam roller
- Corrective exercises to address your particular weaknesses
- RAMP (Range of motion, Activation, Movement, Preparation) exercises
- Core stability and mobility
- Power development
- Strength training
- Metabolic "finisher"

The "progressions" in your fitness routine should be scientifically-designed to ensure that your results are achievable and are reinforced with positive feedback. Pay special attention to these two principals: it's not just how you perform, it's how you improve over time.

MOTIVATION

How can you motivate yourself? First, have fun! Fun stimulates and excites you to stay accountable. Reward yourself and feel worthy. You'll feel competent, be successful and see results!

If your fitness coach takes the fun out of your routine, I guarantee you'll lose motivation. We need to feel good about ourselves, and fun challenges help us do that.

But what happens to our self-worth when we slip? Maybe you missed a training session or splurged too often, and you feel like you've failed. I call these 'speed bumps' and they're part of life.

How do you overcome them?

1. Stop what you're doing and start over. Revisit your reasons for getting fit. A mistake is not a failure if the failure leads to success. Success means achieving YOUR goals.

2. Is your coach helping you stay motivated? A great fitness coach can make a huge difference. What works for one person, may not be a good fit for another. Make a change if you need to.

3. Build in *extrinsic* rewards for your successes. Track your re-

sults and get praise from your coaches, then reward yourself with (for example) new clothes: "After twenty workouts, I'm going to buy myself some new 'skinny' jeans."

4. Recognize the *intrinsic* rewards of working out. Your coach and fitness facility must create the right atmosphere and culture to help you develop an affinity for working out. In the right environment, you will recognize that you love the way you feel when you work out; working out becomes its own reward.

Use all your tools to keep yourself on track. Staying active in your facility's "shape-up" challenges can help keep you motivated when your internal motivation isn't quite there, especially during your initial quest for fitness. Your internal motivation will help you kick things into high gear over the long run, which over time has greater value.

MOTIVATION TOOLS

When you feel yourself slipping, revisit this list and see where you're falling short. Which of these tools can you use to address your lack of motivation?

Set goals for yourself. Can you work your way into your skinny jeans? Do you need to lower your blood pressure or cholesterol levels? Can you lower your body fat percentage?

Build variety into your training program. Make sure you're changing your routine every four to six weeks, not only to keep your body guessing, but also to keep you interested in your workouts.

Train hard AND train smart. If you're not seeing results, you won't be motivated. Spend 80% of your time on the most valuable 20% of your workouts.

Notice your results. Do you have a before/after picture? What health benefits are you reaping from your fitness routine?

Remember your reasons for exercising. Are you doing it to keep up with your kids? To relieve stress? To address a health concern? Use positive cues to remind yourself of these reasons.

Use your journal to keep track of food and workouts. Journaling helps you evaluate where you need to improve.

Look outside yourself for motivation. When your personal motivation falls short, look for inspiration in fitness books and magazines.

Find a reliable workout buddy. Be a reliable workout buddy.

Are you having fun? Remember that fun translates to more feelings of self-worth, which is self-motivating!

Think right. Is your self-talk undermining your ability to take the right actions? Beliefs are powerful, and you can change them if they're not serving you.

Remember: see results, feel successful, feel worthy, repeat! *

(*Note that this copy would work well in a "cycle" graphic.)

ADAPTATION

A good trainer will help you match the degree of difficulty to your skill level, so that your fitness progressively improves. An effective exercise program gradually increases the intensity and volume of work, and is specific to your individual and present fitness levels.

Your program must progressively challenge your body, while not crossing the line into over-training. Training too often or working at too high a level for your individual fitness is counterproductive and undermines your success.

It only takes four to six weeks for your body to adapt to a particular routine! Achieve maximum results and avoid fitness "plateaus" with changes to intensity, frequency, volume and tempo of your workouts.

Training harder does not always equal a higher return. Working out with an effective training program with the right amount of intensity and being consistent will help you achieve your goals.

Adaptation results in:

5. Better heart function, circulation, respiration and blood volume

6. Better flexibility, strength, power, strength endurance and fat loss

7. Better bone and mineral density, tougher ligaments, tendons and connective tissue

8. Overall better health

RECOVERY

Workout all you want, but without good recovery you could be wasting your workout!

First work out, then rest adequately.

Rest allows your body to remake itself in a new form: a fitter, leaner, healthier you. Your routine teaches your body to better respond to physiological and psychological stresses, but without time to rest and recover you're just adding to the stresses of everyday life.

Normal feelings of tiredness and muscle soreness are typical, but if you're lethargic or have the inability to concentrate you may not be recovering adequately.

Recovery techniques:

Get enough sleep. Sleep is the most important form of passive rest. Its value cannot be underestimated. If you're not sleeping enough to feel rested, find out why and correct the situation.

Adequate hydration. Drink plain water throughout the day and during your workouts. Drink half your body weight in ounces to promote healthy functioning of your body's systems, and help carry away excess fat.

Fuel your recovery. Post-workout, consume additional carbohydrates and protein. Immediately after your workout, your body is most receptive to the replacement of glycogen, which helps boost your energy and your recovery.

Make sure you're not overtraining. If you're feeling extra tired, you may be doing too many workouts each week, or attempting to move up too quickly in weight or reps.

Get therapeutic massage. Use a foam roller to help work the kinks out. Your trainer should be able to teach you some great foam roller moves to help alleviate any muscle soreness. You might also want to investigate the use of infrared sauna, if that's available to you.

Meditate or just have quiet time. Meditation, or even just resting quietly, can produce powerful results for improving your outlook on life, visualizing change, and for understanding how to implement change.

Take time for "active" rest. Hiking, biking, swimming and tennis, when done at moderately intense levels can help your body recover from your gym workouts. They're also great stress-relievers!

SUMMARY

As you move through the stages of fitness development, from initial discomfort to having a strong commitment to fitness, you'll begin to see that progress is inevitable and predictable, no matter what kind of shape you're in at this very moment. You can be more fit by following very specific instructions about nutrition, about the structure and timing of your workouts, and about how to best recover from your workouts.

Make time to work out. It really is true that showing up is half the battle. Use these tools I've given you to stay motivated and move forward in your quest for better health and fitness.

Begin by taking just one step towards a better lifestyle every day.

Develop and maintain a positive mental attitude and you can overcome a lot of the challenges you'll face.

"Get fit and change your life!"

About Gary

Gary Steffensen, Peak Results Fitness

During his 25-year career as an alpine ski coach, Gary Steffensen guided elite athletes to their highest results through program design, skill development and motivation. As Head Coach/ Director of University of Nevada-Reno ski team, he led the team to two national championships. Gary was a part of Western Region coaching staff and National Training System for the U.S. Ski Team, during which he traveled the world with many elite ski racers on the United States Ski Team, many of whom are now current Olympians.

He is an International Certified Ski Coach, NSCA-CPT, Fitness Institute of Australia CPT. He earned a Bachelor of Science degree in Sports Science at the University of Nevada-Reno.

Since 2008, Gary has co-owned Peak Results Fitness in Flagstaff, Arizona where he coaches elite athletes and "regular" people who are committed to fitness. His motto is "Get fit, and change your life!"

CHAPTER 11

The Best Way To Hit Your Goals, Really!

By Darren Garland

Knowing how your brain works matters more than knowing how your body works.

In the Fall of 1999, I purchased a book about body transformation that started my personal training journey even though I didn't realize it at the time. The book, which sold over 4 million copies to date, promised dramatic changes in *only 12 weeks*. I remember getting so excited to see a detailed workout plan, menu, and recipes included in an "easy to follow" package, especially since I was told that I could eat whatever I wanted on my one "amnesty" day each week.

I fully expected to get shredded with six-pack abs in twelve weeks. How could I fail with all of the elements detailed with such precision? And, the book included all of those **unbelievable** before and after pictures. Keep in mind, I started my 12-week odyssey at almost 30% body fat and nearly 350 pounds.

Fast-forward twelve weeks and, after irritating all my relatives and peers with my active "crusade", I had lost 35 lbs or 10% of my body weight and felt moderately better. Sadly, I felt like I had failed because I wasn't extremely lean, I had expended a lot of personal energy and I didn't even look like those "after" pictures.

In retrospect, two key factors prevented me from achieving my goal.

First, I did not distinguish between setting "outcome" goals and "behavioral" goals. Second, I completely ignored my logical and emotional underpinnings. I remember learning about the id, ego and superego in school. Yet, I hadn't translated the reality of those parts of my brain into the reality of my "life." Thankfully, the emerging science of behavioral psychology tackles the exact issues which hindered me from achieving my physical goals.

THE TORTOISE AND THE HARE

Leo Babauta in the his book " The Power of Less" notes that in order to create a sustainable habit you need to address **one** habit at a time. His research posits that you can successfully adopt a new habit 85% of the time. But, if you try to make two new habits stick, your success rate falls dramatically to 33%. Focus on three habits and your success rate falls to an abysmal 17%. I might as well have been one of the study subjects identified in the research. Let's look back at my transformation process.

Before starting the program, a healthy meal for me was adding canned mushrooms to my macaroni and cheese. My workouts were pulled directly out of the muscle magazines and my lifestyle included all of the vices and excesses of a recent college graduate.

The program which I tried, at its core, pushed me to change almost all of my bad habits in an abbreviated timeline. Realistically, the only change I truly made was the personal awakening to avoid all muscle magazines hawking "quick fix" supplements. Do we really think we can "Add an inch to your biceps in 1 hour?" I have since come to the realization that changing one small habit would have yielded much better long-term success.

CHUNKY STYLE

Fitness Expert Alwyn Cosgrove often talks about the use of "manageable chunks" or manageable steps when dealing with change with his clients. If I pleaded with you to stop eating "badly" and to start eating "cleanly", it would be confusing, lead to further questioning and you might wonder how I'm helping you, my client. Why?

First, I haven't defined any of the tenets of "clean" eating. Plus, I haven't made it a manageable endeavor, given the amount and complexity of the change. In effect, I challenged your behavior, labeled it as wrong, and expected that you would graciously accept my counsel. Forget the fact that I haven't provided you with any tools or tactics to implement this new transformation.

The better option for success is to begin with an easy step change and repeat until it becomes habit. Then, once it is mastered, continue the habit and adopt a new one.

Fitness Nutritionist expert, John Berardi, has developed a twelve month (not weeks) body transformation program called 'Lean Eating" and he starts every new client with an easy habit. Every day, the client is required to take a multivitamin and the number of grams of fish oil equal to their current body fat percentage. The habit is practiced for two weeks, ingrained in behavior, and then, a second habit is added. This iterative process continues throughout the program. The "Lean Eating" program has produced some of the best long-term body transformations ever seen, and it works using manageable steps and placing the emphasis on behavioral goals and not outcome goals.

EATING THE ELEPHANT

The old question "How do you eat an elephant?" is typically introduced when one faces a challenge perceived to be insurmountable. It is readily answered "One bite at a time." There is much validity to this generic answer when tackling large projects, but this mantra needs to be reevaluated in its actual practice.

Clients consistently ask how they can lose (insert number) lbs and the traditional method usually follows: create a workout, eat a specific diet and check your weight daily/weekly/monthly to measure progress. What is seldom discussed is how the body is going to respond to this approach. People fall into the trap of using "outcome" goals instead of using "behavioral" goals which yield our desired outcomes.

You can't control the outcome, but you can control the behaviors that, when done consistently, will lead to the desired outcome. If you want to sell your house for a good price, you can renovate it and give it a fresh coat of paint. But you can't control the real estate market. If you want to have a nice picnic with your spouse, you can pack a basket and blanket and plan your route to the park. But you can't control the weather.

If you want to lose weight, you can eat well and stay active. But you can't control your fat cells or genetic predispositions. You can't make your body lose 20 pounds on command any more than you can make sure your house is worth a certain amount when you sell it.

In other words, *you can't control the outcome.* But you **can** control the behaviors that *lead to the outcome you want.* So instead of setting "outcome goals," one needs to focus on setting "behavioral goals."

Here are some examples showing the difference between approaches:

Outcome Goals

- Run a 5K race in four months
- Lift 150 pounds on the bench press
- Eat four servings of vegetables a day

Behavioral Goals

- Run for 20 minutes three times per week for the next month, gradually increasing the duration
- Perfect my form on the bench press and use challenging weights
- Write down a list of six vegetables I like and go to the grocery store every week to buy them.

Notice how all of the behavioral goals are a commitment to do a specific set of actions or tasks. Also, notice how the behavioral goals are things you do consistently and regularly.

RIDING THE ELEPHANT

Up to this point, we have covered the logical/analytical idea of change. Now, we must address the emotional side if we are going to be successful. Fortunately, for us, the emerging science of behavioral psychology is exploring how to deal with both our emotional and logical self. The science aptly applied to economics can be utilized equally in analyzing our health and fitness regimens.

Chip and Dan Heath's new book, Switch, contains the subtitled section, "How to change things when change is hard." Since change is never easy, the book's change model and supporting anecdotal evidence encourages anyone needing motivational support.

The book unveils the characters of "The Elephant," the emotional side of change, and "The Rider," its rational side. In the first chapter, "Perched atop the Elephant," the Rider holds the reins and seems to be the leader. But the Rider's control is precarious because the Rider is so small relative to the Elephant. The Switch model instructs us to address the rational side of change (Direct the Rider) as well as the emotional side (Motivate the Elephant). The model then adds a third, crucial step: address the environment for change (Shape the Path).

Most workouts program start with logical progressions and sound science but they lack the realization that humans are emotional creatures. Set and repetition patterns, time under tension, high threshold motor units, and the more complicated exercise jargon have their role in the fitness vernacular. Yet, if a person does not actually complete the workout because they are emotionally and physically drained from the stress of outside life, the greatest analytically-devised workout program fails.

Emotions are a key factor in goal setting and need to be accounted for if we are to be successful. The pachyderm referenced in "Switch", the elephant, is a skittish creature and avoids change at all cost. Our emotional self is hardwired to have a fight or flee response to change. Even though we have updated our brain software from the early hunter-gatherers living 10,000 years ago, our primitive response (hardware) can't be reasoned with.

However, you can make the elephant more comfortable with the change by giving it simple instructions (Behavioral Goals) and rewarding success and laying off the whip of self-sacrifice and will power. Most clients, myself included, failed miserably when attempting to rely solely on will power to make lasting change.

Not surprisingly, long-term change comes from making a plan for the rider (logic) using behavioral goals with time lines and metrics, creating a positive environment for the elephant (emotional) to feel comfortable, and keep on the path to success.

The last part of the successful transformation entails shaping the path or "environment" in which the change occurs. For example, let's focus on how our diet can be affected by our environment.

MINDLESS EATING AND OUR ENVIRONMENT

Research has shown that shaping the path is important because our environment affects our eating habits more than we consciously understand. For instance, research shows that:

- We eat more from bigger bowls than smaller ones. And if the bowl is endlessly refilled, we'll just keep on consuming.
- We eat more from candy dishes that are close to us than dishes that are a few meters away.
- We're more likely to stop for a snack if we enter our homes through the kitchen door rather than the front door.
- We pace our eating speed to other people. If we eat with fast, hearty eaters, that's what we'll become too.
- We'll eat until the dish, package, or container is empty (even if that container is a giant bucket of days-old popcorn).
- We'll eat nearly one-third more food while watching 60 minutes of TV compared to watching 30 minutes.

In other words, we're strongly influenced by food cues and stimuli from the people, things, and overall environment around us. In fact, research shows most of our food decisions have nothing to do with hunger, but are actually determined by what and who are around us, along with our habits and familiar routines.

CHANGE YOUR ENVIRONMENT, CHANGE YOUR BODY

Be aware of what you're seeing, doing, and experiencing. Look around your home and workplace and think about how to change where, how, and with whom you eat.

For instance:

- Sit at a table to eat
- Use smaller dishes
- Keep "problem foods" farther away and healthy foods closer
- Notice when the people around you are encouraging you to over-eat
- Eat slowly (10 minute minimum per meal) without distractions such as TV

- Avoid fast food restaurants — they're designed to get you in and out quickly. (Ever wonder why those chairs are so darn uncomfortable?

FILTERING FOR SUCCESS

In this book, you will be exposed to cutting-edge fitness concepts and training ideas I know you will want to incorporate immediately into your life. Filter all of these concepts through your behavioral psychology lens. Start with the smallest habit that will move you towards your goal. Direct the rider with behavioral goals, praise the Elephant with success and clear the path and make your environment conducive to success.

If I could travel back in time to the early years of my health/lifestyle quest, I wish I knew about the factors determining my success and made the appropriate decisions. I would have started with a small habit like eliminating carbonated, sugar beverages from my diet. For me it turned out soda was a trigger leading me to further temptations. I found drinking soda was just a habitual part of my life.

After making this small change, I noticed a chain reaction of good habits resulting from this simple catalyst. Your challenge is to examine your current habits and pinpoint which one you can change today. That one, small step will yield lifelong success and start you on a path to successfully reaching your goals.

About Darren

Darren Garland is a real world fitness expert who specializes in fat loss and lifestyle improvement for women. Known for his unorthodox ability to get clients results, he has helped thousands of people incinerate unwanted body fat. In addition to being the founder of Emerge Fitness Center, he is also the creator of the "Muffin-Top Meltdown" fitness program, which has been featured on both NBC and ABC. Darren has gone from fat kid to fitness expert. At one point he was 370 pounds, unhealthy, unhappy, and lacking confidence. His personal journey to a healthy body and lifestyle is what sparked his passion for helping others achieve their goals

To learn more about Darren Garland, the real world fitness expert and receive his Muffin-Top Meltdown report please visit: www.emergefitnessnj.com.

CHAPTER 12

Fitness Guidelines For The Busy Parent

By Ryan Jobs, B.H.K.

THE COURAGE TO START, THE STRENGTH TO SUCCEED

Being a young fitness professional, married with no kids, I really had no idea what maintaining my fitness was like while being a parent – let alone having clients pay me to give their lives structure to achieve a desired result. I had many a client sit in front of me and complain that they had no time for fitness. My standard reply was one not from personal experience, but from a hypothetical magic world. I would see the blank stares come back at me, nothing came out, but they were clearly saying, "you've got no clue, buddy." They were right and my clients who were parents were my most difficult to relate to, and subsequently, get results with.

This all changed the day we found out we were pregnant with TWINS! Images of diapers, bottles, toys all over the floor and of course the late nights and early mornings kept me awake at night stressing over what our life was to become. The pregnancy was difficult, my wife's water broke at 23 weeks and for those of you who have had kids you know that this is a serious problem. She spent 9½ weeks on strict hospital bed rest about an hour's drive from our house. The girls were born and they spent another two months in the hospital. Fortunately, two weeks after being born, they got transferred to our local hospital making the commute bearable. After four months of having my girls home, the reality of being a self employed, single income earner had quickly set in. The lessons I learned in the short few months after their arrival home has given me a perspective that cannot be attained by reading any manual or watching any DVD.

The reality is that life is chaotic. We structured our life as best we could, as was necessary with twins, but soon came to the very apparent reality that life was different. I know this sounds obvious, but many parents have this notion that fitness is going to be exactly as it was before kids. This is not my experience with me or my clients. I now sit in front of clients with new understanding; I've traveled their road and walked the walk so to speak. We now relate stories of shortened workouts, lack of sleep, and a total bewilderment about what we did with all of our free time before kids.

This new empathy has empowered Coastal Fitness clients to feel part of a community and know they are not on this 'poor me' island. There are others with whom they can relate to and encourage in their pursuit of health and fitness. None of this was possible before. We now speak to parents with much more conviction, empowering them to be the examples of fitness in their families, instead of spectators on the sidelines. I am going to share with you ***Four (4) Guidelines*** that our very own Coastal Fitness clients employ in their ongoing pursuit of fat loss, better-fitting clothes, increased energy, a revved-up metabolism, improved sleep, decreased stress and overall improved health.

GUIDELINE #1

Upon graduation into parenthood we quickly applied **Guideline #1:**

Expect the unexpected.
The simplicity is the beauty here. You will have late nights, early mornings, cancelled practices, overtime at work, hospital visits and any number of ridiculous reasons your fitness regime can get off track. This takes a bit initially for our clients to get over, as it is easy to use these things as excuses, or worse yet, a full-fledged pity party. The unexpected is life, so we start off with the acknowledgment that there are times that will come up that don't allow for a perfect plan or normalcy. Get over it. Don't dwell. The faster you get back or recover to the plan, the smaller the bump in the road will seem. How we start to expect the unexpected is less actually 'doing something' and more mind set. This mind set is critical to grasping the following guidelines that are more physical and

organisational. The tendency is that once there is a deviation from the norm, the program or goal is shot.

What we really need here is what I call the 'TomTom®' effect. We need to recalculate immediately. There is no time in your day to feel bad about the work out that was just missed. The mentality needs to shift here and fast. It is easy, I know I have done it; to throw your hands up and just keep going down this new path away from your goal. Listen we could dance around this subject in a nice fancy, easy-to-digest fashion, but the truth is, as a busy parent you need to get moving toward your goal again as soon as possible. Imagine for a second (no longer...you're busy, remember?) if you let your GPS take 30 min. to recalculate, you could very easily be one hour off schedule, let alone what could happen on your way back to the route (traffic, run out of gas, pee break etc.). *So you see the negative variables start to compound, the further from the plan you get, and the need to expect roadwork, accept it, and get back on track now becomes crystal clear!*

So, we have learned that there are infinite variables that can throw you off track and seemingly work to keep you there. As depressing as that may seem, we can do a number of things to right this ship.

GUIDELINE #2

The first thing to right the ship brings us to **Guideline #2:**

Know what you <u>can</u> control, and own it.
Let's talk about the things we know for sure that we can control.

1. Your workout plan (exercise order, sets, reps, etc.).

2. Find the minimum amount of time you can give to the gym and guard it like the Fort Knox.

3. 80% or more of your meals.

4. Your effort level in the gym.

5. Your Attitude!!

There are more, but let's start and master these five. With all the information on the internet and in print, of course there are lots of workout fads and gimmicks to follow. Question is, do you have time to find out if the latest one you've read is *your* plan? I would argue no. If you have a finite number of things in your crazy life you control, make sure your plan is simple, straightforward and flexible. Fancy is not necessary here; consistency is. Consistency beats intensity and fancy every time. That is why #2 comes before #4 in this 'control' list.

Simple things Coastal Fitness follows when we make plans for our 'busy parent' clients.

(a). Order Exercises from most dynamic/level of difficulty to less difficult. Reason is, if you get the call for a family or work emergency halfway through the workout you will have gotten the hard, most metabolically-challenging things done.

(b). We do every muscle group every workout. It's just better to know you have it all covered every time. There are many things you can change as your habit sets in, don't worry, simple is better initially. Find the amount of time in your schedule you can realistically allot to fitness and then protect that time like a ferocious guard dog. You may get called away (hopefully not), but at least get started, get moving, get those gym shoes on, make it happen!

Wherever you are doing your fitness thing, please don't lollygag around and waste it. You've successfully defended the time space, now it is imperative you use it effectively. This is time to get business done. Give it 100%, whatever that looks like that day, and trust me I get it, some days you just have more to give, just don't 'wuss' out, go hard.

As a busy parent, having the right attitude is a hard thing to do, day in and day out. It can be especially challenging *when you are not sleeping particularly well or you are not sure which way is up anymore.* At this point, people who are not particularly intrinsically motivated will tend to fold like a cheap tent. You can ward this off first by knowing that you need external motivation, and second, finding it. I like to think more long term as opposed to vacations and new clothes. I'm not saying that those don't work, just not my choice. I like to use my kids as motivation, being able to do fun and active things with them because I made smart choices now is enough to get me to do that extra workout in the week. You need these reminders, especially at the beginning while the habit is still setting. It will keep your attitude positive for those mornings when the kids have woken you up six times in the night and are now in your bed fast asleep while you lay awake with a small foot in your nostril...

You control your attitude; stay positive, it's worth it, they're worth it, you're worth it!

GUIDELINE #3

Realize how important your fitness is to the family unit.
We spend a good chunk of time with parents, like you, going over schedules and possible variables, and we are on the lookout for 'energy leaks'. Basically, this is a nice way of saying, we find wasted time. 45 minutes on Facebook, while interesting, it does not have the payoff a 45 min. full body workout is going to have; not even close. Now, I have heard the excuses and even used them myself, "I need that down time," or "I don't have time to fit that in." Generally, at the very beginning there are scenarios that play out, they genuinely don't have the time, mainly because they have chosen other activities, some of you can identify with that. Then, there is the other group who may have the time, but waste it. They frustratingly always fill the time with fruitless activities that perpetuate the circle of fatigue and lower quality of life. This is a tough one to swallow, but I can tell you time and time again, parents are thankful we find these 'energy leaks,' then direct them towards fitness and spending some time on themselves. The benefits are not just individual. Your fitness has a very large impact on the family as a whole. The result is positive ripple effect on all those around you. The short term couch rest or extra glass of wine and show at the end of the night, while good sometimes (I'm not completely off my rocker, a glass of wine after those crazy days just needs to happen) should not be the norm. It affects everyone eventually; remember that ripple, it can be negative too. Too tired to get up in the morning, short-tempered at work or with the kids, productivity goes down at the office, household tasks seem arduous and insurmountable. Really, there is no magic answer; it starts with you getting yourself moving in the right direction. Soon enough, you are starting to think about healthier eating options, you have more energy to get tasks done and the family bike ride quickly becomes a possibility and not a point of frustration. You are not being selfish, the ramifications of letting your fitness erode may not rear their ugly head immediately, but there is always a price to pay. Model for your kids, telling and not doing does not count here.

GUIDELINE #4

Get a social network!

We're all busy, I get it, and there is someone who has a crazier schedule than you. I have twins, it's chaotic at times, but compared to a family with five young kids, it's relatively easy. Telling us that when the girls were four months old, we probably would have breathed fire on you, but it's true. The point is you are not the only one. At Coastal Fitness we get *results* quicker than others because we understand the power of a strong community environment, an extended family so to speak. Obviously, you are not all going to be able to come up to Vancouver to join us, but the point is: *get others involved.* Some days you will be towing the line and others you'll get dragged. The great thing is, after the days you got pulled through a work out you realize without them it would have never happened. The key is you went; this is the power of a social network in action. I often see it with spouses. One is on the band wagon and the other; well, let's just say they are at the bar as the wagon speeds past. I have seen active spouses struggle with weight loss for over a year, change nothing but have their husband jump on board and 'bam!' – 5 lbs comes off in two weeks. Understanding the psychology is beyond the scope of this chapter, when distilled down: I just know that you need people around you in a positive way to keep the train on the tracks.

Life is crazy, as parents we are busy. Driving to practice, business meetings and deadlines, laundry piling up; it's seemingly unending. While it may be true that we had more free time before we had kids (what did we do with it all?) this is not an excuse to let our fitness slide. If you've had your child(ren) for longer than three minutes you know that the unexpected happens, plan for it. Don't be the parent that wakes up one day out of shape and unable to play with, or enjoy activities, because you have let your fitness slide. You'll have to detour a little more now, but the faster you recalculate the less off-track you'll get. The necessity for us to model a healthy lifestyle to our kids is more critical now than ever. We have control, you have to guard that fitness time with the strong knowledge of how important your fitness and overall wellbeing is to the rest of the family. So put the book down now, call a friend and set up a time you both can meet to go for a walk. It has to start somewhere; it might as well be with you.

About Ryan

Ryan Jobs has his degree in Kinesiology, is FMS Level 2 certified, and is owner of *Coastal Fitness;* a results-based fitness company located in the Lower Mainland of British Columbia, Canada.

Ryan's passion and ability to take information from the best in the industry and provide a fast and effective result to his clients, has quickly established him as the "go to" guy in the region. Having tried numerous solutions, busy parents are turning to Ryan and his team at Coastal Fitness to provide a lasting solution to their fitness goals.

Coastal Fitness was created to empower people in the Lower Mainland, not only to meet, but to *exceed* their health and fitness goals, especially the busy parent who doesn't have two hours to spend at the gym. Ryan and the rest of the Coastal staff strive to give busy parents *the Courage to Start, and the Strength to Succeed!*

Ryan is married to his lovely wife, Joanna, and they have beautiful twin daughters, Kyra and Marika.

For information on Ryan Jobs and Coastal Fitness,
visit: www.coastalfitness.ca
COASTAL FITNESS, Langley, British Columbia
Tel. 604-728-4155

CHAPTER 13

Life Is Not A Perfect Circle

By Lisa Welko

Everything is going your way! You have a job you love that's paying your bills. You're married to a wonderful person who loves and supports you. Your parents are healthy and your extended family seems to be following suit with health and happiness. You work out on a regular basis and you've been able to keep off those 40 pounds you gained after the birth of your two beautiful children...who are on the honor roll of course!

Then...BAM!!!! Life throws you a curve ball. Your great job is in jeopardy. Because of the stress you're not spending as much time at home so you're arguing with your spouse and you've noticed that your kids are playing more video games than you'd like. Your mom's health isn't what it used to be, so you're helping out your father and the time you used to spend at the gym is now spent at drive thru's...and yes, those jeans aren't fitting the way they did a few months ago. So...what do you do? Throw in the towel on the gym and focus on the family, your job, your health, and their health, get your career on track? There's so much to do and NEVER enough time.

Well, friends...Life is NOT a perfect Circle. There will be times when everything seems to be going your way and times that you're carrying the weight of the world on your shoulders! How you deal with THOSE times will determine your outcome! I recently saw a great quote on Facebook..."When you're carrying the weight of the world on your shoulders...DO SQUATS!" This may seem a little too lighthearted for what you're dealing with, but it does make sense, too!

Allow me to share my story, and a few others that may inspire you to turn a corner and get back on track. Ten years ago I was a dental hygienist working part time and raising two young children. My son was in kindergarten and my daughter was only three. Married to a wonderful man and seemed to be a picture perfect model of the American family. Along with living the American dream, I'd blossomed to a size 14 and couldn't seem to get that one part of my life under control. I didn't think I ate poorly and I loved going to the gym, but only to take "aerobics" classes, as those seemed to fit my personality and I didn't really understand all of the equipment that everyone else was using and even then treadmills seemed boring. Well, a friend told me about a class she had taken at a karate studio that wasn't "aerobics", but was done as a group; involved some tubes and weights and kickboxing, and she'd dropped about 20 pounds.

I was hooked! Along with the resistance training classes of tubing and body weight, there were kickboxing classes to get my heart rate up and a simple food guide to follow. From Mother's day to Labor Day in the summer of 2002, I dropped about 40 pounds!

What was it that finally worked? Was it the fact that I'd moved away from "steady state" aerobics classes and got my heart rate and cardio level up with kickboxing—which also created a demand on larger muscles? Was it the fact that two days a week we were using resistance tubing and weights and doing push ups, something I'd rarely tried? Or was it the fact that I FINALLY had adjusted my diet to be higher in lean protein and fruits and vegetables and started limiting my access to refined carbohydrates? Remember Snack Wells?…Well, it WAS 2002!

I think it was this. I'd discovered the secret to fat loss! I'd created The Perfect Storm! Exercise Right, Eat Right, Mindset Right! Weight loss and Fat Loss are like a 3-legged stool. When the three legs are evenly proportioned, your life is in balance, and you'll see the weight come off. When one of those things are "off balance"—you're in for an uphill battle. There's a lot to be said on all these topics. Books, videos and the Internet are FILLED with the next best diet or exercise regime to change your body. But…if your heart's not in it…you'll never win it!

Perfect example...Meet Tiffany:

"My name is Tiffany Holtz, Realtor, and self-proclaimed workaholic who found herself at 235 pounds on a 5'2" frame at only 29 years old. My work in the real estate world fascinates me, and after only 8 years in the business, I had gained 100 pounds due to the fact that my dinner table was my dashboard! Yes, my car had been through every drive-thru that you could list, and I could rattle off which super-sized value basket I wanted quicker than the poor attendant could take my order. This behavior got the best of me and my health was in serious jeopardy. I married the love of my life in July of 2005 and I always tease that he would love me "through thick and thin"! However, a few years later when we tried to conceive a baby, the results were disappointing. After meeting with my physician, he warned me that my weight was an issue with conception and worse yet – I was on the verge of diabetes! I left the office that day crying, thinking that I was not only unhealthy to the point that I was unable to conceive a child, but I was SICK! Time to take control... no problem...I am a control freak by nature!

"In January of 2009, my husband and I joined a local gym and I signed up for an on-line food-logging program to help control the amount of calories that I was consuming. Things were going great as I lost 30 pounds, but suddenly found myself at a standstill. This is when I found Ellipse Fitness and Lisa. I went in to the studio to try a Zumba class, but found out there was a whole lot more to their program. They believe in the 80/20 Rule – 80% is what you EAT and 20% is what you DO. I was all in, I drank the "Kool-Aid," and by September of 2009, I was 125 pounds and 16% body fat...lean and mean! I followed the Ellipse food plan, which is a plan I can follow for life. Plus, I followed the workout format that is set up for me with two days of resistance training and three to four days of cardio training. I found "IT" – a plan that worked for me and one that I could live with for the rest of my life!

"Wow – things are going GREAT! What?? Life Isn't a Perfect Circle?? It was just three short months later and my husband is diagnosed with cancer! This is a heart breaker and definitely a circumstance that could have sent me right back to my dashboard dining days. However, I knew that I needed to stay strong for my husband and see him through his battle. His courage and tenacity was unbelievable and he is stronger than ever. We made it through!

"Enter into August of 2010...It is time to get serious about this family we have always dreamed of! My husband and I started the *in vitro* fertilization process in order to conceive a child and we were successful upon our first attempt! YEAH ....we are pregnant and in 9 months we will be parents. What?? Life Isn't a Perfect Circle?? I am 9 months pregnant, looking at the scale, and realizing that I have a lot of work to do to get back in shape once our baby is born. Yes, part of the process, and she is worth every pound and stretch mark!!

"In an effort to get back to my pre-baby weight, I knew that I need to get back on track with the Ellipse workouts that are planned for me and continue with the meal plans that I already knew worked. After just three months, I had all my baby weight off and I have completed the "Circle" yet one more time. The beauty of it is that I know life will throw me off course many times to come, but I have found my "IT"—the plan that I will stick with for life. Thank you, Lisa, for changing my life forever!"

You've got to balance the stool! You've got to get the three things in line that will change the way you look, think and feel about your body.

- Increase the amount of time you spend MOVING. The first step in getting the body you want needs to be not only finding an exercise you LIKE, but also one that's effective. For example, if you like going for walks, that's a great activity, BUT...it's not the most effective and efficient way to burn fat. You need to add some STRENGTH TRAINING to your routine!

- When it comes to exercise—you have to strength train to see results. Lift something up and put it down. I know this is a funny way to say it, and a simplified statement to a complex idea. BUT...look through this book or countless others. Find a trainer or a coach to guide you if you're new to strength training, or pick up a magazine and give a new workout a try! Life isn't a Perfect Circle, the first thing you try may not work for you...but keep looking, there's a workout out there which involves some heavy lifting that's just right for you!

- Consider this if you're just getting started!
  - A pyramid of tens! Do this for time!
    - ➤ 10 push ups
    - ➤ 10 squats
    - ➤ 10 lunges
    - ➤ 10 bicycles

Then do the same thing for a set of 9, a set of 8, down to 1! At the end you'll have worked a lot of major muscles, your heart rate will be up and you'll have completed a strength workout using your own bodyweight in about 20 minutes or less!

Eat Right:

This also sounds simpler to say than to do! Most of us need to increase the amount of protein we eat every day and also drink more water. This sounds simple, but…if that were the case, 80% of America wouldn't be overweight! When it comes to eating right, the best advice I've ever received is to NOT change everything at once. Make one change to your diet that will have the biggest impact! Stick with that change for a week or two before you add in another. If it's water…drink 8 glasses of water every day. Do this consistently for 14 days before you make any other major changes. Once the water drinking is a habit, perhaps you need to increase your protein.

- Keep a journal. It's hard to gauge "more water," "more protein," "less sugar," "watch the carbs." By keeping a food journal, you will get a black and white picture of what's working or not working in your eating plan.
  - Here's the biggest things to watch for and journal!
    - ➤ Water—are you drinking pure clean water, 8-10 8oz glasses everyday?
    - ➤ Eat Breakfast—starting your day with a proper breakfast jump-starts your metabolism and "breaks the fast" of your sleep, setting the foundation of the start of a healthy day!
    - ➤ Eat protein at every meal and snack. Protein will keep your body full for a longer period of time, fuel your muscles and also increase your metabolism.

➢ Eat 5 meals a day. This is important. Best example on this I ever heard was...eat like a bear, look like a bear... eat like a deer, look like a deer. Don't gorge or save your calories for dinner. Eating several times throughout the day helps stabilize your blood sugar and keep you from making high processed carbohydrate food choices due to extreme hunger.

Mind Set Right:

—Get your head in the game! Remember that Life isn't a Perfect Circle! When life throws you a curve ball, you may need to duck, catch and throw! No one is 100% perfect all the time, so cut yourself some slack! If you miss a workout, go the next day, if you eat a "bad" meal...drink a bunch of water, journal the intake, turn the page and make the next day better...beating yourself up won't burn those calories, and you'll only waste time...which no one has enough of!

• Find a group of supporters! These are people in your corner and on your side when it comes to losing weight! Maybe this is a close girlfriend who joins and goes to the gym with you and goes to class a few days a week, so you don't feel like you don't know ANYONE. Or make friends in a group exercise class and find others who share your love of kickboxing! Having a network of people to rely on will make the obstacles seem easier to overcome! Maybe start an "active living" book club where all the people are reading healthy living books and reporting back on the results!!

• Look for inspiration on Facebook or other social networks! There are so many sites with inspiring quotes or testimonials of people that have overcome small and large challenges! Most likely you'll find something or someone you can relate to, that will keep the journey funny and pleasant, but also personal.

• Keep a Journal and Keep it Real! A great idea is to keep a journal where you not only log your food, but log your mind set! You can jot down a good tip, or a funny quote, or even a new recipe you may want to try. Journaling is a great way to remember your progress and keep your eyes forward. What you learn in the past, when applied to your future...is wisdom!

Define Success!

What is your definition of success when it comes to your body? Only YOU can answer this question and the great news is, YOU'RE RIGHT! Don't let anyone dictate their goals for you when it comes to your healthy body! Will you feel successful when you're a size 4? How about when you're able to carry both of your kids up the stairs at the same time or even go to the park and PLAY instead of watch? Visualize your success EVERY DAY…think about what it will feel like, look like to be in the body you see as your end result. What will the food you eat and the water you drink look like and taste like when you're living that healthy lifestyle? How will you act differently and what choices will you make when you're at that goal? Start now. Choose something right now, from each leg of that tripod stool that will make an impact on your end result and get started!

I'm looking forward to hearing about the Ellipse you create. Sometimes straight and narrow, sometimes a curve in the path…it's yours to create…

Get started!

About Lisa

Lisa Welko is a fitness professional with almost ten years of experience in this fast changing industry! Lisa founded, owns and operates the Ellipse Fitness franchise with corporate offices in Appleton, WI. She still trains and teaches classes in kickboxing, boot camps and strength training – her passion. Ellipse has expanded to eight fitness studios in two states and looking to expand nationally in the next few years. Classes are the backbone of Ellipse and Lisa keeps her eye on trends in group exercise and still oversees all programming.

She has been actively involved in the fitness industry for almost 10 years as a club manager, owner and franchisor. She is regularly featured and quoted in print and television and is a regular featured guest on Real Milwaukee, Fox 6 News.

Lisa is on a mission to help as many people realize that mindset is a major component of weight loss, and is currently writing a book of this chapter's title, *Life isn't a Perfect Circle*, to be released in early 2013. For more information please contact Lisa via email at: lisa@ellipsefitness.com or follow her on Facebook or Twitter. The company website is: ellipsefitness.com where you can find more information and her regular blog feature.

CHAPTER 14

Injury, Rehabilitation, Fitness and Optimum Health

By John Honcharuk, ATC, CSCS

FOUR STEPS TO GET BACK TO OPTIMUM HEALTH

I have been fortunate enough to have been involved in athletics for most of my life. From an early age I was physically active – both with my friends and through organized sports. Understand that my participation in organized sports was something that my family encouraged. I am not sure if it was the benefit of physical activity while working in a team dynamic, or my parents attempts to get us to focus our physicality on someone other than our siblings and/or apparently fragile windows and doors that were prone to breaking.

Lucky enough to have parents that wanted some well-rounded seasonal participation, we participated in whatever the season presented. This is unlike the early specialization that we see as a current trend in youth sports, and as such, I feel lucky to have had that experience.

Truth be told, and trust me, my brother and sister will agree, I did not posses the same level of athleticism as either of my siblings. Needless to say, I actively participated in organized sports throughout my sophomore year in high school. This was a pivotal year for me. It was during this year that it became obvious to me that the combination of my skills, regardless of determination, would no longer be good enough to keep me on the very teams of which I was a member.

It was during this time that my parents began to teach us fiscal responsibility as well – through active participation in free market economy. Simply translated: if I needed money I would need to get a job. Luck would have it that a minor injury freshman year had introduced me to the Athletic Trainer at the high school as well as his minions, the student athletic trainers club. This group of trained students provided first aid services to some of the high school teams. In addition, they had parlayed their first aid knowledge into jobs as lifeguards. Decades prior to Baywatch, the idea intrigued me, and after a long summer of hypothermic life guard training not only had I gotten a job, but I was also then able to remain an active member of the athletic teams at the high school as a student Athletic Trainer.

I will be eternally grateful to those individuals that set me upon the experience that is my life. Working directly with national and state championship teams, as well as professional sports, has provided some excellent training for me. ...And the ability to represent my country. Working with these elite-level athletes provided me a great opportunity and also availed me to work directly with the general public and their injuries as well.

Post graduation, I began work in private practice sports medicine. Typically, this involves working with physicians and physical therapists during the day and then off to a team affiliate in the afternoon. During my work in the clinic at AthletiCo, we identified a common theme in many patients that had the most successful recovery as well as improvement in quality of life. It involved a collaborative effort between the physician, physical therapist, athletic trainer and fitness professional. Moving forward, my "our" refers to all of us involved in their care.

The following steps can be taken for those of you that have an injury, or even those that are deconditioned or have never been conditioned. The same steps can be used to continue your journey to optimal health.

Your injury and/or the circumstances surrounding it are unique. Not only that, but your current level of fitness has also been factored into those events that led to you a physical therapy clinic. For us, there are no typical patients. This is a dangerous over generalization. There may however be some repeating patterns and trends. Let me know if this sounds familiar. You may have had aches or pains that have gotten worse, or, perhaps you had a single event. Either way, your life has been adversely affected. So much so that you not only needed to see your physician, but now your physician wants you to follow up with a course of formal rehabilitation. Next step: seek out the best medical support you can find.

Finding the best rehabilitation you can is a daunting task. Here are a few steps that you can take to locate the best rehabilitation and path to optimum health.

1. Ask your physician whom they like for your specific injury and set of circumstances. Ask for recommendations, and specifically why. Review your long-term goals with your physician PRIOR to getting the referrals.

2. Contact the facility in question. Personally, I would actually visit the locations. If this is not possible, call them directly.

3. Ask about a multidisciplinary approach. What are the types of qualifications and certifications of the staff? You are looking for a facility that has physical therapists, athletic trainers and certified fitness professionals on staff. While these multispecialty facilities may be few and far between, this is where you want to begin your journey.

4. Get aligned around expectations, yours and theirs.

While setting up your first physical therapy appointment, you ought to be informed to wear comfortable, loose fitting, gym-type clothing. Panicking, you immediately rifle through your vast array of current trendy fitness apparel, as you will now be seen in public and want to make a good impression. Turns out your fitness wear would be great for an 80's retro party, but not something you want to wear out of the house. My suggestion at this point would be to wait to make these purchases after your initial consultation with your provider if at all possible.

STEP 1. DETERMINE YOUR CURRENT STATE.

Most patients come into physical therapy in some level of deconditioned state. They come either acutely, with a recent injury, or chronically, in the form of some long-term issue that needs immediate attention. In addition, regardless of injury type, your fitness levels fall into one of three categories:

1. I used to work out.

2. I currently work out.

3. I have never worked out.

Each of you three above present some unique challenges as our patient. That being said, you have made the commitment to attend physical therapy…or at least the first session. So your journey begins, and here are some ways to approach your journey.

1. I used to work out. Great. You have had some experience with exercise! You will no doubt have appreciation for the benefits of physical activity. In addition, you may recall the discomfort that also came with beginning of physical activity. You will excel as a patient as a result of this previous experience – regardless of your what led you to cease working out.

2. I currently work out. This can be a double-edged sword. While you have made the commitment to maintain an active lifestyle, it may be that your injuries are self-induced. This can result from working too hard, too long or just being in the wrong place at the wrong time. In any event, it will be beneficial to bring your workout schedule and specifics with you. This information is useful for the multi-specialty approach, which we know will be successful.

3. I have never worked out. Awesome, you may be the perfect patient. You may have no idea what to expect and only may have read about the benefits of a physically active lifestyle. Oh sure, you may have the idea that this will be uncomfortable and dreadful. I would suggest that you enter into the process with an open mind.

Regardless of your starting point the journey that you are about to embark upon will be life-changing, I promise. Not only can you succeed as a patient, but also your path of fitness to optimal health will continue well past being discharged.

STEP 2. BE CANDID AND TRANSPARENT WITH YOUR GOALS.

Our goal is your goal. Working as a team, our expectation is that we will make some appreciable movement towards your goals. The first step is to write down both short-term and long-term goals. While this may seem a little overwhelming, we are your team, and we will be creating these with you as you progress. Studies indicate that those individuals that actually write down their goals are more likely to achieve them. Not only that, but those individuals that write and review those goals on an ongoing basis will again increase the likelihood of achieving those goals. Use the **SMARTER** acronym when writing out your goals:

S- Specific. What would you like to specifically accomplish? While it may be difficult for someone in the initial stages of rehabilitation, it is important to think both long and short term.

M- Measurable. If we do not actively and regularly measure progress, how will we know if we are actually making progress or not? Every member of your team should be taking measurements and reviewing them with you. This includes doctor, physical therapist, athletic trainer and fitness professional.

A- Attainable. Your goals must be realistic and they must be attainable. During the course of physical therapy, this may be in the form of a specific protocol as it pertains to your injury. The milestones here need to be neither too easy nor too difficult. This can be quite a challenge to some post-surgical cases when simply contracting a muscle may be difficult, or in the case of athletic injuries, getting back for the big game. By getting your health care team aligned around the expectations, you will no doubt create attainable goals.

R- Relevant. Why do they matter to you? Why do they matter to your physician? Why do they matter to your physical therapist, athletic trainer or fitness professional? Communication at the highest level will keep your goals relevant.

T- Time-Specific or Time-Bound. If you are a surgical patient this will be easy. As mentioned above your surgeon will have a set of SMART goals in the form of what we call a "protocol". Your surgeon should have provided both you and your rehab team with a copy of this. We must be steadfast in our resolve to stick to the protocol in order to guarantee a successful outcome.

E- Evaluate: Simply put, evaluate your progress as it pertains to your goals and expectations. There are two questions that need to be asked and answered.

1. Are you making the progress you want?

2. Are you making the progress that we want? aka – "Are you on track with the protocol?"

There are times that these may not actually be as obviously aligned as you would like. In addition, it may be that the answers may be different. This is okay…remember…you are working within the context of a protocol.

R- Re-Evaluate: This is one of the most important aspects of your journey to optimal health. It has been our experience that patients come into the rehabilitation process with one set of goals then, as discharge looms on the horizon, a new set of goals emerges. It is at this time that the patient takes his or her recent bout of rehabilitation to the next level of physical activity with a fitness professional.

STEP 3. INTEGRATING FITNESS PROFESSIONALS.

During your initial evaluation, you should expect to get what is commonly referred to as a Home Exercise Program. Regardless of the number of rehabilitation sessions you are actively participating in during the week, you must be doing some on your own. Don't leave your first appointment without one. In addition, this home exercise program should be updated on an on-going basis. At some point, you will be able to integrate some basic fitness programming into your rehabilitation. While this may sound aggressive, it must not be taking out of context.

If you are being treated for your right arm, what can the rest of your body be doing? Specifically, what can be done that will not first harm the body part you are rehabilitating while improving the conditions to heal. In an integrated team approach, you will be able to use the expertise of the fitness professional. It is imperative that the physician, physical therapist, athletic trainer and fitness professional work together. Again, choosing the right facility will have put you in a position to succeed. As the amount of time you spend with the rehabilitation specialist decreases, your time with your fitness professional should increase.

STEP 4. INVEST IN YOURSELF,
THE JOURNEY CONTINUES...

Invest in yourself. At this point you have been paying a price to get back from your injury. This may be in the form of both your personal time and money. For those of us with a deductible and/or co-pay, you have been regularly handing over your hard- earned money to your rehab team. For the remaining few that may not have had to pay out of pocket, you have still committed 2-3 days per week for 4-6 weeks in order to get to this level of success. Ask yourself: "Does it really make sense to stop now...or ever? I have seen so many patients complete one series of physical therapy only to return with the same issue another time. Stay the course so that you don't have to go back to therapy because now you are on the path of optimum health. And it is a path along a journey, not a destination.

While no one can guarantee results, we know that if you follow the steps outlined above, your quality and quantity of life will no doubt improve and increase. We look forward to working with you.

About John

Born in Chicago, John Honcharuk, ATC, CSCS, has been actively participating in the field of sports medicine for over 25 years.

John is certified by the National Athletic Trainers Association and the National Strength and Conditioning Association. John is also a SPARQ™ certified Trainer and Clinical Sportsmetrics™ Instructor.

John is currently the Facility Manager of AthletiCo in St. Charles, IL. In this capacity, John also serves as Head Athletic Trainer for Fox Valley RFC, Medical coordinator for Predator Rugby Club, and an active member of the USA Rugby Sports Medicine's educational programming.

Committed to continuous improvement, John is studying human movement and how it pertains to injury prevention, rehabilitation and fitness. John is a MovNat Alumnus studying Hardstyle Kettlebell training, TRX suspension training and nutritional coaching in order to better serve AthletiCo's patients, clients and staff.

An expert in the field, John has presented on the local, State, National and International conferences on the topics of injury prevention, rehabilitation and fitness training. John has been published in *Training & Conditioning* magazine as well as *Orthopaedic Excellence Magazine.* In addition, John was featured on ESPN Radio 1000 and Shape online magazine's *Fitness Trends to Watch in 2012.*

John has worked in the National Football League, National Basketball Association, National Hockey League, Arena Football League, National Indoor Professional Soccer League, United States Rugby Team, Midwest Select Side Rugby Team, the University of Iowa and also at the high school level. During this time, he has been a member of State as well as National Championship teams.

John was awarded the American Red Cross Certificate of Merit, the highest honor a civilian can receive, signed by then President Clinton, for "Saving a Human Life."

John brings all of his experience to create an environment from which those that suffer from an injury can actively participate in fitness programming as part of the pathway to optimal health.

To learn more from John, contact him at:
jhoncharuk@athletico.com
www.athletico.com
www.johnhoncharuk.com

CHAPTER 15

Finding Your Motivation

By Ceci Walker

Deb had been a runner in college. Running not only calmed her, but also kept added weight at bay. As the years went on, she had two daughters and lost track of taking care of herself. Quickly, the extra weight showed up on her small frame. As her children progressed through elementary school, middle school and high school, she'd gain some weight, lose some weight – but could never keep it off. Finally, with both daughters in college, Deb decided something needed to change. She needed to take control of her body again and get back to a healthy weight. Being no stranger to exercise she did not hesitate too much to get restarted on working out. She joined a gym. The new routine challenged her and Deb worked out regularly, but nothing drastic happened with her body – at least, not right away. But a few months into the program, her jeans no longer fit. She'd lost two full sizes. What accounted for this change? Deb had been thin in the past, had a good understanding of wholesome nutritious eating and was no stranger to exercise, all of which helped. Still, something held her back. And that's what Deb changed to create her success: she changed her mindset. Deb reworked her success by reworking her thoughts.

If just knowing what to do with fitness and nutrition were enough, so many more people would be where they want to be physically. Having a basic understanding of what to do is necessary, but even with that, the piece that is missing is mindset.

Realizing that your own thoughts will drastically affect the fitness and body transformation outcome you achieve, sets you on the path to success. Finding your motivation, setting your goals and taking actions driven by your adjusted frame of mind constitute a Successful Mindset.

FINDING YOUR MOTIVATION

You're most likely reading this book because you want to change something about your body and your fitness behavior. What is your motivation for that change? What desire got you to pick this book up in the first place? Is it a success you want to achieve? Something along the lines of fitting back into those pants you wore two summers ago. Perhaps it's a failure you want to avoid? Like losing your health and ability to hike, bike and play with your grandkids as you age.

Without an understanding of what is driving you to make a fitness change, sticking with it will be infinitely hard.

Each year in January, a whole slew of folks arrive at the doors of gyms across the country. Hoping to fulfill a resolution to lose weight or to finally get in shape, they sign up for memberships. They crowd the facility for one or two months, but soon most of them have all but disappeared. Why do the majority of those who join a gym as a New Year's resolution fail to complete their goal? What makes that such a common occurrence? Most often, it is the type of goal they set for themselves. Their motivation for action was so grand, so disconnected from the process that chances of success were slim. Large sweeping goals, such as, "this year I am going to lose weight" or "starting in January, I am going to get in shape," *sets one up for failure*. The motivation behind the action doesn't translate into the process. Because the steps to reach that grand ending are not laid out, the goals were not truly created.

Stephanie was a regular gym-goer for years. Despite that, whenever I saw her at social events, she would make comments demonstrating her lack of confidence with how her body looked. She didn't hate it, but she didn't love it. She switched to our gym and began working out in a new way, embracing much of what we teach. Yet she did not achieve the body transformation she was striving for – and that we knew she could accomplish. After about a year at the gym, we began having conversations about her body image.

She wrote down some thoughts about goals she wanted to achieve in the gym. During this process Stephanie expressed that she had always seen herself as a big girl, it was part of her identity. She also realized it was okay that she felt uncomfortable with that perception and wanted to change how she viewed herself. Talk of changing the size of her body and hence the size of her clothing wasn't motivating to her. Yet when she realized feeling fit and confident as she dressed for work in the morning was her true motivation, not the size of the clothes, but the attitude behind her true desires, everything changed. Stephanie dropped multiple sizes in less than three months and continues to change her body to this day.

There are four general driving factors as to why people start on an exercise program:

1. To look better
2. To feel better
3. To move better and
4. To improve some type of performance, such as in a sport

Your motivation to change can be broken down into one of the above categories. These motivations are THE WHY of you reaching your fitness goals. Your goals are THE WHAT. In order to set goals, the what, you must know the motivation, the why. The what and the why will help us to create clearly defined goals, leading to better results.

For example, THE WHAT might be losing two dress sizes and THE WHY might be feeling strong and beautiful at your high school reunion. The *feeling* is the true goal, the motivation.

GOALS: RULES WHEN SETTING THEM

Goals are the driving force behind successful action. They are what will get you to feel the why. When moving to reach your fitness goals, the following action steps will keep your motivation connected with the process leading you toward success. Think through your goals; they are a commitment you are making to yourself.

✓ Be decisive. Goals can't be wishy-washy. As soon as you make that decision, you change the direction of your life.

✓ Set realistic and obtainable goals and when you reach then, update them. If you don't have success along the way, it will be tough to stay on the path.

✓ Write down your goals. Give them a timeline and make them measurable and specific. If you have no specific measurement for your goals, how will you know if you have reached them? Avoid the pitfall of the New Year's resolution crew.

✓ Share your goals by telling others. This builds in some accountability. Associating with those that support you in your goals will increase your success.

✓ Stay focused; use your goal as a focus that you base your decisions on.

✓ Plan thoroughly to help direct your behavior through the goal-reaching process. This includes planning for failure and accepting it when it comes. Failures are what we learn from. Assess what did not work and plan a new strategy.

✓ Maintain your commitment to your commitment/goal.

✓ Take purposeful, conscientious actions based on your plan. That is what will keep you on the path to your goal.

✓ Reward yourself when you achieve a goal.

ADJUSTING MINDSET TO BRING GOALS TO REALITY – TAKING ACTION

Once you have set your goals and made a plan, the next step is actually moving forward with your plan.

Have you ever started on a project, or attempted to start, but became waylaid by the endless list of "I have to's" you associated with getting started? Say your garage has become much more of a storage unit and much less of a place to park your vehicle. You would really like it clean and organized because you really want to park your car in out of the elements. However, every time you think of how much work there is to do in the garage, you end up not starting.

When we think of the finish line, we imagine all we will have to conquer to arrive there. This sort of thinking can overwhelm us and make it feel like there is too much that needs to be done to even start.

To overcome this mindset we need to break things down to a step at a time. Setting your goals in measurable amounts will set the stage for this process.

WHEN WORKING TOWARD YOUR GOALS, DON'T FOCUS ON THE HARD PART

Say you are attempting to start a walking program and you set your goal to walk a 10-mile stretch complete with multiple hills. If you start by climbing up a hill right off, your likelihood of sticking with that first walk and heading toward success is pretty slim. But if you tell yourself all you have to do is stroll along down the flat road for a few minutes, by the time you hit a hill, you're already moving. You'll be in the groove and most likely make it up the hill!

Don't focus on the hard part. The hard part is showing up to start the process. The easy part is the follow through once you are there. Before we start, we create all sorts of stories and ideas in our head as to how difficult something will be. We see the obstacles, the hills. Once we start walking, we can follow through much easier. Don't sabotage the easy part of following through with the hard part of showing up.

✓ Separate getting started with what you perceive as the hard parts of reaching your goal.

✓ Tell yourself all you have to do is the easy part (starting the walk).

✓ Do the easy part.

SET YOURSELF UP FOR SUCCESS BY PLANNING FOR THE DIFFICULT TIMES AND UNDERSTAND THAT THOSE TIMES WILL APPEAR, OVER AND OVER AGAIN

Don't beat yourself up when they do reoccur. What does this mean in practical terms?

If you have to get up in the morning to get to work, do you automatically wake up on your own or do you set an alarm clock? If you set an alarm clock, do you do it just once and then never need to do it again, finding that the one time you use the alarm it changes how easy it is for you to wake up from that point on? Not usually. Most folks set their alarm each night before they go to bed. They have to plan to successfully wake up at their desired time each morning. Just like the setting the alarm, you need to continually plan to reach your goal.

If you are tempted to purchase something sweet every day around 3:00 p.m. then put a system into place to stop before you start. Every day at 2:30 p.m., have a healthy snack, which you packed ahead of time, and fill yourself up with a few glasses of water. Or instead of taking that work break to get the sweet treat, ask a coworker to go for a quick walk with you.

If you know that going to workout after work is always hard for you, then have a friend call you 20 minutes before you leave the office. Their expression of looking forward to meeting you at the gym will hold you accountable to show up.

Our schedules, plus hunger and tiredness are strong factors that stop us from reaching our fitness goals. But these factors are controllable; we just need to plan for them.

ANNOUNCING TO FRIENDS, FAMILY OR COWORKERS WHAT YOUR INTENTIONS ARE

If you tell everyone you are going to the gym that afternoon, you are much more likely to do so.

If you schedule your workouts into your calendar, so they are in front of you, they are harder to skip.

CREATE ACCOUNTABILITY FOR YOURSELF

Use your calendar to schedule the next time you are gong to have your measurements taken or your fitness progress photos taken.

STAY FOCUSED ON THE THOUGHTS THAT MAKE YOU WANT TO MAKE THE CHANGE

What feelings make you want to follow through with reaching your goal? Can you recall a particular incident that brings those feeling up inside you? What can you do to bring to the surface of your mind that which makes you feel those feelings?

Maybe you have the goal of fitting into your jeans from four years ago. Every time you open your closet and see them, you feel it. You feel that desire to wear them again and feel good in them. Instead of keeping them in the closet, take them out and put them where you see them. Keep them at the forefront of your mind.

Perhaps you don't want to end up like your parent or parents who are overweight and out of shape. Place a photo of your parents not looking their best in a spot you see at the time of day that challenges you the most. The cupboard where you tend to graze on unhealthy afternoon snacks. Or on the dashboard of your car where you are sitting as you drive away from work while considering not going to the gym.

KEEP YOUR EYES OPEN FOR WHAT IS TRIGGERING YOUR CHOICE TO NOT TAKE POSITIVE ACTION

Identify what pushes you in the opposite direction of your goal. It is pretty difficult to face something that will affect your goal achievement head on and win. Willpower will fail you. Willpower does not work. Willpower is like brute force.

If your car had a flat tire, you would need to fix that tire before you got back on the road, right? Would you get the spare tire and the lug wrench out of the trunk and use your brute force to lift the car off the ground so you could remove the tire? Would you use brute force to raise the car and then straining and struggling to hold the car up – balanced on your leg – as you loosen the lug nuts? Heck no, you would get out the car jack and assist yourself with lifting the car. Using brute force to change a tire would be pretty impossible. When reaching toward your fitness goal, relying on willpower is like brute force, an impossible way to get a job done. Prior preparation beats brute force every time.

Look at the factors that are under your control and take action on them. If you focus on the pain, the trouble, the tiredness, or the desire to give in, you will set yourself up to fail. This is giving yourself the short-term easy out.

Instead, *commit to yourself*, specifically, to where you want your body and health to be. Identify your goals and write them down. Imagine how you will feel when you reach that goal. Start the process by looking at the easy first step rather than the long road ahead. Plan for the difficult times and put strategies into place to override them, rather then relying on willpower. And then, thinking of your goal, take one easy action today to improve chances that you'll do the right thing tomorrow. Success awaits!

About Ceci

Ceci Walker is the owner of Praxis Fitness in Eureka, California. She and the fantastic team that works with her are constantly looking for ways to improve the success of members through fitness and mindset coaching.

Ceci holds a B.S. in Exercise Science and multiple personal training certifications. Her experience in clinical nutrition, adaptive physical education, swim coaching and the gym atmosphere has helped shape her programming approach.

To learn more about what Ceci and Praxis Fitness are up to,

check out: **praxisfitness.com** or like **Praxis Fitness!** on Facebook.

Special thanks and photo credits to Terrance McNally of Arcata Photo Studios for Ceci Walker's pictures on her biography and on the cover.

CHAPTER 16

Five (5) Strategies to Beat Stress, Blast Fat, and Never Go On a Diet Again

By Shannon Austin

My story starts out like a lot of others in our industry. I was a chubby kid-turned-fit-adult who wanted to help others get fit too. So, I became a personal trainer. Now, thirteen years into my career, I have seen some incredible transformations. I can also recall times when people have struggled to stay on track, some of them quitting all together because changing can be so much harder than staying the same, even when the same means feeling tired, run down, and living in an unhealthy body. I have seen people lose weight, regain it, start and stop exercising. I have also seen many others take control of their habits, remove their own self-imposed limitations, and make lifelong changes that they continue to live by. Change isn't easy, and I have gone through many ups and downs on my own journey towards being my best self. I have been over-weight, I have been an ultra-lean figure competitor, I have lost, regained and lost again the same 20 pounds 3 times, I have competed in endur-ance sporting events, and at times I have struggled to find the motivation to exercise and eat right. It hasn't always been easy for me, but over time I have developed some lifelong habits that have helped me to stay lean and fit, and I did it by following these simple strategies.

STRATEGY #1: BEAT YOUR CRAVINGS AND CONTROL YOUR APPETITE

You can't out train a bad diet. No matter how hard you try, and no matter how much exercise you do, you simply won't get the results you want if your eating habits don't match your efforts in the gym. For me, changing my eating habits was a struggle for a long time because I always felt hungry. A major factor in my personal weight loss success was beating cravings and learning to control my appetite instead of feeling hungry all the time, and I did this by making some simple changes to my diet.

I started by cutting processed foods and sugar from my diet and eating balanced meals, each consisting of lean protein, healthy fats, and fibrous fruits and vegetables. This magic combination has helped me to achieve and maintain a healthy weight by filling me up and keeping me full. Let me explain. You have probably heard that protein helps build muscle. This is true, and protein should be eaten at every meal to help maintain your lean physique. Protein also slows down stomach emptying, keeping you feeling fuller for longer, and suppressing the hunger-triggering hormone grehlin, which is produced by your stomach when it is empty to let you know that it's time to eat. High-fiber fruits and veggies feed your brain and give you energy, and fiber (like protein) also helps to slow stomach emptying.

The right types of fat in your diet support better brain function, may reduce inflammation, and will keep you feeling fuller for longer. When fat enters your small intestine, it triggers the release of cholecystokinin (CCK), telling your body that you are full, so including 1-2 servings of healthy fat with your meals may also help you eat less.

At Mota Fitness, we teach our members this same simple information, and we have some amazing success stories as a result. I have met countless frustrated people who have tried unsuccessfully to lose weight by following an exercise program. By making the same simple changes to their diets that I made to mine, many have seen results immediately and are able to make a permanent change because this strategy is so simple.

STRATEGY #2: PREPARE FOR SUCCESS
AT THE START OF EACH DAY

Have you ever heard the saying "fail to plan, plan to fail"? This is such a true statement, especially when it comes to healthy living. It's amazing how simple it is to stick with a plan when it becomes routine, and how it's even easier to slip down a slippery slope when you get off track. For example, who hasn't gone to bed after staying up too late without packing the next day's meals, then overslept and went to work with frizzy hair after skipping breakfast? Then, later that morning after you have been running around like crazy, you get whatever you can find at Starbucks to go with your coffee, and you make a bad choice for lunch because you're really hungry and figure that you can live a little today because you're bringing your healthy lunch with you tomorrow? That has never been you? Good, me neither, at least not anymore.

Planning is the best strategy I have come up with to avoid this scenario. I plan my meals and prepare them ahead of time so I always know what I am going to eat. I also eat breakfast within an hour of waking up each day. I am a big fan of replacing meals with healthy and balanced shakes, it's something I have done for breakfast just about every morning for the past four years. You can pack a lot of nutrition without a lot of calories into a shake, it's quick, easy to make, and can be helpful with maintaining weight loss. Studies show that people who eat breakfast lose more weight and keep it off than those who don't, and a shake in the morning can make eating breakfast more manageable if you're on the go a lot, or if you just aren't into eating in the morning. You can turn a good thing into a bad one fast with the wrong ingredients, so be aware of what (and how much) you put into your shake. Some things to avoid are fruit juice, yogurt with artificial sweeteners, and ice cream. Yep, somebody once asked me if ice cream was ok to put into a shake. Your shake should taste great, but it's not a milkshake. Here is the recipe I use for my daily shake:

In a blender, mix the following:
- 8 oz water
- 1-2 scoops protein powder
- 1-2 servings of fiber (I use ground flax seed meal or chia seeds)
- 1-2 servings of healthy fat (1-2 tablespoons nut butter or ¼ - ½ cup unsweetened coconut milk are good options)
- ½ -1 cup berries
- ice for desired thickness

You can prepare your shake ingredients the night before along with the rest of your food for the day. If you haven't tried this, you should. It's amazing how easy it is to follow a healthy nutrition plan simply by planning ahead.

STRATEGY #3: MAKE EXERCISE A PRIORITY

Like Rachel Cosgrove says, "to look like a fox, you have to sweat like a pig." If you want to live in a lean and fit body, you have to exercise. Period. I have said a lot here about eating habits, and for good reason. Many experts will tell you that fat loss is 80-90% nutrition and 10-20% exercise. I disagree. Based on my own experience and that of many others, I have found that nutrition and exercise are equally important because neither one is 100% effective without the other. Most of the people I work with at Mota either want to lose weight, or they have reached their weight loss goals and want to maintain their new lean physiques.

The number one reason I hear for why people don't exercise is...you guessed it...time. We're all busy, and really, who has time to spend hours in the gym? If this is you, I have great news for you. It probably doesn't take as long as you think to get (and stay) in great shape. Some of the fittest people I know spend 30-45 minutes exercising 3-5 times each week. I know this because they are members at my gym. At Mota, we teach our members to work out hard and often. We work with men and women of all different ages and fitness levels, and we have found that most of them see great results with 2-3 total body resistance training workouts and 2-3 interval cardio workouts every week, each session lasting between 30-60 minutes.

You can easily and inexpensively set up a home gym and accomplish the same thing if you don't have access to a gym. For me, exercise is certainly about staying in great shape. But, it is also how I manage stress. I find when I work out hard and often, I have more energy, my mood is better, I make better food choices, and I just feel better.

STRATEGY #4: IMPROVE YOUR SLEEPING HABITS

If I had to choose my number one secret to successful and lasting fat loss, it would be this: get enough sleep. It's such a simple thing that so many of us don't do, and a big reason why so many people struggle with their weight. We live in a fast-paced world, and when something has to give to make time for it all, it's usually a good eight hours of sleep. A study from the University of Chicago showed that even when people eat properly and exercise on a regular basis, if they get less than the recommended seven to nine hours of sleep per night, they are at a greater risk of obesity.

Sleep deprivation creates chaos in your body and elevates your stress hormones. When this happens, your appetite soars and your energy level drops. Lack of sleep helps you to store fat and impairs your ability to build muscle. Why? Remember the talk about ghrelin from strategy #1? Well, consider that a single night of sleep deprivation increases ghrelin levels (which increases your appetite) in normal-weight, healthy people. It also decreases insulin sensitivity, and a higher level of insulin (at a fasting level) can shut down your body's ability to burn fat. If you sleep less, you will have less energy and an increased appetite. Simply put, that means you will move less and eat more, and you will put on weight.

Being tired all the time leads to more stress, and the "need" for quick "pick-me-ups" to temporarily boost your energy, like caffeine and sugar. Now you're exhausted, so you caffeinate, you get a brief second wind before you feel awful, and then you crash. Repeat. For a long time, this was my daily existence. I was over-tired and over-fat, and no matter how much I exercised and tried to eat right, I couldn't shed the extra pounds. I also felt like I was constantly fighting my way through stressful days and situations, and my stress level was through the roof. When I decided it was time to take control of my weight and my health, I made sleep a priority, and I could hardly believe how much better I felt in general, and how much easier it was for me to shed the extra fat. Here are a few tips for improving your sleeping habits:

Wind down for an hour before bed. Let your brain relax by turning off electronics, read a book instead of watching the news, and stop stressing over things that are beyond your control. Try sipping on some herbal tea, take a hot bath, or do whatever you do to relax.

Invest in a comfortable bed, get all electronics out of your sleeping space, do not bring work to bed, and make sure your room is dark so your pineal gland can convert serotonin to melatonin, the hormone that helps you sleep.

Wake up at the same time every day, even if you don't go to bed at the same time. Your body will get used to this routine and you will feel better, I guarantee it.

STRATEGY #5: BE ACCOUNTABLE
AND PUT SOME SKIN IN THE GAME

I don't know about you, but when I commit to something with my wallet, my odds for success go way up. I also tend to follow through with my commitments when I report to myself (journaling) and even more when I know somebody else is watching and keeping me accountable. I invest my time and money to work with business coaches, a nutrition coach, and a fitness coach. These are three areas where I want to be my absolute best every day, and I do this by staying focused and investing in the help I need to get better every day. I could probably get by without my coaches, but I know I wouldn't be as successful as I am with their guidance.

As a fitness and nutrition coach, I have seen people make some amazing and life-changing transformations, sometimes just by making some minor adjustments to what they were previously doing, things they were unaware of on their own. It has been my experience that people stay committed to their fitness goals for longer when they follow a program and when they share their experience with others. If you are struggling to find the motivation to exercise, hire a coach to help you. All of our members at Mota have individualized programs specific to their goals and needs, and we offer unlimited coaching to everybody anytime they visit our gym. We also encourage people to participate in our group classes for fun and more frequent accountability.

And remember, what you measure, you can improve. The scale may or may not change much when you are losing fat, so don't use it to measure your progress. Keep score with a pair of jeans you want to fit into. Take pictures of yourself regularly to monitor your progress. Studies show that people who journal lose twice as much weight as those who don't, so keep a notebook with you and keep track of your food intake, exercise, feelings, etc. When it comes to purposeful exercise, I want you to get hot and sweaty, but I also encourage people to get up move and do more in general throughout the day. Try wearing a pedometer and set daily activity goals for yourself. You'll be amazed by how much better you feel and how focused you can be on other things when you get up and move your body regularly.

I continue to live by these strategies myself every day, and I have seen many lives change just by making these small adjustments. If five strategies seem overwhelming at first, just pick one and get started. Then, you can add another, and another, until you are practicing all five consistently. Remember that gaining control over areas in your life where you feel overwhelmed is a process. Your motivation and your success will ebb and flow, and that's ok. If you stay the course and get right back on track if you miss a day, you will be successful in the long run. I wish you great success in your fitness journey, please drop me a line sometime at Shannon@motafitness.com and let me know which strategy has helped you the most.

ABOUT SHANNON

Shannon Austin is the owner of Mota Fitness in Portland, OR. She holds multiple fitness and nutrition certifications and is currently completing a Masters of Science in Human Nutrition. Shannon is committed to bringing the best in fitness and nutrition education to her members and to her community. Her no-nonsense yet kind and simple approach to coaching has helped thousands of people (and counting) to reach their fitness goals and live better lives.

To learn more about Shannon and Mota Fitness, please visit: www.motafitness.com.

CHAPTER 17

The Success Mindset

By Nik Herold & Brian Nguyen

It's a timeworn scenario. New Years day dawns with the idea that, finally, THIS is the year you will work out every day, cut fat, sugar and junk food from your diet, and finally lose those 10, 20, or even 50 pounds you've got hugging your middle like a fat-stuffed fanny-pack. Sure, you've got enthusiasm and a general goal in mind – to "get fit" – but what you lack is direction. All the enthusiasm in the world can't make up for the lack of a solid plan – and a purposeful mindset.

Most people don't know enough about themselves to stay motivated. The weeks tick by, the temptations and pressures of life mount, and, before they know it, that New Year's resolution is a speck in the rear view mirror. Another year goes by, and with it, another failed attempt to change. It's time to ask, "What am I really doing? What are the elements of a successful training program for ME?"

For every method, there is a success story. For every success story, there is a long list of those who gave up, who couldn't cut it. What it comes down to is this: it's not that the program is poor, but that the client doesn't commit to follow it 100% in the first place! Even the worst program in the world would garner far better results, if performed faithfully, than the best program would with half-hearted intensity.

If it's not the program that is at fault, what is the issue? It's MINDSET.

The psychology behind successful training rests on five essential principles.

PRINCIPLE #1: KNOW WHAT MAKES YOU TICK

No one wants to lose 10 pounds solely for the sake of losing 10 pounds. There is always an emotional trigger behind it. Perhaps you feel ashamed that you can't walk up a flight of stairs without gasping for air. Maybe it's the guilt of not being able to run and play with your children. Regardless of the impetus, these emotions must be clearly identified as the reason WHY you embarked on your fitness journey. Your emotions are a huge asset that, when used effectively, can push you through any adversity.

When you feel like quitting, draw on those emotions. Remember the helpless feeling when you couldn't make it up the stairs without wheezing. When you don't feel like working out, remember what it feels like to be at the beach, feeling embarrassed in your bathing suit.

It is these emotions that are going to pick you up and keep you moving toward your goals. Use this all the time to keep you going. Write it on your bathroom mirror, on your refrigerator, and at your computer. Keep it top-of-mind on a daily basis.

PRINCIPLE #2: DEFINE THE DESTINATION

As important as emotions are to drive you, knowing WHERE you are driving is equally important.

Remember your January 1st self? "I'm going to get in great shape this year! I don't know exactly what that means, but I know I'm going to do it!" After 30 days straight at the gym, you're burnt out. Why? You've got nothing with which to gauge your progress. Unguided emotions cause you to float through your fitness journey with no end in sight.

Decide clearly what your objective is. Then, figure out HOW you will know you're on the right path. The goal doesn't feel so distant when you are routinely tracking how much closer you're getting. It also allows you to adjust your course if your routine isn't working. This is where dutifully recording your measurements, weight, strength and endurance comes in.

If one of your goals was to walk up the stairs without gasping for air, time yourself on a set of stairs at the beginning of your journey. Every two weeks, time yourself on those same stairs. It will be clear whether you're making progress or not. You wanted to build muscle? Make sure you track your progression as the weight you're lifting increases over the weeks.

Imagine your goal is to go on vacation. First, you have to get to the airport, right? You'd better know the way to the airport and pay attention that you're following that route or you'll end up driving around in circles. Look for those "road markers" of progress to make sure you're on the right path… and not going in circles, frustrated that you're never reaching those goals.

PRINCIPLE #3: TAKE THE EASY ROAD

We place so much value on "working hard," but what we truly need to value is "working RIGHT."

Valerie Waters said, "Strategy always trumps willpower." No matter how tough you think you are, we all have our breaking points.

Remember how we pointed out how emotions are exceptionally strong? They can push you through anything, right? Well, they can also derail you. That's why, when your emotions swing in the other direction, it's important to have a road to travel on that allows for easy choices. If you put a jar of cookies on your counter, it's very easy to grab those cookies when you feel like quitting or when the journey feels overwhelming.

It doesn't have to be that way. You can just as easily stock your fridge with healthy fruits and vegetables instead of those cookies. It makes the road much easier to follow.

Hiring a coach will significantly ease the path. Your coach is going to keep you accountable, on track, and will help you measure your progress – regardless of how crazy your day is.

PRINCIPLE #4: FOCUS ON ONE CHANGE AT A TIME

Change is tough. We're used to routines, and when we set our minds to changing too much at one time, we're destined to fail. Imagine making five HUGE changes nutritionally, and then a few more for your workouts and then a few more by logging your food. Now throw in work, family and the strains of life in general.

Research has shown that trying to make too many changes at one time ultimately leads to low success rates. When you focus on one change, you're likely to have an 85% success rate, try two changes and your chances drop to 35%, add a third and the odds drop to less than 10%! Multi-tasking changes leads to quitting.

Rather than taking on a huge task, we need to break things down so the project is not so daunting. Improve one thing at a time. If you made one change per week, you'd have improved 52 things in a year! Those small changes add up to big results. Focus and work daily on each goal.

PRINCIPLE #5: CELEBRATE THE SMALL THINGS

Just like you've got to focus on one change at a time, you also need to CELEBRATE those small changes. Most of us only focus on the end results – the BIG finale.

There's a problem with that. Many people can't make it to the big finale because they never reach it! Why? They never focus on the small strides that they make along the way. Those small gains – adding an extra workout each week, doing one more rep, eating one less cheat meal each week – are incredibly important for your long-term success.

If all you see is how far you have to go, chances are the task will be too daunting to ever reach the goal. But if you can slowly check off progress on your map, you will be emotionally-driven, and you'll feel the momentum carry you forward.

Your mind is like a garden. Plant the seed of change. Water it daily. With careful tending, your garden will be in full bloom before you know it. Tend it daily to keep away weeds – also known as mental clutter. Clutter messes with your head and keeps you from starting the day with focus.

Find deep appreciation for yourself. Talk to yourself like a loving parent and you'll grow faster. "I'm impressed with you." "You're a champion." "You can do this!" Document your successes and celebrate by marking them down and rewarding yourself. The more you believe in yourself, the better you'll get. You're reinforcing your own positive behavior.

Don't underestimate the small things. In fact, celebrate them!

A high-quality trainer will help you incorporate all five principles for your optimum success. At BRIK Fitness, we specialize in creating a unique program and approach to every client's needs and goals. There is no one-size-fits-all. You deserve a coach who helps establish your purpose, your goal, your path, your strategy, tracks your progress and changes, and, definitely helps you celebrate the small things! The relationship with our members goes way beyond a wave and a smile as they swipe their membership cards. They become part of our family and part of a team, with everyone working together to accomplish what, before, seemed impossible... one change at a time. Our tagline, "It All Starts With A Little AMBITION" goes right back to working smart, not just working hard. Each letter represents one of our core values:

A – ATTITUDE: The positive self-talk discussed in Principle #5 is key, but along with that is the one change at a time in Principle #4. Every change has to be approached with a can-do attitude.

M – MOVE: Move better and move more often. Each one of us is a conflagration of life events that have taken a toll on how our bodies were originally meant to move. Car accidents, sports injuries, pregnancy, sitting at desks all day – these all take a toll and slowly atrophy our bodies' ability to most effectively move – and to most effectively burn fat and build muscle. A plan with a purpose, performed regularly, will correct these imbalances and improve your strength, energy and overall function.

B – BEST: No matter what, give your best – whatever that is. We all walk into the gym with different abilities and fitness levels. Push yourself to give it your all.

I – IMPROVE EVERY DAY: Look back to Principles #2 and #3. Measuring your progress on your way to your destination confirms you're on the right path and will boost that ATTITUDE! Working with a trainer – and the daily decisions that smooth your path will go a long way toward motivating yourself toward constant improvement.

T – TEAM: Be a team. It's we, not me. Our members exercise exclusively in groups. Studies have shown that we push ourselves 40% harder when we exercise in groups. Even appointments with trainers are semi-private – in groups of two or three. Operating as a team – encouraging each other and building relationships, keeps everyone coming back for more and motivates them to push harder.

I – INSPIRE: It's the job of our entire team to inspire members – from trainers to office staff. We also stress to our members that they must take an active role in inspiring their fellow members.

O – OVER-DELIVER: Go above and beyond. We do this for our members every day, setting us apart from the rest. From that place, we see and expect our members to give that extra measure of effort and dedication.

N – NO EXCUSES: The only person limiting you is yourself. You can exercise aimlessly and wonder why you're not getting anywhere. You can set up your own roadblocks and hinder your progress. You can blame the program, the weather, the tough day at work, a stressful relationship, cupcakes jumping out in front of you every time you go to the grocery store, etc. But that emotional reason that prompted your fitness journey that we talked about in Principle #1 has to push through all those excuses to remind you of those feelings you never want to have again. *That's where excuses got you in the first place. Dump them. They have no place in this life change.*

About Nik and Brian

Nik Herold created Ambition Fitness, now Brik Fitness, in 2007 to provide an alternative to health clubs that do not help their clients reach their goals with *PERMANENT solutions* for a fit and healthy body. With workouts that are fun and easy to follow (and without fads or crash diets), Brik Fitness specializes in helping real people with busy lives reach their fitness goals.

Nik has appeared on *CBS' The Doctors*, and his work has been featured on *ESPN*, *NBC's Today Show, NBC's Biggest Loser, Southbay Magazine* and the *LA Times*. His resume includes: pre and post natal certified coach, NSCA Certified Strength and Conditioning Specialist, Russian Kettlebell Certification, head fitness coach for Cenegenics Medical Institute in Beverly Hills/Redondo Beach, former head fitness coach for Dr. Murad's Inclusive Health Center in El Segundo and was named Results Fitness Business Owner of the Year in 2010 and 2011. *The Daily Breeze* awarded then-named Ambition Fitness as having the "South Bay's Best Bootcamp" in 2010 and 2011.

Brian Nguyen joined Ambition Fitness as co-owner in the Fall of 2011 and Brik Fitness was born. His skill in training both amateur and professional athletes brings a new dimension to Brik's offerings.

Oscar nominee, Mark Wahlberg, found Brian's skills indispensible and hired him to be part of his now-legendary entourage as his personal Director of Human Performance and Health. Brian spent six years with the actor and was a key player in more than eight films, including last year's Academy Award-winning, "The Fighter." Other celebrity clients include Adam Sandler, Will Ferrell, Dwayne "The Rock" Johnson, and NBA Star, Derek Fisher.

Brian spent five NFL seasons as a trainer for the Jacksonville Jaguars and was Head Athletic Trainer and Head Fitness Coach for the Los Angeles Avengers of the Arena Football League. Brian comes from an athletic training and strength and conditioning background with an emphasis in sports medicine and human movement. He is certified as an athletic trainer by the National Athletic Training Association, as a strength and conditioning specialist by the National Strength and Conditioning Association, and as a functional movement specialist. He received his undergraduate degree in Physiological Science from UCLA with a minor in Biomechanics. Brian served as a student trainer for the university's athletic department for four years.

Contact Information:
Brik Fitness, Redondo Beach, California
Visit: www.brikfitness.com

Tel: 310-529-4094 Or 310-908-3834

CHAPTER 18

IT'S ALL IN YOUR HEAD…
—Using Brain Science and Basic Physiology Principles to Hack Your Exercise Plan and Guarantee Results, Faster!

By Andy Clower, ATC & Carmela Lieras, CPT

Does this story sound familiar? It's most likely happened on more than one occasion. Whether it be a New Years resolution, a tropical summer vacation, or a competition between friends, something planted a seed in your head that it was time to get in shape and finally get the body you always dreamed of having. You clean out the fridge, buy new workout gear, find the old weight and cardio routine you used last year, and set the alarm clock for 5am so you can get to the gym before work. The next six weeks are going to test and challenge you, but you're totally up for it.

Day one of the new you has arrived and it's off to the gym you go! You begin with a light 5-minute stroll on the treadmill to get your blood pumping, then head upstairs to tackle the weights. In the next 30 minutes, you complete three sets of ten leg presses, seated hamstring curls, bicep curls, tricep kickbacks and shoulder raises. Feeling pretty darn good, you head over to the elliptical, pull out your magazine and burn some more calories for another steady 30 minutes. To finish, you head to the stretching area and do two sets of twenty abdominal crunches, stretch your hamstrings and quads, and call it a day. This is your routine for the next six weeks, five days out of the week. You don't miss a day! This is finally going to be your year! You can't wait to get on that scale, and this time be rewarded for all your hard work, consistency, and dedication.

You get up early on the day after you finish your six-week "body transformation contest," and hop on the scale. This can't be. How could you have possibly gained four pounds? Maybe it's the scale. You step off, let it reset and step on again. Same thing! Maybe it was the two slices of pizza you ate last night as a reward for completing six weeks of hard workouts. Yes, it had to be that. So you do what seems reasonable, and "fast" the entire day to make up for the bad food you ate yesterday. You still stay hydrated, and have a piece of an orange and a few salted almonds as a snack. But that's it! Then, you decide to wait until early the next morning to weigh yourself again.

5:00 am rolls around, and you wake up feeling lethargic, cranky, and light-headed. But it will all be worth it to see that number on the scale drop! You head to the bathroom, de-clothe, and step on. WHAT???? Another two pounds? Ok, that's it. DONE. It's pointless. You've come to the realization that you are ultimately stuck with the body you have. No one can help you, not even the entire personal training staff at your local gym. Defeated, you immediately go into "self-sabotage" mode and resort back to your old eating habits, skipping the gym altogether and your weight hits an all-time high.

This is an all-too-familiar scenario for fitness professionals, but trust us, you're not alone! We've had the opportunity to help our clients in this situation get back on track and pinpoint exactly what needs to be tweaked. Typically, it isn't just nutrition that is holding a client back, nor is it their workout schedule (days per week). This may be surprising to a lot of people, but a culprit is usually the actual workout! Not necessarily the exercises themselves, but more the way you work out. Let us try to break it down for you...

We've spent countless hours researching and learning in hopes to find explanations and new techniques and tools to fast-track the process and guarantee results. Based on the most current findings about the body and how it works, and as the title of this chapter implies, we *have* to discuss the brain; but we'll do our best to keep it simple. There are two amazing processes in the body that should be taken advantage of in every program:

1) *Myelination and Neuroplasticity: Your brain needs and wants a new stimulus!* If you look in any strength training or exercise book, there's one rule or "principle" that should drive every exercise program: the SAID Principle (Specific Adaptation to Imposed Demand). The simplest way to describe this is, "You *always* adapt to *exactly* what you do." This process (and every process that happens in the body) starts in the brain. This adaptation happens as a result of two amazing processes that happen in the brain: "myelination" and "neuroplasticity." Every time we do something, the brain creates a *physical* pathway, or "circuit," of that activity that instructs the body to do exactly what we are trying to accomplish - *neuroplasticity*. The more we do that activity, the stronger that circuit becomes. With repetition, a fatty substance called myelin is laid down and wrapped around that circuit to "insulate" it (think the rubber coating around an electrical wire) - *myelination*. The more insulated that circuit is, the faster and more efficiently the signal that instructs the body to perform that activity travels and makes it happen - faster, better, and easier! This principle applies to everything: from simple instructions for muscles to fire at exactly the right time, to instructing your metabolism to speed up and produce more energy, to instructing your pituitary gland to release Growth Hormone for repair and rebuilding of your muscles so you can do it better next time.

This process happens at an extremely fast rate. The brain is constantly craving more challenge and stimulation that you may no longer be giving it. For example, if you're now able to complete 30 minutes of elliptical machine "running" while reading a magazine, it's obviously not challenging enough for your brain to pay attention and change your body at all to make it "easier" or better-- you're already there! *Take advantage of the principles of myelenation and neuroplasticity and add a new challenge to every workout.*

2) *Metabolic Flexibility: Make your body a fuel-burning machine!* Metabolic flexibility is an attribute we are all striving for without even knowing it! What is it? Some great research from the

University of Minnesota has shown that when our body is at it's healthiest we are able to metabolize fats and carbohydrates for energy easily and actually able to switch from one to the other when needed. (When we're working out hard, we mainly use carbs for energy; when we're exercising at a leisurely pace or just going through the day we're relying mostly on fat for energy.) Metabolic flexibility occurs when we put our body through enough activity that our metabolism increases and more efficiently digests the calories we feed it. (Remember when you were young and playing all of the time and were able to eat anything you wanted?) What happens when we don't move or exercise enough? We become metabolically *in*flexible - our ability to properly handle carbohydrates or fat declines, causing all sorts of health issues, including more belly fat!

As our health improves, our ability to digest and use more diverse sources of calories without causing more damage and improving health and performance expands. Depending on where you started, it takes time to rebuild that flexibility, but it can be done! According to research, it takes at least 5 hours of *activity* per week, with a continual load increase of 5% to improve your metabolic flexibility. If you're not continually changing and increasing the difficulty of your workouts and activity, you're not giving your brain and body the stimulus it needs to adapt and transform!

This sounds complex, but it doesn't have to be! Keeping it simple keeps you motivated and more willing to continue to try things out until you find what works best for you. Just follow these steps:

FIVE EASY STEPS TO APPLYING THESE PRINCIPLES AND HACKING YOUR EXERCISE PLAN:

1. ***Pick a specific goal.*** What specifically do you want to be able to do or to look like? Tony Blauer once said, "The clarity with which you define something determines its usefulness." If you don't know exactly what *your* dream body looks and feels like, how can anyone design a program to train for it? It's hard to aim without a target! A good tip: Pick an athlete who looks and moves like you would like to look and feel and move like. Then, train like that athlete. What attributes do you need to accomplish

that goal? ...strength, speed, mobility, fluidity, stamina, posture, structure (big muscles!)?

2. ***Pick your exercise movements, sets, reps, and weight based on accomplishing one of these attributes each phase, week, or workout.*** In order for your brain to pay attention enough for adaptation and myelination to occur, every training session should have a goal. Training with a specific goal and purpose gives your brain a reason to pay attention and adapt to what you're doing at a much faster rate. Every exercise should be challenging enough that you have the opportunity to make *and correct* mistakes. If it's so easy that you can complete every rep perfectly with almost no challenge (put away the 5 lb. dumbbells!), it will take hundreds of reps - when fatigue actually finally sets in - to get your brain to really pay attention enough to change. If it's too hard and you're unable to "correct your mistakes," you won't improve either. You'll just learn how to move poorly with bad alignment and shaky knees.

Pick 2 to 3 movements that are related to your goals (squats, lunges, push ups, pull ups, rows, deadlifts to name a few that should be staples of most programs) and train for one of the above attributes each session. Hypertrophy (muscle growth) occurs at any weight that's above 60% of your one rep maximum, so you should be getting that with every workout anyways. Want to work on posture? Make sure you have perfect posture with every rep - use a mirror! Fluidity? Use a sufficient amount of weight to challenge you, but try to make every rep *look* smooth and easy. It may be hard, but look bored! Building stamina requires you to push yourself a little, and to continually increase the difficulty as you improve. Stamina is very much a slave to the SAID Principle, so you have to pick what type of stamina you'd like to achieve: run for hours; do high rep sets (15-20 or more); do multiple bouts high intensity/short time intervals (like what most sports require).

3. ***Increase your load by 5% every week.*** Load can be increased four ways: weight, volume, speed, and attention/intensity. Adding weights is easy enough, – just add 5% more weight to what you're lifting. Increasing your volume by 5% is easy as well: add

more reps to each set; add more sets; increase your interval time or the length of your run; add more movement patterns (for maximal learning and adapting, most brains can only handle working on 3-4 movement patterns per session until you become more advanced). You don't need to add exactly 5% speed- how would you quantify that? Just do your reps faster, or to really change up your workout, do them slower! Your brain learns more when you're moving at a slower speed than what's *comfortable*. Do a few sets of 5-6 slow reps (8 seconds per rep) and you'll learn this quickly! As you continue to advance and improve, you can also increase your volume by increasing your attention – get picky with yourself! Only allow *perfect* reps. Pick a body part that's been problematic for you, and focus on making that part move or hold perfectly in each rep. Increasing your mental load is at least a 5% or more increase!

4. ***Variety!*** As you've seen in every athletic body you desire to have, there are multiple attributes they possess that give them that body. Don't limit yourself to only one method. Every comprehensive exercise program includes variety and daily activity (recovery included!). Strength train, do *some* endurance work, run sprints for speed, walk/hike on your off days, and take time to play! Most likely you don't want to look like the beefed up, stiff body builder type; but more like the strong, fit, fast, and fluid great athletes you see on TV who have the perfect body and make everything look easy. They have multiple skills and attributes, and didn't obtain them by doing just one thing (the best athletes don't "specialize" until later in life (Tiger Woods being one of the exceptions!). They developed playing multiple sports, training and practicing for each of them, and building overall athletic skill.

5. ***Nutrition***: Following an 80/20 rule: 80% good/20% "splurge" should set most people up on a good, healthy way of eating. As much as possible, eat organic, fresh, whole foods. In general, most meals should involve plenty of healthy fats (fish, grass-fed meats, coconut oil, butter- yes, butter!, olive oil), plenty of vegetables, and add some carbs if you're still hungry (white rice, sweet potatoes). Get 3-4 servings of fruits and berries daily. Allow for some splurges, but remember: You can't out-train a bad diet!

The science is complex, but the principles are easy! Steps 2 and 3 above give you a template for endless opportunities to continually adapt and get results from every workout. Of course there are always exceptions. Having a professional assess you and guide you towards the plan that will work for you is always the best option.

So, here's the bottom line. You *can* transform your body, but it's a process that's going to take not only hard work and dedication, but also enough NEW stimuli to your brain at the right time. Using an old routine isn't necessarily wrong. However, your brain will surely need a NEW way of structuring your workout with those particular exercises. Change your load, change the sets, change the order or the pairings, and combine it with high intensity cardio. Instead of hopping on the stairclimber at the gym, go out to a track and run the bleachers! Changing from an indoor setting to an outdoor setting will be a welcome surprise to your brain and will actually make you work harder than being on a stationary piece of equipment.

Eat healthy, organic, whole foods, drink plenty of water and if you have the means, hire a nutritionist or trainer to help you in the areas you aren't so sure about. Lastly, don't give up on yourself. Even on the days when you feel like throwing in the towel, just make one NEW change with your workout and see how quickly your brain says "thank you." Trust us, we've seen it happen, and it's one of the reasons why we do what we do. Now get out there and make it happen!

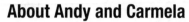

About Andy and Carmela

Andy Clower and Carmela Lieras are the owners of Fitness Evolved, the San Francisco Bay Area's most "cerebral" gym. They use the latest research and techniques from neuroscience and exercise physiology to design the most cutting-edge exercise programs targeted directly at getting clients to their functional and fitness goals quickly and safely.

Instead of waiting for the mainstream fitness industry to catch up with the latest research, they sought out those who are already applying it well - the world leaders in fitness and performance training - and spent thousands of dollars and countless hours being mentored by and learning from them and applying their principles. They are members of the Results Fitness Biz Mastermind group, mentored by Alwyn and Rachel Cosgrove - recognized world wide for their cutting edge business model and unmatched program design for fitness and fat loss. They have spent the past two years studying under and learning from Dr. Eric Cobb, creator of the world-class brain-based training system of Z Health.

Their training system helps put their clients back in control of their own performance; continually making lasting breakthroughs in all areas of performance including pain relief, injury prevention, and mindset. They are most often sought out by clients who have "tried everything else" with no results.

Carmela received her Bachelor of Arts degree in Exercise Science and is a certified personal trainer through the National Academy of Sports Medicine (NASM). During her collegiate education, she also served as a student athletic trainer for 3 years when she was not competing in cross-country and track and field. She is a Z Health Level 3 Certified Rehabilitation and Integrative Exercise Specialist, and also has a certification in TRX Suspension Training.

Andy is a Certified Athletic Trainer (ATC), with 10+ years of experience in Orthopedics and Physical Therapy, as well as sports performance and athletic rehabilitation. He is a Z Health Level 4 Certified Trainer, specializing in rehabilitative, therapeutic, and integrative performance exercise.

For more information about Fitness Evolved's services or to contact Andy and Carmela, go to: www.fitness-evolved.com

CHAPTER 19

Making Changes
To Your World

By Aaron Benes

The tension in the room was so great you could almost cut it with a knife. With nervous hands and butterflies filling my stomach, I sat there with my two little sisters as the three of us contemplated what was ahead. What did our parents need to share with us that could possibly be so important? Astonishment spread across our faces as the words "I am pregnant" fell out of my mother's mouth for the fourth time. Hundreds of thoughts raced through my mind while I secretly started to pray for a baby brother.

The third Benes girl was born a few months after my tenth birthday, leaving me to grow up in a house full of girls. Within a few years, our residence became the number one place for female social events ranging from soccer parties to late Friday game nights. My childhood could best be described as a nearly all female version of The Brady Bunch. Although back then I desperately wanted a little brother, today I would not change anything. Constantly being surrounded by girls at such a young age has made me the person I am today. As a consequence of these countless female interactions, I have developed a special fondness for the opposite sex.

On the whole I am very grateful to females. Because of them I've become a better listener, have more patience and am more understanding. Women have also taught me to be kinder and gentler while still remaining strong and a more compassionate leader. I've found women on the whole are better at balancing the many areas of life. As men, many of us tend to work too much, play too little and do a poor job of taking care of ourselves. I feel I've gained much in the way of balance with many of the women in my life keeping a watchful eye on me, and gently reminding me when they see the scales beginning to shift too much.

I believe it is important to view life from the perspective of the bigger picture, which in essence is that life is all about the journey and not the destination. I consider myself a life-long student to learning about as much as I possibly can (including about women). Due to my gender difference I realize I'll never completely understand them. However, I'm very grateful to females and all that they've given me and due to the rarity and depth of my experiences, I would like to think I do know just a little something about females. It is safe to say that my love for women is about as old as I am and carries much weight in my decision to specialize in working with females.

Growing up with three sisters in a household where athletics and sports played a significant role in our family lives laid much of the early foundation for me becoming a coach. During the many years of coaching, I began to see the bigger picture by looking at why people do the things they do and what ultimate desire they were seeking. It is here that I aim to open your eyes to your own inner workings and ideally prompt a lasting change in your life.

For real permanent change to occur, we must 'first off' really want it. Unfortunately it sometimes takes a life-changing event like losing a loved one to a disease or having the doctor tell us that we won't be around much longer to watch our kids or grandkids grow up to prompt us to make some heath and lifestyle changes. On the flip side of the coin, sometimes it's not one specific event that sparks the movement toward change but often a long and painful regression of the body, mind and spirit. From what I've seen, many women reach a dark place where things look very grim and often it is from this place that real change begins to occur.

Once the acceptance of wanting something better has happened, the next part of the journey towards transformation includes looking deep into one's self and exploring what you want to achieve and why it's important to you. It is in this process I've seen that all people are essentially seeking the same things: greater self-esteem or inner pride, love, freedom, peace and greater self-confidence – all of which lead to more happiness. Two ways people go about attempting to achieve these ultimate goals are through extrinsic or intrinsic methods. Most choose the former because it requires no need to look within ourselves and the sense of gratification is immediate.

EXTRINSIC VS. INTRINSIC & THE REAL ISSUE

Extrinsic: _According to Merriam-Webster, extrinsic is defined as "originating from or on the outside."_

For the purpose of this chapter, my definition is anything which is external or an outward attempt toward achieving an ultimate desire. This is different for all women - it may be visiting the tanning salon, purchasing a new pair of shoes, new purse, or a new outfit, having your hair/ nails done, or getting plastic surgery of some form. Other times it may be with food, alcohol or even drugs. Maybe you've had a tough day at work and think to yourself, "I deserve a treat, I've worked hard and I just need to relax" – so you have a glass or two of wine. This is also commonly done with food, "I've been really good on my diet all day so I deserve to splurge" and so you have a piece of chocolate cake or some ice cream. In every example here, you wanted something good for yourself – whether it's to feel good about yourself and have more self esteem, peace, or freedom doesn't matter. Regardless of the method the ultimate desires for all of us are always the same.

However, the extrinsic approach possesses two challenges. First off, the core issue is never realized or addressed, and as a result we do not gain the priceless knowledge of learning more about who we are as an individual. Secondly, this method often turns into a bad habit without the benefits of any healthy lifestyle changes. This is a short-term, temporary attempt toward a solution, commonly referred to as the "band-aid" approach. You want to feel better about yourself, and buying a new purse, visiting the tanning salon, or drinking a bottle of wine gives you those 'feel good' feelings you desire. But what do you do when those feelings wear off? After a week has passed and the thrill of the new purse is gone, then what? Most go buy another purse, pair of shoes, outfit etc. The same thing applies with the glass of wine or sweets to relax. It starts as an occasional thing, then it turns into a nightly event, and before you know it, it's a needed part of your day. Let me be clear: there is nothing wrong with buying a new purse, having a glass of wine, eating a cookie or visiting the tanning salon.

Action step: Before you do one of those things, you may want to first consider why you're doing it and then really look at what ultimate desire you hope to get for yourself with the purchase or action.

Intrinsic: *Intrinsic is defined as "originating and included wholly within an organ or part." (Merriam-Webster)*

For the purpose of this chapter, my definition is *change coming from within*. This is where the ultimate desires of having more happiness, peace, freedom, love, self-esteem etc, are sought through the means of an internal change. This is certainly the harder of the two methods, which I believe is why it is chosen significantly less frequently. Intrinsic methods to achieving ultimate goals have to do with looking at the root cause of one's unhappiness and then making a physical, mental, emotional and or spiritual change toward fixing the issue. There are a variety of approaches for achieving ultimate goals through intrinsic methods and the benefits are significantly greater than through extrinsic methods.

The first and most important benefit is that it addresses the reason why the individual so desperately wants the change. Taking the time to slow down with our busy lives and reflect inwardly is incredibly powerful and rewarding. It has been said in many cultures that the greatest gift is to know oneself. Secondly, through the process of intrinsic methods, real internal, lasting change begins to occur. The most common approach of achieving an ultimate goal through an intrinsic method is by that of a physical means. For example, if you want to feel better about yourself because you're no longer fitting into your size 8's and you just noticed last week that now your size 10's are becoming uncomfortable you could go to the tanning salon (everyone knows, tan fat looks better than white fat) to feel better about yourself, and this might last for a day or two. Or you could address the real core issue which is the fact that you are unhappy with the added weight gain, you really want to feel good about yourself, to feel sexy again and this might prompt you to make some lifestyle changes.

You know that your body always feels better when you're on a consistent exercise program and when you eat foods that are good for your body. Some individuals might choose to achieve their ultimate goals through mental and emotional changes and they could begin working with a counselor or therapist. Others choose the spiritual route and they might begin by working with a spiritual teacher, reading spiritual texts, and/or through prayer. Personally I've found in my own life and in working with clients that the changes of the greatest magnitude occur when the physical, mental, emotional and spiritual realm are all concurrently addressed.

Action step: 1) First, take some time to inwardly reflect and look at what it is that you are unhappy about. 2) Secondly, pick an intrinsic method which is best suited to achieve your goals.

SOLUTIONS

At this point I'm hoping you've had a couple of a-ha moments. Maybe you now realize that the reason why you do most of the things you do is because at the root level you are seeking something good for yourself. We all are seeking greater self-esteem, love, peace, freedom etc. You may have also realized that you too are like the majority and typically use the band-aid approach in an attempt to fix your issues and achieve your desires. My hope here is that you've learned a little something about yourself and have actually taken a good look inside which has provided you with some insight and ultimately changes your behavior.

The behavior modification is the most important part because otherwise the theory is just that, and without a plan of how to make some lifestyle modifications, it is likely that very little transformation will take place.

Life Style Solution - Action guide:

1. The first and most important thing you can do as a woman is let go of the false perception of perfection being attainable. All human beings are constantly changing, evolving, growing and learning – therefore we are not capable of attaining perfection. I suggest you consider giving up this notion of attainable perfection, forgive yourself and your body for not being perfect and also forgive yourself for any wrong-doings in your past. Find the good of your past, realize the lesson you learned from the experience and then move on. The truth is, you would not be who you are today if it wasn't for your past; you have always done the

very best you could in every moment – with the tools you had available at that time.

2. The second step is to take some time and figure out what you want. For example you may want to reduce your clothing size and get back into your size 8 jeans. Great! You know what you want. Now figure out why you want it. Once you get back into your old jeans what will that ultimately give you? Probably something along the lines of more self-esteem/self confidence, happiness etc.

3. The third step is to figure out what has stopped you in the past from attaining this ultimate desire. Quite possibly it may have been the fact that your sole method of achieving the desired good feelings was through an extrinsic method. What was your old band-aid approach to achieving your desired state? Was it food or alcohol-based by eating or drinking too much? Or was it shopping or the tanning bed?

4. The fourth step is to figure out what mode or modes of intrinsic behavior are best suited to attain your ultimate goal. If your desire is to lead a healthier life, have a toned figure and get out of a constant state of aches and pains which will ultimately provide you with more freedom, self-esteem and happiness. The right approach may be to work with a professional that offers fitness and nutritional coaching.

5. The fifth and final step is to take immediate action! Now that you've given up on the silly idea of being perfect, you've learned the lessons and forgiven yourself for your past. You've done some inner work and figured out what ultimate goal you desire and what unsuccessful mode of behavior you were using in your past. You now know the right intrinsic method or methods to achieve your goal so there is only one thing left to do. Take action right now! Avoid waiting for tomorrow, or for everything in your life to be just right. Avoid putting it off any longer.

The truth of the matter is you as a woman deserve better. You deserve to be happy, lead a fulfilling life and to have all of your dreams come true. This begins with you making the decision and taking action toward putting yourself first. As a woman and a natural nurturer you've probably always put others first. The trouble is when you're always putting others first you get left behind and your needs go unfulfilled. It is not possible to do an excellent job caring for others when your needs are not being met.

I hope you will now consider taking a little time by putting yourself first and addressing your mental, emotional, spiritual and physical needs. In conclusion, it is my hope that in some way this chapter has left a positive and powerful lasting impression on you by leaving you feeling empowered and changed your life for the better. Visit us at: www.imagineiffitness.com/resultsfitnessbook for the rest of this chapter and the amazing journeys of women just like you. I wish you the very best of luck on your journey and look forward to having our paths cross someday!

About Aaron

Aaron began his career as a coach at the very young age of 14, and has continued coaching a wide variety of clients ranging from AYSO soccer players to college and professional athletes. Having a strong thirst for knowledge and a desire to enhance the lives of others, Aaron graduated with a BS in Kinesiology with honors and then became a Certified Strength and Conditioning Coach with the NSCA. Aaron is also a certified Sport Performance Coach (certified to coach Olympic style weightlifting) under United States Weightlifting and a Functional Movement Systems (FMS) and Corrective Exercise Specialist (Level 2). He continues to study under some of the top strength, fitness, health and nutrition experts in the country.

Having spent the last decade being coached by and training with many world champions in Power-lifting, Olympic weightlifting and professional Strongman, his under the bar experience and knowledge is rather extensive. Along with his far-reaching knowledge in the fitness industry, Aaron is also a Destination Coach (certified life coach) and currently working on his doctorate in spiritual studies at Emerson University.

On a mental and spiritual level, Aaron's diligence toward understanding the human condition and human mind is rather apparent in his approach towards individually addressing each and every person he works with. Several years ago, on a quest to find inner peace and happiness, Aaron set out to heal his wounded heart. Having to deal with issues of abandonment, anger, regret, his parent's divorce, major conflicts, trauma, and a broken heart, forced him to seek help outside of his field. In doing so, he became not only a more compassionate person, but was so motivated by his own personal transformation that he now employs the tools of his mentors. This journey enabled him to see with compassion, listen with empathy and produce incredibly effective and lasting change for his clients.

Aaron's strong desire to help people become fit, healthy and happy is apparent in the passion he puts into his work. His compassion and understanding for the human spirit reveals itself in the manner in which he helps each client not only meet their physical goals, but also grow mentally, emotionally and spiritually.

Aaron works with clients from all different backgrounds and believes in treating each person as the unique individual they are. Every journey at **Imagine If** starts with an initial Strategy Session and a Body Blueprint so that a customized program can be written to address each individual's particular needs. Each client receives a personalized fitness program, nutritional counseling, and life coaching that reflect his or her needs to accomplish their goals. The client's progress at Imagine If is fueled by the customized programs that adapt and grow as the client does. Because Aaron is equipped with a wide variety of knowledge, he specializes in a holistic approach and addresses each client on a physical, mental, and emotional level; essentially helping them become their best self while allowing them to live the life of their dreams.

You can reach Aaron through his website: imagineiffitness.com or call (949)475-5555 or email: aaron@imagineiffitness.com. He is available for a variety of services including fitness coaching, life coaching, nutritional counseling, consultations, speaking engagements and workshops.

CHAPTER 20

Fitness On The Go

By John Farkas

"Yes, three days a week is plenty of time to get you into the best shape of your life." I swear I have said that hundreds of times when I first meet a new client. It sounds like a perfect scenario for about 20 seconds until they throw that first curveball at me... "By the way, I am going to be gone on the following dates." From there, I slowly see that perfect workout program starting to develop holes in it.

I preach on a daily basis that consistency is key. I don't care how hard you workout or how great of a program you are following, if you aren't sticking to it consistently, it is going to be very hard to see noticeable results.

I learned early on in my fitness career that you are going to have to get a little creative when it comes to keeping busy clients active on a consistent basis. Lets face it, in today's world, people are always on the run and travel seems to be a part of everyday life for many individuals. It is not uncommon for me to see someone on a Monday morning only to send them off with a checklist of activities to do throughout the week. I am not sure how some people are able to pull it off living out of a suitcase, but you have to play the cards you are dealt.

If living out of a suitcase isn't challenging enough, hours of back-to-back meetings may leave you with little time in your day to workout. Throw on top of that the business dinners (which tend to be on the unhealthy side) and the constant sitting while you are on the road and you have a recipe for disaster.

Fortunately, there is a solution. A little planning, commitment and creativity can go a long way when it comes to staying on track while you are traveling. With the right plan of attack, you can even make some major improvements when you are faced with these complicated times.

If you or someone you know is one of those individuals that can never seem to stay in one place for a very long period of time, I suggest you keep reading as I have put together a list of seven key tips that have helped many of my clients stay on the right track.

1. It all begins with proper planning.
Yes, I know that you may not be able to predict certain happenings that will occasionally come up, but at least give yourself a fighting chance. Make sure before you leave you at least have the basic necessities. Athletic shoes and exercise clothing are an obvious must unless you plan on starting a new fashion trend and working out in your business attire. If you are anything like me, you also better remember to bring the music and headphones as well.

2. Do your homework.
Call ahead to the hotel. It isn't going to hurt to know ahead of time what kind of facilities your hotel has to offer. Before leaving, I have all of my clients check with their hotel to find out this information. Often times, if hotels do not offer an exercise room, they might have an affiliation with a nearby gym for a small fee (or even better sometimes free!). It never hurts to ask.

3. Keep it simple.
Traveling can be stressful and rushed. There is no need to worry about setting aside an hour or more of your day to fit in some complicated exercise routine. I have heard too many times, "I didn't have enough time to exercise." Stop looking at it as "all or none." 10 minutes is great if that is all you have to spare. If you won the lottery would you say, no thanks, I only wanted it if it was the Powerball mega millions or would you be OK with winning $50,000? Same rules apply here, I will take something over nothing any day!

4. Get creative.
You do not have to have access to tons of gym equipment to get a great workout. Last time I checked, most hotel rooms have a

bed and it has been awhile since I was in a hotel without a desk and chair. Be innovative with what you have. For example, just within your hotel room, you can use your chair to perform dips, push-ups (incline or decline), step-ups, rear foot elevated split squats, planks, one-legged squats and hip extensions (and I'm just getting warmed up). Couch cushions or pillows can be used to create instability to perform a number of exercises such as one-legged dead lifts, push-ups (placing your hands on the cushions) or squats. This is just 'the tip of the iceberg' because we haven't even talked about using the best piece of equipment money can buy... Your body!

(PS- If the exercises I just mentioned sound like a foreign language that is perfectly fine. You can find video demonstrations of all of them on my blog at: www.BlueOceanFitness.net)

5. Pack your own tools of torture.

Let's just say you don't heed my previous advice and fail to check into the hotel fitness options and don't consider yourself a very creative person. You can alwaysguarantee you have exercise equipment if you take it with you in your suitcase. Now I don't expect you to pack around a set of kettlebells everywhere you go but, a resistance band, suspension trainer, jump rope or val sliders will fit just about anywhere. This is one option that I give to my clients often because that ensures that they have enough equipment to get an awesome workout. I am not even going tobegin on the unlimited number of exercises you can perform with any of the above-mentioned equipment. I think the best part of all is that you can take them anywhere inside or out. Now it is going to be even harder to come up with an excuse, when you know you have everything you need to workout on the beach or wherever else suits your fancy.

6. Make sure your workout is effective.

If you are still training one body part every time you walk into a gym then you need to step out of the 80's and find a new role model. The days of training like Arnold have come and gone. Unless of course you are interested in getting all oiled up, standing in your underwear and flexing next to others of the same gender. Yes I am referring to the cult of bodybuilding. I think it's safe to say that most people do NOT want to look like the person that you are probably envisioning right now. The facts are that training your whole body more frequently will result in better fat loss and bigger muscle and strength gain which is what most of us are after. The beauty of it is, rather than spending 5 to 6 hours in the gym each week just to perform your strength training, you can actually get much better results working out in about half the time. Who wouldn't that sound good to?

7. Use mult-joint exercises.

This one relates very closely to #5. Once again, you can thank the bodybuilding cult for leading everyone down the wrong path here. Isolation exercises working one muscle in one plane of motion such as leg extensions, bicep curls and leg curls areout. Yes, while performing these exercises you might feel like you are really accomplishing something because of the immediate burn you feel in the specific muscle, but that doesn't mean they are more effective and providing a muscle-building stimulus. If time is ever going to be an issue while you are on the road, you can't go wrong with multi-joint movements such as lunges, step-ups, push-ups or squats just to give you a few examples. Not only will these allow you to target moremuscles with fewer exercises, they are also greater for calorie burning and fat loss.

8. We can't forget about food.

Now what would any talk about staying on track be if we didn't at least touch on the nutrition side of things. This is often the big killer. I have heard horror stories from clients that fell off the bandwagon while traveling. Although it isn't the end of the world, finding a happy medium will be well worth it when you step on that scale after returning from your trip. Personally, I am not about to haul around a gigantic cooler so I wouldn't expect you to either, so lets focus on items that are pretty much safe anywhere.

Almonds, walnuts, cashews and seeds are all staples that I never leave behind. A protein shaker and some powder in a zip lock bag will also go a long way, although it has raised questions a few times when passing through security. One word of advice I recently learned: you might be better off traveling with chocolate flavored protein powder. The vanilla tends to draw a little more attention, especially when traveling internationally. Protein bars, granola bars and fruit are also all great options as well that will easily fit in a carry-on. If you have good intentions of buying healthy food at your destination, make sure you at least pack something for the trip. I don't know how many times I have forgot to pack a snack and ended up in line at the nearest airport fast-food stop. Lets face it, when your stomach starts to get hungry, your fitness goals can get put on hold.

SAMPLE PROGRAMS

Here are two different programs that you can use just about anywhere. Both are set up as "density workouts." Density workouts involve a series of five exercises done without rest for 20 consecutive minutes. The goal of the program is to complete as many sets as possible. This is my favorite way to get in and get out in record time.

Sample 1 (using a resistance band):
- Mountain climber - 8 repetitions with each leg
- Reverse lunge - 8 repetitions with each leg
- Resistance band chest press - 8 repetitions
- Resistance band squat to row - 8 repetitions
- Resistance band chops - 8 repetitions on each side

Sample 2 (using a chair)
- Step-ups - 8 repetitions with each leg
- Decline push-ups (feet on chair) - 8 repetitions
- Rear foot elevated split squats - 8 repetitions with each leg
- Dips - 8 repetitions
- Plank (elbows on chair) - 30 seconds

About John

John Farkas is a St. Louis-based fat loss expert that has helped hundreds of individuals look and feel their best. He is regularly sought out by the media for his opinion on fitness trends and fat loss strategies. John is the founder and owner of Blue Ocean Fitness, where he is known for his effective group personal training programs. He has also become one of the leading authorities in online fitness coaching.

John provides fitness workshops to both the general public and area businesses where he educates groups on effective workout methods and more efficient ways to reach their fitness goals. He is the author of *The Metabolic Breakthrough,* an E-book designed with short and effective metabolically-demanding workouts for clients to do while traveling on the road with minimal equipment.

To learn more about John Farkas, Blue Ocean Fitness or *The Metabolic Breakthrough* – Visit: www.BlueOceanFitness.net
Or call: 314-952-9496.

CHAPTER 21

Knee Pain? No Problem: Stop Limping and Start Lifting

By Kari Negraiff, CSCS & Steve Di Tomaso, CSCS

At age 29, Ziad is a recreational motor sports enthusiast with a successful engineering career. At a glance he seems to have everything going for him - with the exception of the lean and muscular physique he's desired since college. Long hours in a sedentary job combined with indulgences of convenience food, and social dining have softened his waistline. One day, tired of his flabby mid-section, Ziad decided to hit the gym.

Unfortunately, during his quest for the "ultimate athletic physique" his progress was hampered by chronic knee pain. Frustration mounted as traditional multi-joint lifts renowned for their hormone-stimulating and fat-burning metabolic prowess such as squats; step-ups and lunges caused intolerable knee pain. Despite exhaustive efforts at rehabilitation and manual therapy, his achy joints were non-compliant. Ziad needed a unique approach to training in order to produce the jaw-dropping results he sought. Ditching the age-old cliché of "no pain-no gain" his trainer implemented a pain-free and "joint-friendly strength training" (JFST) approach which included single and multi-joint exercises. Finally able to build strength in his legs and intensify the metabolic affect of his workouts, JFST allowed Ziad to train his way to 20 lbs of fatloss in just three months.

Ziad's story is compelling, but perhaps you're wondering how this concept of JFST can help you with a performance-related goal. Meet Zana, a Division I basketball player and junior national standout. At age 18, before her freshman year at Utah State, Zana was faced with a difficult decision. She had been suffering for years from a painful condition called jumper's knee that had degraded both of her patellar tendons. In the off-season, Zana had debridement surgery on both knees to reduce pain and promote healing of the tendon. Unfortunately her knee pain returned with a vengeance by the end of her basketball season with Utah State. She returned home to Vancouver unsure if she'd ever be able to play the game she loves again. Zana was dejected, her knee pain was intolerable, but she was determined that she was going to live a healthy lifestyle. She began seeing a trainer that applied the principles of JFST. Through knee-friendly training she was not only able to build strength in her legs and reduce much of the pain she had previously experienced, but she was able to do the unthinkable and return to play university ball on a full scholarship just one year later.

WHAT IS JOINT-FRIENDLY STRENGTH TRAINING??

The term "joint-friendly strength training" was coined by strength coach and educator, Nick Tumminello. Though the concept of avoiding pain while training is not new, the JFST difference is that it shifts focus to maximizing your results despite limited and painful joints. JFST goes against the grain in a fitness industry that has shifted much of its focus to corrective exercise. Rather, JFST is a safe way to gain strength and improve performance while managing pain of compromised joints, whether it is due to injury or chronic condition.

What if you were able to build bigger and stronger legs despite having sore knees? That is exactly the value of JFST. So you can't squat without knee pain? No problem. By adjusting your program to include knee-friendly exercises, you CAN be successful in reaching your fitness goals while sparing your knees.

The following are a list of our top nine knee-friendly exercises that we have seen great results from:

1. <u>Barbell Hip Thrust</u>

Start Position: seated with shoulders resting against bench.

Movement: drive the hips up to full extension while pushing through the heels.

Tips: the head, shoulders, and hips should all move together. Knees should NOT be less than 90 degrees at the top of the lift. Use a bar pad for added hip comfort during the exercise.

2. <u>Supine Hip Extension with Leg Curl</u> (SHELC)

Start Position: lying on back with hips fully extended and knees bent at 90 degrees.

Movement: slowly extend knees through full range of motion. Flex knees to return to start position.

Tips: Maintain extended hip position throughout entire movement.

3. <u>Reverse Lunge</u>

Start Position: standing tall.

Movement: slowly step back controlling the movement with the front leg and maintaining a slight forward lean until your back knee is close to touching the ground. Return to start position.

Tips: the spine and the front leg's shin should run parallel throughout the movement; both the knee and trunk should be angled forward with the lowest rib making contact with the thigh in the bottom position of the lift. Maintain the weight on the front heel throughout the movement. Push through the heel at the bottom of the lift to return to the start position.

4. <u>Romanian Deadlift</u> (RDL)

Start Position: tall standing position with knees locked out and shoulders locked into position and pelvis pushed forward.

Movement: push the hips back with relatively straight legs in a neutral spinal position. Once a forced stretch is achieved in the hamstrings (back of thigh), return to the start position.

Tips: the key to maintaining a neutral spine position during the bend portion of the lift is to keep the shoulder blades pulled down and back.

5. <u>Rack Deadlift</u>

Start Position: feet shoulder width with shins aligned vertically one half inch away from the barbell. Hands grip the bar slightly wider than the knees while pulling the scapula down and back. Hip hinged with a neutral spinal position and tension on the hamstrings.

Movement: push the heels through the ground and stand tall. Finish standing tall with the pelvis pushed forward. Return to the start position by hinging at the hips.

Tips: the key to a neutral spinal position is to keep the shoulder blades pulled down and back throughout the duration of the lift. Adjust the rack height to the limit of your hamstring flexibility. Have a look at your profile and ensure that back is in a neutral position at the bottom of the lift. Though knee flexion is encouraged it is necessary to align the shin vertically to keep undue stress off of the knee.

6. Split Stance RDL

Start Position: tall standing position with the working leg's knee locked, pelvis pushed forward. Place the toe of the non-working leg slightly behind the working leg.

Movement: Identical technique to the RDL with the exception of having one leg used only as a point of balance.

Tips: The non-working leg is a point of balance throughout the movement and should not be used to bear weight.

7. Rear Foot Elevated RDL

Start Position: tall standing position with the working leg's knee locked, pelvis pushed forward. The non-working leg's foot is placed laces down on a bench.

Movement: Identical to the RDL with the exception of having one foot on a bench.

Tips: The majority of the weight should be supported on the front/working leg.

8. Plate Push

Start Position: hands on plate with one foot forward.

Movement: Push plate forward by stepping one foot in front of the other

Tips: can also be performed with a towel on a wood floor.

9. Kettlebell Swing

Start Position: with the kettlebell placed in front of the user keep a neutral posture, grab the kettlebell, feel a loaded stretch in the hamstrings, put weight on the heels, and swing the kettlebell back between the legs to start the movement.

Movement: drive the hips forward explosively causing the knees to lock out and the pelvis to push forward. The hip 'snap' should lead the movement of the arm swing.

Tips: stay tight in your abdominals throughout the movement. 'Compress' your breathing and exhale at the top of the movement.

Use what works best for you. If there is pain in a movement, use common sense. DON'T DO IT!

A-B-C'S OF HOW TO MAKE JFST WORK FOR YOU:

Simply providing you with a list of knee-friendly exercises is helpful - but not enough to get you the results you want. We are going to provide you with our coveted four-step system for maximizing your results using the JFST approach.

Step One: Run through the above list of exercises, first with body weight only, then again using a load that allows you to complete 8-12 repetitions without maximal fatigue. Most importantly, ensure proper alignment of the kneecap with the second toe when performing the above exercises. Alignment is central to reducing unwanted joint forces that contribute to painful movement. While performing the exercises, note any positions or movements that cause discomfort or pain (for consideration in Step Two).

Step Two: Organize the exercises you performed in Step One into three categories:

Category A: Pain free

Category B: Mild but tolerable discomfort that can be managed with load, joint position and/or movement range of motion

Category C: Painful

Step Three: From your list of exercises in Categories A and B, prioritize them from highest to lowest, in terms of their specificity toward your goal. For instance, first determine whether you are you training for fat-loss, muscle building or performance. Fatloss and muscle building goals will give highest priority to exercises with the most metabolic demands and hormone stimulating/strength stimuli such as rack dead lifts and RDLs. Whereas a performance-related training goal might give highest priority to exercises that most closely mimic the force-producing patterns required for performance-enhancement in sports, such as reverse lunges or kettlebell swings for vertical jump improvement in basketball players.

Step Four: Design your knee-sparing training program, while honoring good form and progressive overload. Use our sample training programs outlined below as a template to create individualized programs. Keep in mind that the exercises trained first in the session will receive the most benefit, so this is where you want to perform your highest priority exercises determined in Step Three.

SAMPLE TRAINING PROGRAMS:

Order	Exercise	Sets	Reps	Tempo	Rest
	Power Development				
1	KB swings	3	6	X	60s
	Resistance Training				
2a	BB Hip Thrust	4	6	Mod	90s
2b	Reverse Crunch	4	8	Slow	0
3a	Push-up	3	8	Mod	60s
3b	Reverse Lunge	3	8	Mod	60s
3c	Chin Up	3	8	Mod	60s
3d	RFE Deadlift	3	8	Mod	60s

Table 1. Performance Program

Order	Exercise	Sets	Reps	Tempo	Rest
	Combination				
1	BB RDL + bent over row	3	10	Mod	60s
	Resistance Training				
2a	Rack Deadlift	4	10	Mod	0
2b	Alt. Overhead Press	4	10	Mod	0
2c	Split Stance RDL	4	10	Mod	0
2d	Inverted Row	4	10	Mod	0
2e	Side Plank	4	30s	Mod	90s
	Metabolic Circuit				
3a	KB Swing	2	15	Fast	0
3b	Push-up	2	15	Mod	0
3c	Plate push	2	20s	Fast	0
3d	Bent over DB row	2	15	Mod	120s

Table 2. Fatloss Program

CONCLUSION

Painful joints cannot always be resolved but applying the principles of JFST will maximize strength, size and performance gains without causing further pain. JFST will enable you to realize your potential with exercises that have been adapted to provide critical training stimuli while working within your limitations. We encourage you to experiment with the techniques offered in this chapter to enhance your training and to help reach your performance and physique goals.

Remember - use common sense; if it hurts, don't do it!

About Steve & Kari

Steve Di Tomaso of Vancouver, BC, is distinguished as being the most sought after fitness professional in his area. He is highly educated and certified through top fitness governing bodies including the NSCA. Always setting goals for himself, he believes that pushing his own limits will help him to be a better business owner, coach and leader. With a passion for the human body and continuing education, he strives to empower his clients with knowledge so that they may constantly improve throughout their lives.

Kari Negraiff, also of Vancouver, BC, is a highly-qualified fitness coach with credentials from several top internationally and locally recognized institutions. She is known for her relentless drive, and her passion for coaching others to success. Kari is locally renowned as her area's most successful and desired fitness coach. She attributes her success as a fitness coach and business owner to her commitment to core values of teamwork ("we, not me") and bringing her best every day.

Kari and business partner, Steve Di Tomaso, are proud owners of their highly popular, hybrid fitness club, Envision Fitness. Specializing in fatloss, their gym has revolutionized the way fitness is done by consistently providing above average results using a semi-private and group training system adapted from industry leaders in fatloss training, Alwyn and Rachel Cosgrove. Kari and Steve attribute the success of Envision Fitness to its family-like culture and collective emphasis on expert coaching via fun and innovative training techniques.

Personal credentials:
Steve Di Tomaso, CSCS
Kari Negraiff, CSCS

For more information on Steve and Kari or how you too
can realize your fitness potential:
Visit: www.envision-fitness.ca
Or call 1-604-568-4243.

CHAPTER 22

Ultimate Fitness:
It's In The Bag!

By Joshua Henkin

Whether you're a couch potato or a dedicated gym rat, you probably know you should be doing some kind of exercise just to stay healthy, never mind to look and feel your best. But with so many options and opinions out there, it can be hard to know exactly what you're supposed to be doing to get the benefits you need.

Core-strengthening programs like Pilates are popular with a lot of people – particularly women – but while they're great for working core muscles, they don't provide much of a cardio-boost – or calorie-burning power. Strength training with weights or the machines at the gym can work your muscles, but again, it doesn't do much in the area of cardio. On the other hand, cardio workouts like spin classes or running on a treadmill burn calories, but they don't provide many of the important benefits strength and core training provide.

Of course, you can do all three different types of workouts – and as a personal trainer, I definitely know some dedicated people do. But I also know that doesn't leave you much time for a life outside the gym.

That's what makes The Ultimate Sandbag such a great exercise tool.

WHAT IS THE ULTIMATE SAND BAG?

A bag of sand might not sound innovative, however, it is the secret that athletes such as martial artists and wrestlers have used for centuries. Hard to argue with the amazing all around fitness of these athletes. Revolutionizing the design and purpose of the sandbag training brings us into the needs of modern fitness programs. The weight is ideal for strength training, the instability of the bag helps strengthen core muscles, and the entire workout burns up to 30% more calories than with other strength training methods.

But it's more than just a piece of exercise equipment – it's also an entire fitness system, designed entirely around this one piece of equipment and designed to work for anyone at any fitness level. From dedicated couch potatoes to serious gym rats, The Ultimate Sandbag evolves with them as they get better and stronger.

THE BIRTH OF THE BAG

When I invented the Ultimate Sandbag in 2005, I didn't realize the full power of this new system of training. I was looking to improve my own health. Back during my high school basketball career, I badly herniated low-back discs. And while I was able to recover enough so that I could play in college, a second injury cost me my spot on the team, as well as temporary use of my right leg.

Although the loss of use of my leg was temporary, the pain seemed to be permanent. It stuck with me no matter what I did. I was still in school at Arizona State University studying exercise physiology, which gave me access to just about every method of rehabilitation that was available. I made myself, and solving my problem, part of my studies, and started my own path on sort of a "self-journey" trying to figure out what I could do to stop the pain.

But nothing worked.

Then one day a colleague suggested I stop looking for the "latest, greatest" thing and go back to basics. He suggested I read about what old-time strongmen did, before the days of physical therapists and specialized surgeries and exercise as a science.

I figured I had nothing to lose. So I checked a few books out of the library and started reading.

As I researched, I kept reading about one common practice that all of these tremendous athletes shared – they all mentioned using odd objects in their training. One of the objects that kept popping up was a sandbag, and since it was pretty easy to make my own, I decided to try one out. I got hold of a duffel bag and filled it with sand, and I started experimenting with it. And almost immediately, I realized I had hit upon something special.

Lifting the sandbag was unlike anything I'd ever experienced before in the world of fitness – and as an exercise physiology major and lifelong athlete, that's saying a lot. I've used just about every tool you can find at a gym, and while a lot of them claim to be different and are designed to do different things, at their core, they're all pretty similar. They're hard – they're fixed in position – they stay where and how they are when you grab them.

The sandbag, on the other hand, had a feel and use that was profoundly *different.* The sandbag moved and shifted the moment you began to lift it. Unlike a barbell where the center of mass is through the middle and the weight is perfectly balanced, with the Ultimate Sandbag you could never predict the movement — making more muscles come into play. Unlike any piece of equipment I had used up until this point, the sandbag was "non-cooperative."

And it was just that lack of cooperation that helped me more than anything I had tried before.

Working with the sandbag challenged my body in completely different ways. It worked all the usual muscles I always tried to work, but it also worked those little connector muscles in my core that I needed to rebuild my strength, forcing me to engage them to keep my balance and coordination while lifting the constantly shifting sandbag. Before long, I could see and feel the benefits, and my back was finally seeing improvements, and became better than it ever was – even when I was a high school athlete.

As I moved into personal training, I brought my sandbag to sessions and started using it with my clients. This exposed the not-so-miraculous side of my homemade fitness miracle. Yes, it produced results like nothing

I'd used before. Yes, it challenged my clients in a whole new way. But as great as it worked, it was still, in essence, a duffel bag full of sand. It was messy and dirty – it leaked sand and kicked up clouds of dust when it hit the ground. The rough surfaces of the bag scratched some people's skin. Plus, it was difficult to make the sandbag progressive – once people got as far as they could with it, there was no way to make the exercises harder or more challenging.

Since that's a requirement of any successful training system, I assumed my sandbag and I had gone as far as we could go. I figured it was time to abandon the system and go back to the old ways of doing things.

That's when a friend asked a question that changed my life. He asked me, "If you could create something that would solve those problems, what would it be?"

That one question really laid the foundation for The Ultimate Sandbag and the system that I still use today.

Inspired by my friend's question, I re-imagined my sandbag as a solution to people's fitness needs – durable and leak-proof, made from skin-friendly materials, with a variety of handles that can be comfort- ably gripped and additional components that can easily be attached and removed.

I developed an entire workout system around the sandbag, with programs for everyone from hardcore lifters down to complete newbies.

And I watched it become a fitness revolution.

WHO IS THE ULTIMATE SANDBAG FOR?

A lot of people ask if The Ultimate Sandbag is really only designed for fitness fanatics like me – and in the beginning, that's certainly who the system attracted. But there are programs within the system that work for everyone, from reforming couch potatoes who are new to exercise to seasoned gym rats. We work with a lot of people who exercise at home, and a lot of trainers like to use The Ultimate Sandbag in their gyms, because they take up less space than bulky exercise machines. You can even take them with you when you travel. The best part is, wherever you go, you get a gym-quality workout.

It's easy to get started with The Ultimate Sandbag – we have a whole exercise routine specifically designed for beginners. Not that it's easy – you instantaneously find out that it's a lot more fatiguing than other exercises, because every repetition is different. With most exercise equipment, once you get used to it, you start to do what I call "grooving" the exercise a little bit. As you get more used to an exercise, you gain efficiency at it, and when you gain efficiency, the results you get from the exercise decrease.

The Ultimate Sandbag, however, is not so easy to master, which is a very good thing. The constantly shifting weight means your body constantly has to fight for stability – every time you lift The Ultimate Sandbag, you have to use your core or you'll be too unstable to lift the bag at all.

Now, add in the strength training provided by the weight, plus a very effective cardio workout – we've had people achieve heart rates that are very close to the heart rates they'd reach during sprinting – all at the same time. And what you get is a true, all-in-one workout that makes really great use of your time. A lot of programs tell you that you get "everything at once," but we've actually measured it and been able to prove it. And you'll be able to progress further without injury, because those core muscles you're strengthening protect your back and other sensitive areas from injury.

ONE SANDBAG – HUNDREDS OF EXERCISES

Once we designed the sandbag as a fitness tool, it opened up a lot of doors as far as what we could do with it. Our program currently includes over 300 drills that are a mixture of upper body, lower body, core, strength and stability – and the best part is, a lot of these are integrated all at once into a single exercise. That's why people find after a while that the program is really challenging, because you're not just working your arms, you're not just working your quads, you're using the whole body through most of the exercises, so there's a big "bang for your buck" kind of return on your workouts.

And it's not just about lifting. Some of the exercises are very unique, and that's kind of an exciting aspect for people too. You work at very different postures and positions which hits more muscles, builds faster fitness, and provides some really innovative exercises. A lot of people – maybe you're one of them! – don't like to exercise because they think it's boring. With this program, suddenly your body is doing things it's never done before. A lot of people start smiling, or even laughing, because they're moving in athletic ways they've never experienced at a gym – or anywhere else!

Because of the way the equipment and the program are designed, there are also all kinds of ways to progress from beginner all the way to expert level with the very same piece of equipment. With a typical fitness system, you either increase the weight or the reps - that's about as far as your options go. With the Ultimate system, the possibilities are almost endless. You can hold the bag in different ways – we have 12 different holding positions that range from very easy to very difficult, and different body positions that can make the exercise more stable – and easier – or more challenging and difficult. You can also change the weight and/ or dimension of the sandbag by adding on various attachments. More possibilities not only allow for incredible variation in workouts, but more importantly almost always put you in a positions to succeed. All of a sudden it is no longer about a "bag of sand"!

A typical workout can take only 20 minutes and almost always is less than your standard gym workout. This is due to the full body getting trained at once and the fact the Ultimate Sandbag is such a challenging fitness tool. We know the challenge because we see workouts that can burn anywhere from 400 to 700 calories in one workout! We recommend working out from three to four days a week, depending on your current level of fitness – newcomers should take it a little more slowly, because the exercises will ask your body to do things it's never done before. Remember, a little can accomplish a lot, especially at first.

When you're ready for more, you'll know it. And The Ultimate Sandbag can provide it.

SUCCESS STORIES

My wife is a physical therapist who was once almost an Olympic-level swimmer, until she herniated five discs in her back. She couldn't squat carrying only her body weight without pain. Like me, she used all of her expert knowledge as a professional to search for a way to feel better, and was unable to find anything that worked – even with everything she knew about physical therapy. But after working our program for a year, she can not only squat without pain, she can also do it while carrying an 80-pound sandbag.

And The Ultimate Sandbag doesn't just work for athletic types, as this story will illustrate:

All my life I have been overweight due to poor diet and nutrition. In November of 2010, I was 27 years old and the largest I had ever been at 336 pounds. I was told by several doctors that I would develop Diabetes and was in very poor health. I decided to change my diet and started exercising, but once I was down about 40 lbs, I got stuck. Then I saw an ad for The Ultimate Sandbag on a fitness site – it seemed more interesting and more versatile then traditional weights or workout equipment. I got the Strength Package and I can honestly say it was some of the best money I ever spent on my health. USB bags are built to take any kind of punishment you can dish out – it's rock solid, and it will make you rock solid! 6 months went by and now a full year after I started I am at 246 lbs (I've lost 90 pounds) and am working my way toward 100 pounds. The sandbag is one of the only pieces of fitness equipment I recommend to others and use over and over and never get tired of it. It's waiting for me in the gym, like a good friend, wanting to challenge me and help me to become the best I can!

~ G. Duff

The Ultimate Sandbag works for all kinds of people, in all kinds of situations. I still train individual clients every day, and I also travel all over the world teaching professionals and organizations how to implement the program in a way that suits their needs. Most recently, we taught The Ultimate Sandbag program to the U.S. Army Special Forces recruiting battalion, and I just got back from Missouri State University, where I taught the program to their athletic training department. It's been featured on TV shows like "The Biggest Loser," and in a wide range of magazines including "Men's Fitness." And it just continues to grow. Why? Because it flat out works!

Way back when this all started, I wasn't looking to start a revolution. I was just looking for relief. But I have to admit, I'm proud of where The Ultimate Sandbag has taken me, and how many different kinds of people it has helped.

I'm incredibly excited to see who it helps in the future.

About Josh

Josh Henkin, CSCS is known as innovator of Dynamic Variable Resistance Training (DVRT) and has become one of the most sought out fitness professionals for his revolutionary fitness programs. Josh has taught his DVRT program to over ten countries worldwide as well as instructing some of the top fitness associations in the U.S.

In 2008, Josh was commissioned by the US Army Special Forces Recruiting Battalion to create "SELECTED". A unique fitness program specifically designed to help recruits successfully pass the Selection process. His programs have been used by NBA, NFL, NHL, UFC, and Division I athletes as a means to get an edge on the competition.

His DVRT program is not just for the elite, being used by top fitness facilities in more than 70 counties worldwide. Josh's DVRT program has been used on "The Biggest Loser," featured in "Details Magazine," demonstrated on "Access Hollywood," and he has been a contributor to "Men's Health."

Josh's creation of The Ultimate Sandbag has completely revolutionized how exercise programs are performed and designed. In 2005, Josh released his Ultimate Sandbags and DVRT program that allowed anyone to achieve incredible results without the need for expensive gyms or equipment. With over 400 exercises, Josh's DVRT Ultimate Sandbags offer the most complete fitness experience.

You can learn more about Josh's DVRT program and the success of his Ultimate Sandbag System by visiting: http://DVRTFitness.com or call 1-800-698-2556

CHAPTER 23

The Tough Love of Self-Myofascial Release

By Heather Binns, CPT

Whether you're an athlete, a casual exerciser, a stay-at-home-parent or an office junkie, Self-Myofascial Release (SMR), aka foam rolling, is a cost-effective treatment for muscle pain, inflexibility, injury prevention, physical imbalances and relieving stress – doctor's visit <u>not</u> required ☺. Most people think only athletes are the ones requiring therapy for overactive/overused muscles. However, sitting at a desk all day causes various muscle groups to shorten and tighten while underutilized muscles grow weak. Effects of this physical discrepancy cause injury, especially if you perform movements with improper form. All of this results in muscle imbalances and incorrect functional movement.

I have been a runner and athlete my entire life and always refused to stretch before and after cross country and track practice in high school. I don't know why; just me being stubborn I guess, which probably comes from my spicy Puerto Rican side. Either way, I was a runner (no more than a 5K [3.1 miles] back then). As I got older I continued running and increased the mileage up to 10Ks (6.2 miles), half marathons (13.1 miles) and full marathons (26.2 miles). I started getting shin splints more often and began having knee pain, hip pain, ankle pain and more. When I ran my first marathon in October of 2006, the Long Beach Marathon, it was a great but extremely painful experience! You can read my recap of the race written the very next day at: www.FullOfLifeFitness.com. Who knows, you may have faced some of the same trials and tribulations I did in that first marathon and can fix them now.

It wasn't until I became a Certified Personal Trainer that I learned about Self-Myofascial Release and started foam rolling regularly. The changes in my running were unbelievable! I was able to run longer and faster without pain, and run more efficiently, all the while getting stronger and more fit than ever before! My muscles were finally happy, elongated and refreshed.

Self-Myofascial Release is a soft tissue therapy and stretching technique used to improve flexibility and function of tight muscles, inhibit overactive/overused muscles, reduce inflammation, improve joint range of motion (ROM) and more, by focusing on the body's neural and fascial systems. Self-Myofascial Release is based upon two principles:

1. Breaking-up fascia within the body, and
2. Manipulation of various neuromuscular receptors to release muscle tightness.

Self-Myofascial Release uses the concept of autogenetic inhibition to improve soft tissue extensibility, thus relaxing the muscle and allowing the activation of the antagonist muscle (opposing muscle responsible for returning the limb to its initial position). When you increase this pressure/tension in the muscle to the point where it is at risk of injury, the Golgi Tendon Organ (GTO) responds by relaxing the muscle (autogenetic inhibition). By stimulating the GTO, you are able to cause relaxation of the muscle and consequently the fascia surrounding it to achieve a proper stretch and increased range of motion.

For various reasons including disuse, lack of stretching and injury, the fascia and underlying muscle tissue can become stuck together, which is called an adhesion. Adhesions result in restricted movement, cause pain and soreness, reduce flexibility, and inhibit range of motion. By applying gentle force to the adhesion, or trigger point, the collagenous fibers are changed from a bundled position into an alignment that is more parallel with the direction of the muscle and/or fascia. Together, muscle and fascia make up the myofascial system within the body.

Fascia is the soft tissue element of the connective tissue that offers protection and support for most structures within the body, which is located between the skin and the underlying structure of muscle and bone. It consists of three layers:

1. Superficial fascia
2. Deep fascia
3. Subserous fascia

Fascia is one of the three types of dense connective tissue (the others being ligaments and tendons) and extends without interruption from the top of the head to the tip of the toes. It covers and connects the muscles, organs and skeletal structure in the body.

Muscle is a tissue consisting primarily of highly specialized contractile cells used to produce force and cause motion and movement. There are three types of muscle:

1. Skeletal muscle
2. Cardiac muscle
3. Smooth muscle

These muscles are a mass of musculus fibers attached at each extremity, by means of a tendon, to a bone or other structure. The muscle origin is the more proximal (closer to the midline of the body), or more fixed attachment. The insertion is the more distal (further from the midline of the body), or more movable attachment. The caput or head is the narrowing part of the muscle that is attached to the tendon of origin.

Cardiac and smooth muscle contraction occurs without conscious thought and is necessary for survival such as contraction of the heart. Skeletal muscle contraction occurs voluntarily and is used to move the body. Examples are smaller movements of the eye and larger movements of the arms and legs.

When muscles become fatigued and overused due to acute physical trauma, poor posture, repetitive movement mechanics, over-training, inadequate rest and poor nutrition, trigger points (tender spots/painful areas) accumulate in the muscle. Trigger points are created in muscles that must remain contracted for very long periods of time without rest. Some of these muscles are commonly used to support the neck and shoulder joints.

Examples of common overuse situations are holding one's arm up on the steering wheel while driving, using a computer keyboard and mouse, drawing and painting, building small objects, and any other repetitive movements. The body attempts to maintain the contraction of the muscle in these situations, but over time the muscle is damaged or develops trigger points. However, if given a chance to rest, the muscle may be able to repair itself.

As in most tissue, irritation of the fascia and/or muscle causes local inflammation. Chronic inflammation results in fibrosis, or thickening of the connective tissue, which causes pain and irritation resulting in reflexive muscle tension that causes more inflammation. This cycle can result in ischemia (inadequate blood supply to an organ or part of the body) and somatic dysfunction (impaired or altered function of bodily structures). Self-Myofascial Release aims to break this cycle.

WHERE AND WHEN TO USE SELF-MYOFASCIAL RELEASE

Self-Myofascial Release is most commonly performed on the calves, shins, hamstrings, adductors (inner thigh), quadriceps, hip flexors, iliotibial (IT) band, glutes/buttocks, chest and lower/mid/upper back. The mid/upper back can be rolled by lying on top of the foam roller, the glutes/buttocks by sitting on top of the foam roller with your legs partially crossed, and most of the other muscles require sitting or lying on the floor with one or two legs, or an arm, propped-up on top of the foam roller.

Self-Myofascial Release is hard work and sometimes painful. By far, the most painful area for most people is the IT band. When I first started using Self-Myofascial Release in the latter part of 2006, I would almost cry while being on the foam roller, especially on my IT bands. I could only handle it for a few seconds at a time before collapsing on the floor.

By performing Self-Myofascial Release a minimum of three times a week in conjunction with strength training, cardiovascular exercise, and various other forms of stretching, you can reduce muscle pain, correct imbalances, and minimize future injury no matter who you are and what type of lifestyle you live.

BENEFITS OF SELF-MYOFASCIAL RELEASE

- Relieve and decrease muscle pain and soreness
- Reduce inflammation
- Improve flexibility and function of tight muscles
- Correct muscle imbalances
- Improve joint range of motion
- Relax sore muscles
- Decrease recovery time
- Reduce neuromuscular hypertonicity
- Inhibit overactive/overused muscles
- Maximize recovery time
- Enhance extensibility of musculotendinous junction
- Increase neuromuscular efficiency
- Reduce injuries
- Increase training efficiency
- Reduce muscle spasms
- Improve posture and balance
- Maintain normal functional muscular length
- Relieve joint stress
- Improve circulation
- Improve overall performance

Self-Myofascial Release has been shown to relieve various muscle and joint pains many athletes and runners, such as myself, commonly experience:

- IT band syndrome
- Shin splints
- Piriformis syndrome
- Tendonitis
- And more…

EQUIPMENT FOR SELF-MYOFASCIAL RELEASE

Self-Myofascial Release, aka foam rolling, uses a cylindrical piece of extruded hard-celled foam called a foam roller. Foam rollers are inexpensive and come in various sizes and densities. The most common foam rollers are 36 inches long and 6 inches in diameter. However if you travel with a foam roller, which I highly recommend, you should consider one that is approximately 12 inches in length.

The heavier the person, the denser the foam roller should be, unless you are new to foam rolling and/or have severe trigger points. For example, large muscular athletes do better with a very high-density foam roller whereas an older individual can use a less dense foam roller. Most often the color of the foam roller can help distinguish the density. White foam rollers are typically the softest and the least dense, while blue and black foam rollers tend to be harder and more dense.

While the high-density foam roller may be uncomfortable at first, especially to a the new user, it is important for the foam roller to be stiff in order to be aggressive while trying to relieve sore and damaged muscles. It's a love – hate relationship with Self-Myofascial Release. You may hate it while doing it because it can hurt like hell as you roll over the adhesions, but once you're done, you feel like you're in Heaven! Just like with deep tissue massage…it hurts when the therapist digs into the adhesions, but you feel like Jell-O when you leave.

High-density foam rollers, which I recommend, have a smooth surface and will not lose their shape, deform, or compress easily with heavy use like the white and blue foam rollers do. High-density foam rollers are molded, which means they do not have pockets of empty space, and last much longer under long-term use. I use a black, high-density 36-inch foam roller (found at: www.FullOfLifeFitness.com) and an orange, 13-inch Trigger Point® foam roller called The Grid.

HOW TO PERFORM SELF-MYOFASCIAL RELEASE

You perform Self-Myofascial Release by using your own body weight on a foam roller to 'massage' or 'roll' away trigger points (tender spot/ painful area). The feel of the foam roller and the intensity of the self-massage/rolling should be properly geared to the age, comfort, and fitness level of the individual. One of the advantages of foam rolling is that you can control the intensity with your own body weight.

The pressure you apply while foam rolling should be sustained on the trigger point until the discomfort is reduced by 75%. This process should take approximately 30 - 60 seconds, or longer depending upon the individual's ability to relax. Roll the full length of the muscle to capture every trigger point. Keep the abdominal muscles engaged and tight to provide stability in the lumbo-pelvic-hip complex during foam rolling. Remember to breathe slowly as this will help reduce any tense reflexes caused by discomfort.

Self-Myofascial Release usually is slightly to moderately uncomfortable and sometimes painful, however, if it feels too painful you will tense up and get the opposite of the desired effect. Remember, the goal is to help relax and relieve tension in the muscles just like a massage. Make sure the surface you are lying or sitting on is comfortable and fairly soft (exercise mat, carpet, etc.). This softer surface reduces the pressure the foam roller is exerting on the muscle.

Self-Myofascial Release should ideally be performed 1-2 times daily including pre- and post-workout. There is no excuse not to foam roll. If you watch television at home, perform Self-Myofascial Release on the floor while watching your favorite shows! Below are a few examples of commonly foam-rolled muscles groups.

Calf Muscles (Gastrocnemius/Soleus/Peroneal):

Preparation:

1. Sit on the floor with one leg extended in front of you on top of the foam roller and the other leg crossed over at the ankle of the lower leg. For the gastrocnemius and soleus muscles, place the foam roller under the mid-calf. For  the peroneal muscle, turn the foot outward so the foam roller is under the lateral (outside) part of the calf.

2. Placing some weight on your hands and on the lower leg, lift your hips off the ground (calf pressed into the foam roller).

Movement:

1. Draw in your abdominal muscles and activate the glutes (buttocks) to prevent low back compensations.

2. Slowly roll the calf area to find a trigger point and hold until the discomfort and the pain eases (up to 75%).

3. Proceed to the next trigger point and hold again.

4. Continue foam rolling your calves in search of all the trigger points and repeat the process on any you find.

5. Repeat on the opposite leg.

Quadricep Muscle (Anterior Thigh):

Preparation:

1. Lie in a prone position (face down) placing some weight on your forearms with the foam roller under the anterior (front) part of the upper thigh.

Movement:

1. Draw in your abdominal muscles and activate the glutes (buttocks) to prevent low back compensations.

2. Slowly roll from the pelvic bone to just above the knee to find a trigger point and hold until the discomfort and the pain eases (up to 75%).

3. Proceed to the next trigger point and hold again.

4. Continue foam rolling your quadriceps in search of all the trigger points and repeat the process on any you find.

5. Repeat on the opposite leg.

Note: Refrain from foam rolling any injured areas and over any bone or joint such as the knee, elbow, etc.

For more information about Self-Myofascial Release and to receive a copy of Heather Binns' **Self-Myofascial Release Guide for the Human Body**, please visit: www.FullOfLifeFitness.com.

About Heather

Fitness expert Heather Binns is the Owner/Founder of Full of Life Fitness in Southern California. Heather has had a passion for health and fitness for more than 20 years. She holds multiple fitness certifications including the National Academy of Sports Medicine (NASM), Apex Fitness, Equinox Fitness Training Institute (EFTI), TRX Suspension Training, Kettlebells, Functional Movement Screens (FMS), Special Populations (obesity/health/joint problems), ViPR, and the Power Plate. Heather specializes in fat loss, metabolic and interval training, physical imbalance correction, resistance/strength training, functional movement, athletic/sport training, corrective stretching techniques, core/stability training, and Self-Myofascial Release. Her training philosophy focuses on proper form and functional training styles, in addition to healthy nutrition to safely and effectively reach one's fitness goals.

Heather is very athletic and is a former professional athlete. Her background includes running and football. She ran cross country and track & field, which then progressed into races from 5Ks to marathons, triathlons, century rides and adventure competitions. She is a Running/Triathlon Coach and has led many training programs/ teams for Nike, The American Heart Association, The Leukemia & Lymphoma Society, Runnergy and Full of Life Fitness. She has worked for some of the top clubs in the industry such as the Sports Club/LA and Equinox Fitness and instructed group fitness classes at Disney, Nestle, Paramount Pictures, Power Plate North America and Plus One. Heather was also a professional football player (Defensive End) for the Los Angeles Lasers in the WPFL and the WAFL. Her love for sports and fitness subsequently carried on to her daughter who is a high school track star.

Heather holds a Bachelor of Arts degree in Communications from Chapman University and two Associate of Arts degrees in Fire Science and Liberal Arts. Heather enjoys volunteering and raising funds for charitable organizations such as The American Heart Association, The Leukemia and Lymphoma Society, Susan G. Komen Foundation, Train 4 Autism, The Epilepsy Foundation, and more. In her spare time she enjoys running, dining, painting, hiking, reading, spending time with friends & family, working out, maintaining her health, and writing heath & fitness articles for various media outlets.

To learn more about Heather Binns and receive her *Self-Myofascial Release Guide for the Human Body*, visit: www.FullOfLifeFitness.com or call (818) 925-LIFE (5433). Heather helps you find your athlete within!

www.FullOfLifeFitness.com

CHAPTER 24

Fit And Fabulous Forever

By Cecily Casey

A year ago I was faced with turning the big 5-0. Wow, it had crept up on me really quickly...where had the last 10 years gone? Where had the last 20 years gone? When I think back to my early thirties I recall diapers, bills, opening my retail stores and barely making ends meet. It was a decade of give and take. Taking from myself and giving to others. Not that I minded, it was just what I did to make things work, just as many mothers do throughout their lives. We give to our families and our work so that life can happen.

My early forties were like my thirties, but on a larger scale. More little ones came along. Yes, I have four kids. Along with our growing family came a larger home, and much larger bills. Every ounce of me was invested in growing my family and my business. I was living the "American Dream." I had a beautiful family, home and a successful business. By all appearances, everything looked great, except me. The years of nurturing everyone but myself were starting to show.

Around this same time, my Mother became sick with cancer. She had invested much time and energy in many different causes throughout her life, but as much as she invested in others, she never reinvested in her own health. Even in the last year of her life, she continued her philanthropic work instead of focusing on herself. You can only give of yourself for so long, until eventually nothing is left. I think of it like a savings account, if we continually withdraw and never make deposits, we end up bankrupt.

After my Mom died, I made a promise that I would start reinvesting in myself so that I could live the second half of my life with joy and appreciation of all of life's possibilities. I spent endless hours reading everything I could find about health and wellness. I attended health and wellness seminars, and eventually returned to college to educate myself for a career in the field.

The process changed me forever. I became the woman that I had dreamed of, I looked fit and healthy, and felt ten years younger...I had my fabulous back! My friends and family began coming to me for advice. Because I loved sharing what I had learned and helping other women, I outlined a simple plan for other women to follow. I call it the **Fit and Fabulous Forever Plan.**

If you are feeling the way I was...drained, dull and a little dowdy, follow the steps outlined in my plan, and you will rediscover your fabulous self no matter *what* your age. My plan will successfully get you your sexy self back so that everyone, but most importantly yourself, will discover the irresistible you!

Our motto is..."Women in the prime of our lives, having the time of our lives!"

THE FIT AND FABULOUS FOREVER PLAN

THE GOAL:
Every successful plan starts with a clearly defined goal. Create deadlines for your goals based on life events such as birthdays, anniversaries, weddings, and reunions. My goal was to be fit and feel fabulous by the time I turned 50.

For me, fit means strong, **not** skinny, As we age, skinny starts to look frail. Lean muscle gives our bodies shape and keeps us looking sexy into the prime of our life. Lean muscle also helps to crank our metabolism, allowing us to eat more and burn more calories throughout the day.

Being fit also allows us the freedom to face challenges without asking for help. Of course, it is fine to ask for help when needed, but to need help less often is pretty awesome. Imagine how empowering it would feel to throw a 40-pound bag of dog food over your shoulder and march confidently out of the pet store!

A fit body will also promote higher energy levels and keep us focused throughout the day. Imagine...no more multiple trips to Starbucks to refuel ourselves. Our bank accounts will love us!

Outlining our goals at the onset of the plan is important; we must know where we are going with a concise set of directions to get there.

Your goals may differ from mine, just be sure you know what they are and write them down. Be sure to list reasons why those goals are important to you. In moments of weakness, it will be helpful to have your goals clearly stated.

Remember to embrace the process. We are becoming a new and improved version of ourselves. If you embrace the notion that we are always in the process of becoming who we were meant to be, then you will be open to change and growth in your life. Enjoy the process of becoming!

THE TOOLS:
Our Fit tools will help us chisel away the old you and uncover the new, fabulous you!

Fit Tool #1: Photos
Be sure to take before pictures. They serve as tangible evidence of progress. When I am feeling down or discouraged, I find it very encouraging to look back on my 'before' pictures. I continue to take pictures because I still enjoy the process of becoming a more fabulous version of me!

Fit Tool #2: Journal
Track your progress daily in a journal. Just as pictures will provide evidence of your outer transformation, journaling will provide a testament to your inner transformation. It is empowering to open your journals and re-read your words. Expressing our thoughts and actions in words solidifies our journey in a concrete "forever" medium. It provides evidence of how far we have progressed.

Fit Tool #3: Your Team
Enlist an accountability partner. This *may* be a family member or friend that understands your goals and can lend support when needed.

Fit tool #4: Your Mirror

It is imperative that you get off the scale. Learn to gauge your progress by the way you look. Because lean muscle weighs more than fat, you may actually gain weight on the scale, but you will still be losing fat. The scale does not tell us the truth about what is happening within our bodies, but standing in front of the mirror in your favorite jeans does.

Fit tool #5: Kettlebells

This fabulous chunk of iron will allow you to get the most amount of work done in the least amount of time. What once took an hour in the gym now takes 30 minutes with kettlebells. Too busy to be fit is no longer an excuse This cast iron ball with a handle is equivalent to a handheld gym. When used properly, Kettlebells will promote strength, endurance, cardiovascular health and flexibility.

Kettlebells helped me reach my goals quickly, but it wasn't love at first sight. When I was first introduced to the kettlebell I was hesitant, but I found a certified kettlebell instructor (I highly recommend an RKC), who taught me proper technique. I fell in love with the way kettlebell training made me feel.

The cornerstone movement of the kettlebell training is the Swing. This movement quickly changed my physique and as an added bonus, its fun. I was so taken with kettlebell training that I went through the RKC and became a Russian Kettlebell Challenge instructor.

KETTLEBELL SWING WORKOUT

Here is a fun kettlebell swing program that I teach at my gym: Do this quick 30-minute workout 3 times a week. Please visit my website: www. FitandFab4Ever.com for more on how to train safely with Kettlebells.

Weeks 1-4:

Women should start with a 10 kg or 12 kg kettlebell depending on your fitness level. Set an interval timer for 30 minutes with 15-second work intervals and 1-minute rest intervals. Swing as many times as you can in the 15 seconds and then rest for 1 minute. As soon as you can get 2-3 more swings in the 15-second work interval, move up to the next size kettlebell.

Weeks 5-8:
Increase your work interval to 20 seconds and decrease your rest to 45 seconds. Because you are increasing your work-to-rest ratio you might have to go back down a bell size the first few sessions, but don't be discouraged, you will quickly build enough strength and endurance to step back up to the bell size you finished week 4 with. If in weeks 7 or 8 you can increase your swings by 2-3, move up to the next bell size.

Weeks 9-12:
Increase your work interval to 30 seconds and decrease your rest interval to 30 seconds. Again, use a lighter bell at first if need be, and move up a bell when you can get 2-3 more swings in a set.

By the end of this 12 week swing program, you are well on your way to becoming fit and fabulous!

Fit Tool #6: Beautify Your Body With Whole, Healthy Food

It wasn't until I started to replenish myself with knowledge and strength that I discovered the most important part of the Fit and Fabulous equation; *healthy nutrition*. We no longer have to starve ourselves to look fabulous, in fact the case is quite the opposite. We must eat to keep ourselves fit and feeling fabulous. Good nutrition can account for 70% percent of our success. Don't sabotage all your hard work in the gym with poor food choices!

I now think of food as a way to nourish my body. It wasn't until I started to trace where our food comes from that I became very particular about what I allowed in my body. I now try to eat as naturally and simply as possible. By simple, I mean whole foods from the earth. This will beautify you from the inside out. Think before you eat!

THE NUTRITION PLAN:

(a). Replace grains with colorful veggies.

Eliminate all grains? I'm not fond of the word eliminate...its harsh. Instead let's use the word replace. Replace grains with colorful vegetables. Yes even whole grains. I know many of you will be thinking...what??? How will I survive without my carbs? I did and you will too. Vegetables will provide you with plenty of carbohydrates in addition to many more vitamins, minerals and fiber than grains. I successfully ran a marathon and numerous half-marathons without any starchy, processed carbs!

Our goal is to eat at least 2 different colored veggies at every meal. Some tricks I use to get enough veggies throughout the day. Every Sunday I make a chopped raw veggie slaw. Any colorful raw veggie that is in season goes into the mix. I use this as a base throughout the week to build my meals on. For example, breakfast might be a few ounces of poached salmon placed on top of a few scoops of my veggie slaw...delicious and easy. Also, invest in a juicer; it will allow you to concoct all sorts of fun, healthy veggie and fruit drinks to keep you nourished throughout the day.

(b). Say NO to Dairy!

Dairy can contribute to inflammatory responses reeking havoc on our system. It is estimated that over 60% of the world's population is allergic to dairy. Many of us develop dairy allergies later in life.

Replace cow's milk with coconut milk. I'm coo-coo for anything coconut! Coconut milk is loaded with medium chain fatty acids. These are goods fats, which are quickly used by our bodies, instead of, stored as fat deposits. Medium chain fatty acids may also help to maintain and even speed up our metabolism, helping us lose stored fat at a higher rate!

(c). Eat Plenty of Protein.

Protein is important in repairing body tissue, which is important after our strength training. We must eat enough protein everyday to aid in creating lean muscle. Remember, it is the muscle on our bodies that is going to give us our new, fit shape and keep us feeling fabulous. Good sources of protein include wild-caught fish, grass-fed beef, bison, free-range chicken, turkey, and eggs from free-range chickens.

(d). Good Fats.

Good fats are Gods gift to fit and fabulous forever women! Instead of craving sugary sweets, I now crave good fats such as olive oil, flax seeds, avocado, nuts and nut butters. Good fats will keep us looking and feeling young. As we move into our prime time years, they help to hydrate our skin and plump the fine lines as well keep our hair shiny and manageable.

Make sure you are taking a fish oil supplement in order to get DHA, an Omega 3 fatty acid. DHA works to keep our memories strong and accurate. Below-normal levels of DHA have been associated with Alzheimer's disease.

(e). Eat every 3-4 hours.

In order to keep our metabolism revved, we need to eat every 3-4 hours. I'm not talking about huge meals here, but strive to have a small fruit or 1-2 servings of veggies along with a lean protein and good fat every 3-4 hours. In addition, be sure to drink enough water throughout the day. Water will flush toxins from your system as well as keep your skin looking fresh and hydrated.

Managing Menopause:

Every woman manages menopause differently. As estrogen and progesterone production begins to slow some women experience symptoms that include anxiety, dry skin, fatigue, headaches, heart palpitations, hot flashes, insomnia, irritability, decreased sex drive, lack of concentration, mood swings, night sweats, reduced stamina, urinary incontinence, weight gain, cold hands and feet, joint pain, and hair loss. When we live a healthy lifestyle, we help to free ourselves from hormone fluctuations associated with peri-menopause and menopause.

When we do enter menopause (menstruation has ceased for 1 year) most of the unpleasant symptoms stop as well. I like to think of menopause as a time of freedom. After 35 years or so of menstruation, we are no longer tied to a monthly biological cycle and all the constraints and struggles associated with it.

TOOLS TO HELP THE TRANSITION

- Follow the Fit and Fabulous strength and nutrition plan!

- Drink a glass of water every two hours. You will flush out toxins and avoid dehydration from fluid lost during hot flashes or night sweats.

- If you enjoy a glass (or two) of wine, keep it to once a week. This is not only good advice for transitioning into menopause, but limiting alcohol will keep your metabolism from slowing down as well.

- Cut back on caffeine. Like alcohol, caffeine can intensify hot flashes.

- Anise, black cohosh, fennel and sage are all herbal remedies that promote natural estrogen production.

- Try acupressure to minimize headaches, smooth tension, and strengthen the urinary tract.

- Massage therapy works wonders in relieving stress. Treat yourself to a good massage once a week. Remember…give back to yourself!

- Educate your family about what you are experiencing and ask for their help in minimizing your stress.

FABULOUS BY DESIGN

Design your future. It would be a shame to grow old and not realize what your body is capable of. Be proud of your years! In the months leading up to my 50th birthday, I found every excuse I could to tell people my age, because I knew I was the best I had ever been!

When we take care of ourselves we empower ourselves to be better mothers, partners and 'fit and fabulous forever' women.

About Cecily

Cecily Casey is a mother of four children ranging in age from 11 to 24 years. After a twenty-year career in retail, Cecily created a new life plan and now owns and operates RealFit Gym in Highland Park, Il. with her business partner and daughter, Lucy. The two specialize in helping women of all ages reach their fitness and nutrition goals.

Cecily earned a Bachelor of Arts degree from DePaul University and completed a college certificate program specializing in Health and Wellness Promotion with a concentration in Personal Training. In 2009, Cecily earned her Russian Kettlebell Challenge (RKC) certification, and in 2011 assisted as an instructor at the 10th anniversary RKC hosted in Chicago. In 2010 Cecily earned her USA weightlifting (USAW) Performance Coach certification. Cecily is a certified personal trainer with the American College of Sports Medicine as well as a functional movement specialist.

Cecily continues to travel and learn, attending workshops and seminars in order to bring the best to her clients, Cecily believes that through empowering women we can build a stronger, healthier community.

Websites:
www.FitandFab4ever.com
www.realfitgym.com

CHAPTER 25

SPEED DEVELOPMENT: COMMON MYTHS THAT ARE HOLDING YOUR ATHLETES BACK
— And The Secrets To Unleashing Their Potential

By Travis Motley

As sports performance specialists who have trained hundreds of athletes ranging from the NFL to the local youth soccer league, the overwhelming desire every athlete possesses is the "need for speed!" You know, that thing that separates the great athletes from the recreational ones, the missing piece of the puzzle that holds thousands of kids back from receiving a Division 1 scholarship. Speed not only "Kills" as they say, but it also "creates"…**opportunity,** that is. And for decades, the art of developing speed has been so watered down with garbage that I am making it my mission to unleash the secrets and shed light on the methods that truly produce the life-changing results we're all looking for.

Now, before I dive into this, let me give you some practical experience that started my quest to find the secrets of speed training.

In high school, I was a tall and skinny football player with big dreams and an even bigger will. I had been told I had all the tools but needed to work on my speed if I wanted to play Division 1 ball. Now when I say I was tall and skinny, I am talking about being 6'2" weighing in at a whopping 160 lbs soaking wet; I remember having to hide small 2 ½ lbs weights in the pockets of my shorts just to get a decent weight next to my name in the program. Anyways, I was hell bent on playing Division 1 football, so every chance I could get I would be on the computer in the library at school researching everything and anything I could find on speed training. Since I didn't have a computer in my home, I would often skip class just to research while I had the resources, at least that's what I told myself to feel better about skipping class. I even subscribed to all those hokey "decrease your 40 yard dash in 2 weeks" websites that ironically, I still get spam from to this day. Unfortunately and unbeknownst to me at the time, the Internet was saturated with fallacies and terrible information on the topic of speed. Ultimately, I was reading all the wrong crap that was actually leading me away from the truth, and further away from my dream.

So I started putting all of the information I was "learning" into practice, ...speed ladder drills for hours, ...Seated hamstring curls, ...quick feet drills and hundreds of jumps trying to "stimulate my fast twitch muscle fibers." The workouts were horrible, but I was convinced I found the fountain of youth for speed training. Now fast forward a couple of years and I am playing at a small Division 1 college, despite not training properly, but still doing a lot of the same stupid training on my own time. Throughout college I was still very interested in the subject and wouldn't you know it, was still reading and applying a lot of the wrong information! Now my college career is over and it's time to get ready to workout for the NFL scouts at what's called a 'Pro Day.' This is where I come face-to-face with reality and my first taste of the truth.

Of course, by this time I'm feeling like a freakin' guru on the topic of speed, so I take the privilege of training myself for the pro day. I train hard and specifically for my 40. I feel amazing going into the big day; finally it's here, "time to blaze." Except I didn't really blaze anything but my ego after I ran. Don't get me wrong, it was still a good time. However, how fast I thought I was, was different to what the clock said. I remember asking myself, "What happened?" I thought I followed everything perfectly. I thought to myself, "I look faster than that on game film" and "I ran and covered guys who ran much faster than I just ran, plus my feet move so quickly there's no way that can be right." In hindsight, I now see that I was more interested in how fast my feet were moving than how much ground I was covering.

When I got back home, I heard about a performance coach...in our area and started to train with him for my next few workouts and tests I had coming up. This man changed my life! He is still one of the smartest performance coaches I have ever been around, and I give him a lot of credit in my development as a coach. I took advantage of him training me as an athlete and used it as a form of a mentorship program to also train me as a future performance coach. I started reading the books in his library now, started following some of the godfathers of the performance world, traveling to seminars and even picking up the phones and giving some of these gurus a call to pick their brains. All of this really shifted a lot of my thinking and got me realizing that I had been defining speed wrong the entire time!

Now that the epic fail that got me here has been established, let's get down to the meat and potatoes. We're going to break down a couple massive mistakes and myths that are probably keeping you from improving speed and overall performance. I can think of at least three to five more myths that are keeping most athletes slow, but in order to fit everything in this chapter, I picked the three most common errors. If you are thirsty, like I was, to learn more about speed development, shoot me an email and I'll get you and your athletes on the road to success.

Anyways, on we go...

Myth #1: Speed is only linear.

What is speed? Webster defines it as a "high rate of movement or performance."

The first of many problems most people have is that they believe speed is only in a straight line. Most people who believe that would also tell you that anything that is non-linear is agility and not speed. Although there is some truth to that, speed is still a high rate of movement or performance and that definition doesn't restrict it to one direction therefore speed is absolutely multi planar. In sports we often see that it's not always as simple as who can get from point A to point B the fastest, but its really more like point A to point D with a couple different changes in direction on the way there.

Myth #2: Running track will make you faster.

This is a huge Myth! The biggest one in my book, no pun intended. Just to be clear, you can get faster by running track but normally it's just a result of lowering your body fat % and getting in better general shape than it is anything specific or unique to track and field. Outside of indoor, the shortest race is 100 meters. Because of this, track coaches are focused on top-end speed, running form and mechanics. All three are elements that have zero translation in any other sport. It takes the average elite Olympic sprinter 60 meters to get to top-end speed, how often will an athlete be asked to still be accelerating 70-80 yards down the field? And even if they had the ability, who cares? They could play their entire career and never have to use it.

In almost every sport, top end speed doesn't do much for you. Running form goes out of the window when you take into consideration the amount of chaos that is going on in a given game/match or duration of an explosive movement. Track sprinters run in a straight line and have the advantage of being able to go over the mechanics in their head as they're running. Good luck dribbling a soccer ball or running between the tackles and making sure you have proper knee drive. Let's just say you would be finding some real estate on the closest bench near you if you took that approach. What athletes are really looking for is explosive acceleration and bursts of 5-20 yards. If you look at some of the best athletes, they have the ability to decelerate and accelerate extremely fast. I have played with and against several Wide Receivers that would absolutely blow my doors off in a 100-meter dash, but on a football field where they're being asked to do a lot more than run in a straight line, they are just as easy to cover as an offensive tackle – because track doesn't do anything to improve functional speed. Lastly, Track has zero emphasis on deceleration. Again, sports are chaotic and require high levels of stopping, starting and changing direction and are often based on reaction – none of which Track can help improve. There is simply no correlation or carry over from Track to any other Sports.

Myth #3: You don't have to be strong to be fast / Heavy lifting will make you slower.

This one drives me crazy!

A lot of coaches and parents think that strength training would cause athletes to become muscle-bound and would be counterproductive to speed. It has been proven that athletic performance depends either directly or indirectly on qualities of *muscular strength*. We must remember that strength builds the foundation for *ALL* other athletic qualities. For example, if you do not possess great relative body strength (strength in relation to your body weight), you will never be able to run fast, jump high or change direction quickly. This is due to the fact that all aspects of movement at high velocities require high levels of muscular strength. In other words, if you can't achieve the proper push-off to accelerate or the proper loading mechanics for deceleration, you can't be fast! And this is just one example. Many university studies have also found a high correlation between an athlete's jumping ability and agility in relation to their relative body strength. What this means is that an athlete who is strong for his/her bodyweight will possess the ability to jump higher and move quicker, when compared to their weaker counterparts.

The other half to the myth is where most coaches and parents will fall into. "Heavy lifting will actually make you slower because you're moving the weight slowly." I mean where do people come up with this stuff?

First, in order to truly improve strength you must lift heavy. According to the National Strength and Conditioning Association you should lift at 6 repetitions or lower to get stronger. This equates to about 85% or higher of your max. Contrary to the science, most coaches are having their athletes lift the typical 3 sets of 10 of a weight that's around 70% of the athletes max. The funny thing about this one is most people try to avoid lifting heavy in an effort to "not bulk up," yet science shows us that hypertrophy (increase in muscle size) is best gained through set/rep schemes closer to what they're actually doing.

Back to why heavy lifting and gaining strength helps with speed. Multi-directional speed will always require an element of deceleration, in order to be efficient and quick during deceleration you must have the ability to stabilize under momentum and velocity. One of the only ways to mimic stabilizing under high levels of velocity and/or momentum is to lift heavy crap. If an athlete weighs 150 lbs and is running full speed and must stop on a dime (decelerate) to change direction, that athlete has to stop and stabilize their own 150 lbs multiplied by the force being created by the momentum. If you convert those variables into lbs it's a lot, hence the importance to lift heavy weight. Here's another example, a simple analogy of acceleration in cars will prove the point. You have two full- sized vans that are fully loaded. Everything in this test is equal but the engine. One van has a V8 engine and the other a four cylinder. Which do you think is going to accelerate faster? The V8 of course. It is science that dictates why the van with the V8 gets off faster. Unless you have figured out how to trick science I would go with the V8. How do you develop a V8? Get stronger, how do you get stronger? Lift heavy. Nuff said!

THE OPTIMAL WAY TO DEVELOP SPEED

Now that we covered what's holding people back, lets talk about what actually works! When we train athletes at IMPACT, everything is trained in all three planes of motion: Sagittal(Linear), Frontal(Lateral) and Transverse(Rotational/Diagonal). We develop strength, mobility, power and speed in each plane as well. This is extremely important due to the multi-directional demands in sport. I'm not saying that we should simply mimic the exact moves in the sports we play, but its important to understand the fine movement patterns and demands in ALL sports and train them appropriately. Cutting, accelerating, decelerating, reacting, jumping and landing must all be addressed through every plane of motion. If you are not doing that, you're leaving a lot on the table and I advise that you find a professional near you that can implement such strategies with your athletes.

Lastly, and probably most importantly, in order to understand a big part of our philosophy at IMPACT, lets go back to some science. Newton's third law states that for every action there is an equal and opposite reaction. That's it! If you understand that, which I'm sure you can, you can drastically improve your athlete's speed. For every action there is an opposite and equal reaction, this means if we want to produce force, power and speed then we need to be driving all of that into the ground. In other words if an athlete can't drive a lot of force into the ground, then according to science, they won't be able to produce a lot coming off of the ground.

How do you improve this ability? Get stronger in all three planes through squat variations, multi-directional lunges, deadlifts and unilateral training. Use functional equipment like bands to do various deceleration drills that help mimic momentum and teach athletes how to properly decelerate, load (stabilize) and drive force into the ground. Sled sprints and heavy-car and prowler pushes are great for improving force production into the ground. Throw the speed ladders away and stop the quick feet drills; speed is about the force we can drive into the ground from multiple planes.

Just remember this, like everything else in life, when it comes to the relationship between speed and the ground, you get whatever you put into it.

About Travis

Travis Motley is the co-owner and director of athletic development at Impact Strength and Performance in Bellevue, Washington. He is one of the most sought after sports performance
coaches in the Northwest. His expertise in athletic development
and speed enhancement has led hundreds of high school, col-
legiate and professional athletes from the NFL, NBA and MLS into his facility. His
thirst for knowledge has led to the development of the most cutting-edge and results-
driven programming.

He serves as the director of sports performance at three different high schools and
is in high demand to local club sports as a performance consultant and performance
coach. Despite his success, he is most proud of the relationships he creates with his
athletes, normally training them for their entire competitive career. As a former Professional athlete, Travis understands the physical and psychological demands placed
on athletes, which gives him a very unique insight and ability to not only relate to his
athletes, but also produce results – to which Travis attributes his incredible retention
rate.

When Travis isn't coaching or watching one of his athletes compete, you can catch
him standing by the nearest grill, barbequing for his family and friends and spending
as much time as possible hanging out with his wife and son.

CHAPTER 26

A Brief Breakdown Of Fiber Or...Get Your Sh-- Right and Tight!

By Ben Dearman

When I was asked to contribute to this book I was both honored and stunned! What the hell am I going to write about that won't already be covered?

Business. Check.

Weight loss. Check. (*Frankly, boring to talk about. How many times can we regurgitate "eat protein, fruits and/or veggies at every meal, drink lots of water and cut out processed foods"*? If these ideas are new to you then we have trainer problems!)

Personal motivation. Check.

Business success. Check.

As with all of my best ideas, the topic for this chapter came to me while I was talking to a client (who happens to be a holistic chiropractor) about his bowel movements only happening once per day. (*Hey, at our gym we hit all aspects of health.*)

"Isn't that normal?" he asked.

"Of course it is! And that's the problem!" Voila, I had my topic!

If a holistic chiropractor with 8+ years of formal education, advanced certifications, and who lectures nationally on supplements and nutrition doesn't 'understand shit', then chances are, very few in my profession do.

(That was the only poop joke. Promise.)

See, my friend shares a problem with almost 99% of the population:

He doesn't get enough fiber.

Fiber is a catchall term that includes:

1. Soluble – dissolves in water and therefore your stomach and forms a thick gel. Soluble fiber will be the main topic of this chapter.

2. Insoluble - does not dissolve in water and therefore is not broken down in your belly. Think of insoluble fiber as a scrub brush for your intestines.

Both fiber types are essential and are always paired naturally with very nutritionally dense and calorically light foods.

INSOLUBLE FIBER

Insoluble fibers main benefits are (this list is not all encompassing):

1. Remove waste from the colon by removing stuck debris. That can be upwards of 15 pounds! Some spas charge big bucks for cleanses' and people pay out the wazoo (figuratively and literally) for these services. Switch it around so they pay that money to you for a lifelong cleanse, instead of a 30-day one.

2. Help to keep an optimal pH balance in the intestines thus helping to reduce toxins in the body.

3. Move bulk through your intestines, speeding up bowel movements and preventing constipation. A healthy digestive system is lively. If you're eating 4-6 meals a day with a good fiber intake, it's not unreasonable to expect 3-5 healthy bowel movements.

4. Help tone the muscles of the bowel by providing something to "push" against, enhancing bowel movements. Insoluble fiber is

like a prowler for your bowels. And really...who wouldn't want stronger bowel movements?

There is an ancient saying that goes, "Strong bowels leads to strong bones that support a strong body that houses a strong mind."

Actually I just made that up for this chapter, but it does sound pretty good.

SOLUBLE FIBER

If weight loss or improving health is your goal, including soluble fiber-rich foods in your diet is a no brainer. Benefits of fiber are many, with some listed below:

1. Fiber helps reduce calories via a coupling effect.
2. Fiber-rich foods are naturally loaded with phytonutrients, anti-oxidants, vitamins and minerals.
3. Fiber slows down the digestion of carbohydrates – reducing rises in blood sugar.
4. Fiber helps with satiation.
5. Fiber helps reduce total cholesterol and LDL.

Let's look at each point closer. The above list is far from an exhaustive list of the benefits of fiber, but it does hit the relevant points.

1. Fiber helps reduce calories via a coupling effect referred to as Fecal Energy Excretion (Sexy, I know) or Fiber Flush. Because your body cannot digest fiber easily, it binds to other nutrients preventing the intestines from breaking down and absorbing them. Small amounts of soluble fiber (depending on the type) can be digested in a process called fermentation, which yield 2 calories of short chain fatty acids per gram. Short chain fatty ac-ids are a great thing because your body utilizes them for energy as well as helping to reduce inflammation.

One study done by the USDA found that women who ate 24 grams of fiber a day absorbed 90 fewer calories. Which translates to 10 fewer pounds on your frame over a year.

Another study showed a coupling effect of between 8 and 12 calories per gram of fiber.

Any way you look at it, adding fiber to your diet could help you from gaining extra weight.

Not too bad for just eating fruits and veggies!

2. Fiber-rich foods are loaded with vitamins, minerals, phytonutrients and anti-oxidants. Since most people don't get enough nutrients in the first place, ensuring you get lots of fiber in your diet through natural sources will help to erase that deficit. Being low in key minerals/nutrients (such as vitamin C which helps to synthesize carnitine, a key chemical in fat metabolism, or chromium which enhances the effects of insulin as well as assisting in glucose and fat metabolism) is detrimental to not only health goals but physique goals as well.

Incidentally – Vitamin C is found in all green leafy veggies (roughage! a great source of insoluble fiber), broccoli (which also aids in increasing testosterone) and citrus fruits (bonus points if you can pick your own) to name a few all-natural sources. Chromium is also found in broccoli (it's safe to say you should add 1-2 cups of broccoli to your daily diet) as well as apples – two great sources of insoluble and soluble fiber!

Phytonutrients are nutrients derived from plant material that have been shown to be necessary for sustaining human life. Read that again – NECESSARY.

Antioxidants are compounds that scavenge free radical oxygen, the leading cause of signs of aging. Eat your fiber, look younger!

3. Fiber affects the absorption of carbohydrates through our gastrointestinal tract by slowing it down. Taking longer to metabolize carbs is essential for reducing rapid rises in insulin.

If you receive money for any health service and you don't understand insulin then you are doing a disservice to your clients and should be fired. Insulin is THAT important. It helps to control blood sugar and determines where nutrients get delivered (among other things). See below for a brief run down of insulin and weight loss:

As carbohydrates are digested glucose floods the bloodstream. The body attempts to lower blood sugar levels by producing insulin, which takes sugar out of the bloodstream and pushes it to be stored (in muscle or liver), used (by muscles) or converted (into fat and stored). The higher the concentration of sugar in the bloodstream, the greater the insulin release. If blood sugar remains chronically high (preventing glucagon from influencing fatty acid breakdown) eventually fat mobilization comes to a screeching halt and conversion/storage in fat cells becomes the dominant role of insulin. We get fatter. The body responds by producing more and more insulin and eventually the system falls apart. That's called insulin resistance and eventually leads to diabetes.

Fiber slows things down, reducing how much glucose enters the bloodstream thus causing insulin to be released slower. Instead of blood sugar being shunted off to fat cells, it can be utilized as sustained energy.

Remember, the slower insulin is released the longer your blood sugar remains elevated, providing us with sustained energy, preventing our bodies from storing excess fat because working muscles are able to burn that sugar off.

4. Fiber helps with satiation via the hormone CCK, which in turn is influenced by volume in the stomach. Cholecyctokinin is a hormone that is responsible for telling us we're full as well as stimulating the release of enzymes that digest carbs and fat. Keeping levels of CCK high, thus increasing satiety, is vital for controlling hunger. CCK production is stimulated by the walls of the stomach stretching, and since it only sticks around for a few minutes and is released in quantities relative to the volume of the belly, if we can keep the volume in the belly up (via water intake, foods and fiber) we prolong CCK release. It takes 15-20 minutes for your stomach to tell your brain you're full. So if you are eating fast and digesting low-fiber foods, you will eat more food – thus consuming more calories before CCK tells you to stop eating.

Note: If your goal is weight gain or adding muscle mass, you may not want to increase fiber levels too much as a lot of fiber will prevent you from potentially getting the calories in you need due to fiber's increase satiety effect.

5. Fiber also helps with reducing total cholesterol and LDL in the bloodstream thus reducing the risk of heart disease.

Understanding how to reduce LDL and total cholesterol is not really THAT important if you're a health professional trying to deliver leanness, sexiness and a longer life, while charging $90 an hour. <u>Note the sarcasm in that statement!</u>

It's important to understand that fiber is what causes a reduction in cardiovascular disease — *not* Cheerios®. Nothing pinches my nuts more than foods that tout they are "Heart Disease" fighters because they have fiber in them. Because most of our foods are now processed, refined and then fortified, there are now "Functional Dietary Fibers" such as those found in Splenda® (sorry folks, unless you're sucking the sugar out of sugar canes, there should be no fiber in sugar). Fiber is the fighter, not your processed, enriched, wheat bread.

The exact mechanism of how fiber helps to reduce the risk of heart disease is way beyond the scope of this chapter. But, I'll clue you into one way:

> Fiber interferes with absorption of bile in the intestines causing more bile to be released in the feces. That's good because the liver makes bile salts out of cholesterol, and in order to obtain the cholesterol necessary for this process, the liver increases the amount of LDL (the "bad" type) to be pulled out of the bloodstream.

HOW MUCH FIBER SHOULD I INGEST?

Intake recommendations vary:

- The United States National Academy of Sciences, Institute of Health, National Cancer Institute, U.S. Surgeon General's Office and the ADA all recommend 20-35 grams of fiber.

- Precision Nutrition (probably one of the best sources for almost anything related to nutrition) recommends 30-35 grams per day for women and 40-45 grams of fiber for men.

- See below for a ridiculous and outlandish table that the Institute of Medicine came up with:

MALE

Age	Average Daily Calories	Fiber intake in Grams
1-3	1404	19
4-8	1789	25
9-13	2265	31
14-18	2840	38
19-30	2818	38
31-50	2554	38
51-70	2162	30
70+	1821	30

FEMALE

Age	Average Daily Calories	Fiber intake in Grams
9-13	1910	26
14-18	1901	26
19-30	1791	25
31-50	1694	25
51-70	1536	21
70+	1381	21

Source: Institute of Medicine. Dietary Reference Intakes for Energy, Carbohydrate, Fiber, Fat, Fatty Acids, Cholesterol, Protein, and Amino Acids. 2002. Washington, D.C.: The National Academies Press. Retrieved August 15, 2007 from http://books.nap.edu/openbook.php?isbn=0309085373

The average American, according to Harvard School of Public Health, gets around 12 to 18 grams of fiber per day. Since most processed foods have very little fiber, a diet high in those would have very little fiber.

So, it's a safe assumption that we should be consuming a MINIMUM of 35 grams of fiber per day. Why do I use the upper end of the recommended dosages?

Because the government shouldn't be trusted! I kid, I kid...kind of.

Just as the government takes a conservative view on vitamin and mineral recommendations, they most likely will also take a conservative view on fiber recommendations.

Which is understandable. Nothing worse than a government that encourages the people they are supposed to protect to consume poor quality foods in abundance that may lead to disease, physical issues and early death. Oh wait a minute...

So, let's shoot for the upper end! Plus, in the book "The Fiber35Diet" 35 grams is recommended and in Cassandra Forsythe's awesome book called "Perfect Body Diet Plan" she encourages 25 grams of fiber.

CAN YOU 'OVER FIBER'?

The studies are hazy on that one, but most organizations recommend keeping intake below 60 grams per day.

There are some negatives to drastically increasing fiber intake; mainly gas, bloating and constipation due to fermentation and the body being unprepared to handle the extra load. If that happens back off on fiber a little bit until it subsides, take some probiotics/digestive enzymes and drink LOTS of water then start to gradually increase the intake again.

WHAT'S THE BEST WAY TO GET FIBER IN?

Fruits, veggies and beans! I don't recommend relying on grains for your fiber intake. I never really encourage anyone to consume something that may cause health issues due to allergies/sensitivities, increase inflammation and poor digestion. If you do decide to use grains as supplemental fiber intake, do it sparingly, and try to use grains will very little/no gluten.

Plus, the government recommends you consume a minimum of 8 servings of grains per day. *Not - To - Be - Trusted*.

Below is a brief description of where you can find some good sources of fiber. For a more complete list, please visit: www.kdrfitness.com and sign up for our newsletter where you will get a phenomenal breakdown for good sources of fiber and serving sizes, as well as some sample menus for various caloric intakes.

RELIABLE SOURCES OF FIBER

FOOD	TOTAL FIBER (G)
1 c black beans	15
1/2 c fiber-rich cereals	12-14
1/2 c pinto beans	11
1 c peas	9
2 Tbls Flaxseeds	8
1/2 c kidney beans	8
1/2 c Shredded Wheat cereal	5
1 apple with skin	5
7 prunes	5
1/2 c chickpeas	4
1 pear	4
1 c blueberries	4
1 sweet potato	4
1/4 c Brussel sprout	4
1/2 c corn	4
1/2 c lentils	4
1/4 c sesame seeds	4
1 c oatmeal	4
1/2 c whole grains	3
1/2 c vegetables with skins	2-3
1/2 c fresh or frozen fruit	2

THE FINAL PITCH

As fit pros, we live in a slightly more educated world than our clients. It's our job to make the gap of ignorance between what works and what doesn't as small as possible. Assuming you follow the dogma of fruits and veggies at each meal getting 35 grams of fiber in daily should be a cinch by subbing in a few servings of beans, flax seeds and some extra fruit/veggies.

Oh no! Not more stuff of what I should be eating a lot of anyway!

SUM IT UP!

Fiber will help you live longer:

- By reducing free radicals - essential to aging gracefully.

- Reducing internal physiological stress – poop more, live longer. Pretty simple.

Fiber is a natural cleanser. You want to cleanse and save your money? Poop more! There is no better cleanse than a bowel movement!

Fiber will help you feel better:

- Bloating sucks. Fiber helps bind to noxious chemicals that may be causing your gas and helps to move them out of the body.

- We understand the chemical and physiological process of inflammation in the body, and eating more fiber via increase in veggies and fruits will 100% help you reduce inflammation both directly (increasing intake), and indirectly (helping you stay away from the crap that causes inflammation).

Fiber will help you look better:

- Through the mechanisms listed above, and also by:

  • Reducing hunger pangs.

  • Keeping us full and thus less likely to cheat.

  • Fiber's propensity to hang out with great friends like essential vitamins and minerals.

  • Coupling effect – the good ole Fecal Energy Excretion – helping you to cut back on calories.

  • Controlling insulin – arguably the most important hormone to manipulate if weight loss is your goal.

About Ben

Ben Dearman started his career in 2000 working as a student athletic trainer while attending Bloomsburg University. He graduated in 2004 with a B.S. in Exercise Science with a concentration in Athletic Training. Ben was fortunate enough to work with Shawn Windle (Internship at Rutgers University) as well as Jerry Shreck (assistantship at Bucknell University).

After Bucknell he worked as the Head Strength and Combatives Coach for the 75th Army Ranger Regiment and 3rd Army Ranger Battalion where he received the CO's Medal of Excellence and Excellence Plaque (the only strength coach in the history of the 3rd BN to receive both awards). While at Fort Benning, he was instrumental in developing physical readiness programs for the elite Ranger Recon Detachment (RRD) as well as assisting in the development of the early Ranger Athlete Warrior (RAW) Program. He was also on the Modern Army Combatives (MACP) Competition team lead by Matt Larsen "Father of Modern Combatives" and was integral in helping the 75th Army Ranger Regiment in securing the All Army Combatives Championship.

While working with the Army Rangers, he was also vital in developing, teaching and training Navy SEALS in the O.P.E.C. (Operator Physical Evaluation Course) program, where he worked closely with world-renowned physical therapist Gary Gray, the "father of function" and the developer of Functional Transformation, Applied Functional Science and the Gray Institute for Functional Transformation.

In addition to his undergraduate degree in Exercise Science, Ben holds certifications from:
NSCA – CSCS
USAW – Sports Performance Specialist
PN – Precision Nutrition
FMS – Functional Movement Screen Certified
IYCA – Youth Fitness Specialist
MTS – Movement Training Specialist

Today Ben Dearman and Jamie Crowe own and operate KDR Fitness in Lebanon, NH – specializing in weight loss and post-physical therapy progression. They started KDR in 2008 after Ben attended the Results Fitness Mastermind and Mentorship program led by Alwyn and Rachael Cosgrove. There he realized there was a better way to help his clients and at the same time increase revenue while working less hours and leveraging his time better.

He has taken his extensive knowledge of exercise, rehabilitative and nutrition sciences, coupled with the education and assistance he receives from Results Fitness University and created a real world fat loss and corrective exercise system.

"At KDR Fitness, we know how to help our clients lose fat in the safest, fastest way possible without starvation diets or exercise gimmicks. All of our programs are scientifically progressed to ensure any past or current injuries are eliminated on the way to a healthier, happier and more functional individual. We use a real world, tested, proven and realistic system for weight loss. Our name says it all - Knowledge Driven Results."

For more information on this topic and to see how KDR orchestrates increasing fiber intake in member's diets, send Ben an email at: KDRFitness@aol.com.

CHAPTER 27

Cutting Out the Drama Via Shortform Improv

By Laura Clancy

I take an improv class to learn how to recruit my funny bone in less than a moment's notice. One of the games that we play is called "*Fairy Tale.*"

That game works as follows: The audience picks a fairytale. The improv actors then act out a scene from that whimsical tale in about 45 seconds.

Once the scene is performed, the referee insists that the fairytale was NOT FAST ENOUGH. So, he asks the audience if they want to see it faster. Always eager to please, the audience shouts "*FASTER*" and the game begins anew, with only half the time to do the scene. This repeats several times until the scene is done in about 6 or 7 seconds. Whew!

Sound easy? Well, it is when you cut the fairytales into fewer distinct "beats".

You then minimize the beats each time and the scene is done in half time. I'd love to show you how that works through an example. Let's take the fairytale, Jack and the Beanstalk.

Here is the first 45 second scene as enacted by four improv actors:

Jack walks onstage and greets his mom. "Hi mom. What's up?"

She replies sarcastically, "I'm just great Jack, whaddaya think? We are poor and have no money. Did I mention that I'm hungry? Take our last cow down to the market and trade her for as many greenbacks as you can get for her."

"Okay, mom", he replies, grabbing the imaginary cow by the invisible rope. He then skips to the other side of the stage where he quickly hands the rope over for something that he cups in his hands.

After gleefully skipping back "home" to mom, Jack says "Lookie what I got, mom! I traded our cow for a bunch of beans."

Jack's mom takes her imaginary broom and hits him upside the head while berating him, "Jack, what were you thinking? Are you a simpleton? You take after your feckless father's ilk. Now, we'll starve."

Jack retreats from the "broom" to center stage and plants his "beans".

Soon Jack's astonishment is seen on his face. Lo and behold Jack watches his beans take root and grow UP in front of his eyes. He then begins his imaginary climb up.

The giant is stomping around while bellowing, "FEE-FI-FO-FUM, I smell the blood of an Englishman." This eleven word phrase is repeated several times in his quest to find a pint-sized Limey.

By flapping, honking and grimacing, the goose leaves little doubt that she is having trouble laying a golden egg. Regardless, Jack shimmies down the beanstalk with the goose.

The giant follows "FEE-FI-FO-FUMM..." -ing. Jack pulls out his "ax" and chops the "stalk" down. The giant falls down dead.

The scene is over.

The referee says, "Yes, that was good, but it wasn't fast enough, was it audience?" The audience loudly concurs! Here is that scene again in cut time... 22.5 seconds on the clock:

Jack: "Hi mom. 'Sup?'"

Mom: "Take this cow to market and trade her for greenbacks."

"Okay," he replies while running to the other side of the stage. He hands the rope over for something that he cups in his hands. He races back "home," shouting because he is only halfway home but saving time, "Look beans."

Jack's mom "brooms" and berates him: "Feckless father-like simpleton."

But Jack doesn't hear her or feel the broom because he is not there.

He is planting the beans that have already grown to the ceiling BEFORE he even planted them.

He climbs and hears..."FEE-FI-FO-FUM."

He sees the squawking goose and having no mercy for its misery laying eggs, grabs her. He leaps down goose in tow.

Giant chases him: "FEE-FI-FO-FUM...."

Jack chops down the vine and the giant falls down dead.

But, it's not fast enough! "Faster" the referee and audience yell... so the actors invoke their inner Edward Scissorhands again...11.25 seconds on the clock.

Jack: "Mom"

Mom: "Cow for bucks."

Jack: " 'kay!" sprinting across the stage and back with cupped hands. He yells to mom while planting beans, "Beans"....

She yells: "Simpleton"

He climbs.

Giant stomps and bellows: "FEE-FI-FO-FUM"...

Jack leaps down with long suffering goose...

"FEE-FI-FO..." is heard as the giant falls dead.

But, it's not fast enough! "Faster"...it's trimmed one last time to 6 seconds. The audience primes itself for hilarity watching four crazy people running around trying to convey the entire story using a few important beats.

"Mom"

"Cow "

Sprint.

"Beans"

"Simpleton"

Climb, squawk and grab.

"FEE – die!"

Endgame.

I love this game. It is so simple and cuts the non-essential boring bits out of the story.

What is this scenario doing in the nutrition section of this book?

Well, since I am the author, I thought that you might find it fun and funny. Since I have artistic license, I put it in to whet your appetite to "fun" nutrition...but, *that's* not important right now.

What *is* important is that I hunger...

– to find a way to give the basic yet boring information of "what to eat," "why to eat" and "how lean people eat" into a compressed 6 to 7 second format.

– to find the important 'beats' of nutrition when there really is no easy or quick answer.

Tightening your nutrition belt is not easy for most people who are reading this book. Weight loss, specifically fat loss, is not fast acting relief; it's more like a slow release formula(ic) response to daily action taking. Fat loss is something that takes time to achieve (you can see some real results in 6 to 8 weeks and amazing results in 12 weeks). That's pretty incredible because when the time essential for significant weight loss is contrasted to the shorter length of time required to gain that weight, weight loss is a "quickie" (:-)

Nutrition seems to be so, SO, so many of my clients sticky point and it is one of the top keys to fat loss, I need to figure out how to communicate the information in a way that is not boring to you and not grueling to me.

How?

I dunno, but here's what I am gonna do:

I have already come up with a teaching point: The story of basic nutrition is boring, fact filled and LONG. But, since nutrition is the primary key to fat loss, it must be understood and adhered to. I am going to pull out my inner Jack and chop the facts down to smaller tangible "beats" that are more digestible.

Ready?

The Story of Good Nutrition the 45 Second Version:

Food is fuel for your body. Nothing more/nothing less. It nourishes your body with the things that it needs to be healthy. It is not your friend, lover, or closet dwelling buddy.

Eat a diet consisting of fewer calories than you metabolically burn. I know, I know...duh. Here's something you may not know...do not ingest so few calories that your body shuts down metabolically. Go figure. Yet another balancing act in your life. You must ensure that you are taking in the proper nutrients needed to fuel your body.

In addition, I believe that special consideration should be taken with regard to the type of foods that you eat (ratio of protein/fat/ and carbohydrate). Many experts have found that eating a diet consisting of 30% protein/30% fat/ and 40% carbohydrate lends to quicker FAT LOSS. I suggest two quick method guesstimators of your caloric intake.
Method 1: Women ingest between 1500-1750 calories per day and Men ingest between 3000-3500 calories per day to lose weight.
Method 2: gives a slightly more personalized number of calories based on your lifestyle:

Activity Level	Recommended Caloric Intake per Pound of Body Weight for Weight Loss	Recommended Caloric Intake per Pound of Body Weight for Weight Maintenance
Sedentary (no exercise)	10 to 12	12 to 14
Moderate (3-4 days of exercise per week)	12 to 14	14 to 16
Active (5-7 days of exercise per week)	14 to 16	16 to 18

(As an added information bonus, 18-20 calories per pound is recommended to gain weight...I am sure that YOU wanted to know that).

Eat breakfast every morning, preferably within 15 minutes of waking up.

Eat 5-6 "meals" daily, ingesting every 2-4 hours. Don't let your food energy dip, that wreaks havoc on fat loss. The calories for these meals can be spread evenly over the day or a 3 "meals" and 2 "light snacks" approach also works well for fat loss.

Have a complete protein source at every meal. A good guideline for your daily protein intake is 20-25 grams of protein at each meal. This means that you will never eat carbohydrates by themselves.

Limit eating any food that does not come from nature and is not considered a whole food. Whole foods are foods which are free from additives and other artificial substances and have been refined or processed as little as possible. Here's a great guideline ~ Let's say that you did not ingest the food in a timely manner and the Mayan Calendar has run out. If *you are gone* and the *food item still remains*, that is NOT the right stuff to have in your cabinet to eat. We all know that Twinkies are not real food; but please consider that neither is pizza a real food. Lesson here: Do not eat processed carbohydrates.

Eat a piece of fruit or have vegetables at every meal.

Only eat natural starchy carbohydrates after a workout or for the first meal of the day. Starchy carbs are foods such as sweet potatoes, barley, beans, oatmeal, brown or wild rice, whole grain bread, etc.

Eat healthy fats every day (for optimum fat loss, this can be 30% of total daily calories).

Write down EVERYTHING that you eat.

Eating a wide variety of whole food is better than bars and shakes, except after a workout. However, bars and shakes are better than nothing.

Eat within the lines 90% of the time. If you eat 5-6 "meals" per day and multiply that by 7 days, you are eating 35-42 meals per week. That means that you get 3 to 4 "cheat meals" outside of the line PER WEEK.

Don't skip meals. A skipped meal is outside of the lines.

Drink water (and lots of it – I suggest drinking half your body weight in ounces). Keep coffee and black tea intake low. Green Tea is allowable and even suggested for fat loss. No sugary drinks (including alcohol) past your gullet unless you realize that it's a "cheat." I personally do not subscribe to or recommend "diet drinks" which have chemicals that are the understudy of nature.

Take a Multivitamin and Omega-3 Fish Oil (3-6 grams) daily.

Drink a workout shake during or within 10 minutes of finishing your workout.

Create a realistic goal(s).

Have a plan A, and a plan B...and if you are a little OCD'ish, go for plan C and D. Prepare for the inevitable misadventure.

Honor self-promises to achieve those goals and follow that plan without fail.

If you do fail, reset, sight your goal and again follow the plan. Do this GUILT FREE.

Only hang with supportive friends and look for a support group or support forum.

**Yeah, that's about it. But was it fast enough? Nope..."FASTER!"
Let's see how this goes...*alla breve*...2/4 time signature...cut time...**

FOOD IS FUEL

- Eat fewer calories than you burn.
- Eat breakfast.
- Eat 5-6 "meals" every 2-4 hours.
- Have a natural source of protein + carbohydrate at every meal.
- Have fruit or vegetables at every meal.
- Eat starchy carbs only after workouts and for breakfast.
- Eat healthy fats every day.
- Write down what you eat.
- Eat right 90% of the time.
- Don't skip meals.
- Drink lots of water.
- Take a Multivitamin and Fish Oil daily.
- Drink a workout shake during or within 10 minutes of finishing your workout.

SET GOALS

- Have a plan A, and a plan B...and consider having a plan C and D. Fail to plan, plan to fail.
- Honor self-promises and learn to trust yourself.
- Reset, GUILT FREE, in the unlikely event you fail.
- Have only supportive friends.

Fast enough? No Way...FASTER!!!

Nutrition - just beat it 'cause no-one wants to be defeated. The following are the smallest marching orders of nutrition that I can give and still have meaning:

- Food=Fuel
- Reduce Calories.

- Eat Breakfast.
- Eat every 2-4 hours.
- Complete Protein + Fruit or Veg carb at every meal.
- Limit starches to breakfast and/or after workouts.
- Eat healthy fats.
- Journal food ingestion.
- 90% proper nutrition.
- Don't skip food.
- Drink water.
- Take a MV and FO daily.
- Goal set.
- Plan.
- Trust yourself.
- Guilt free reset.
- Have Supportive Friends.

There you go!

Follow these rules and prepare for a fairytale in which your happy ending is living happily ever after in your little black dress.

About Laura

Laura Clancy is the proud owner of Muffin Toppled™ Fitness Coaching (www.Muffintoppled.com), writer of Wit and Fit™ and creator of the 12 week "Laugh, Cry and Lose Weight™" program.

In another life, Laura counted beans; she holds a B.S. (that's telling) in Accounting from George Mason University. Until 1999, the only weight that she had ever lifted was a fork fully overloaded with sweet food. In 1999, she began lifting weights with a personal trainer to lose weight between "birthin' babies" and found that she was no longer "between birthin'." After lifting weights through her entire pregnancy, she found lifting to be the magic potion to getting back to pre-pregnancy weight. Lifting ensured that she would not be fat for her 20th High School Reunion, but life interfered and lifting stopped after that reunion was done.

Realizing the short lived success of the High-School Crush Diet Plan, Laura got serious and re-toppled her own muffin in a leap-of-faith step when she became a Certified Personal Trainer and Certified Nutrition Consultant at the National Personal Training Institute. She has never looked back.

Laura is not only a trainer, she walks the walk! Laura is a competitive power lifter and holds two world records. She proudly lifts with the team, www.teamforcepowerlifting.com

As a fitness professional living, loving, and laughing in Northern Virginia, she has found a few stories in her humor arsenal that she would like to share in order to inspire women everywhere to weight train and eat well.

Currently, Laura trains clients of varying levels and consults on nutrition; but her real passion lies in giving seminars and workshops. She is also busy writing another book..the flood gates of words just will not stop. She finds the most joy in inspiring women that THEY CAN DO IT TOO... if they just step into the "man section" of the gym and believe in themselves.

You can reach Laura at: Laura@muffintoppled.com

Or by calling 703-209-3085.

CHAPTER 28

Your 4 Step Blueprint to Metabolic Training For Women

By Cameron Makarchuk

Picture this:

You've just gotten home after a long day at work and are exhausted. You sit down on the couch and flip on your favorite T.V. Show and the last thing on your mind is hitting the gym.

Then you remember: you crushed a killer metabolic training workout in the gym yesterday at lunch time and guess what... you're STILL getting the fat-burning benefits from that workout!

Your metabolism is still humming away, working hard to rebuild the muscle tissue you worked yesterday, all while you sit on your couch watching T.V. relaxing. As a matter of fact, you're going to burn calories tomorrow from that workout also.

Pretty cool, eh? That's just one of the many benefits of incorporating metabolic training into your fitness program.

Over the next few pages I'm going to take you with me through the exact system I use to design our metabolic training programs at BOOM BodyShaping Studio. At the end, you will have a complete blueprint for designing your own metabolic training program so you can accelerate your results in a fraction of the time!

STEP 1: GET YOUR GOAL IN YOUR MIND

I'm not going to spend too much time on this area because that's not what this chapter is about, but the first thing I talk about – when designing a program for a client – is to take a few minutes and make sure they figure out where they want their metabolic training program to take them.

Another area to think about during your goal setting time is: how many days per week you can commit 100% to your metabolic training program. With our clients at BOOM BodyShaping Studio we see the best results in the people that can commit approximately 30-45 minutes at least 3 days per week to their program. Ideally these days would be split such as Monday-Wednesday-Friday or Tuesday-Thursday-Saturday, but you need to decide which days are going to work best for you and schedule them so you have that appointment. Even if it's an appointment with yourself, you'll still have better success if you put it in your schedule and make the appointment.

Once we have a schedule in place we can move onto the next step in the system.

STEP 2: METABOLIC TRAINING OPTIONS

After you schedule your workouts and decide how much time you can commit during the week to your new metabolic training program you can start to look at your options.

Metabolic Circuit Training

At BOOM BodyShaping, we use mostly time sets with our metabolic training and have seen fantastic results with our clients. So if you only have 3 days and 30 minutes per day to get your training in, you could do a lot of damage to that waistline with three total body metabolic workouts using timed sets.

The most basic example of a timed set would be a circuit. Our circuits are usually 5-8 exercises using a 30 seconds WORK, 30 seconds REST set up and typically doing 4 or 5 rounds trying to keep the total workout time between 20-30 minutes.

An example workout for this type of training might look like this:

1. 2 Hand Kettlebell Swing

2. Push Ups

3. Wide Grip Pull Downs

4. Split Jumps

5. Mountain Climbers

6. Stability Ball Leg Curls

So you'd do each of those exercises for 30 seconds with 30 seconds of rest between until you completed all 6 exercises, resting 1-2 minutes between rounds. If you're just starting out, take the full 2 minute rest between rounds, and then decrease that rest time every week until you get down to 1 minute.

Another variation of metabolic circuit training we utilize is to use 3-5 supersets instead, which is kind of like a mini-circuit consisting of 2 exercises each. Our clients love this style of training because once you're done the time at one superset you never have to come back to it like you would with the circuit above. When you're done, you're done!

What we typically do with these is to have 2 opposing exercises grouped together in a superset. For example, push ups and kettlebell swings would make one superset. We then alternate between the two exercises for 30 seconds of WORK and 15 seconds of REST until we have completed 4 rounds/sets of each exercise. Once we've completed this we rest for 1-2 minutes and proceed to the next superset. Typically, total workout time for this structure will be between 25-35 minutes because of the increased rest time, but it allows you to push even harder for your WORK intervals!

The main thing to keep in mind with these two metabolic styles is that we are trying to get as many GOOD repetitions as possible during the WORK intervals. Keyword being GOOD (read: perfect form, under control). We typically want to be explosive on the concentric phase (i.e., the "lifting" part) and a little slower, more controlled on the eccentric phase (i.e., the "lowering" part). Keep track of your reps each round/set and try to either beat it or stay the same for the remainder of the workout, then try to beat your reps the following week.

Density Training

I first read about density training in a book called Cardio Strength Training by Robert dos Remedios and it immediately opened my eyes to an entire new style of metabolic training.

In the density training model, you'll have a group of exercises and complete a set number of repetitions for each, trying to complete as many rounds/sets as possible in a predetermined time, resting only as needed. So instead of trying to get as many good reps as possible in a timed interval, you're trying to get as many ROUNDS as possible in the total workout time.

For example, you're density training workout might look like this:

1. Burpees – 10 reps
2. Barbell Straight Legged Deadlifts – 12 reps
3. Kettlebell Goblet Split Squats – 12 reps each side
4. Low – High Cable Chops – 10 reps each side
5. Dumbbell Incline Bench Press – 10 reps
6. Bent Over Dumbbell Row – 10 reps

You would then set a timer for somewhere between 12 – 30 minutes depending how much time you have and what fitness level you're at (beginners start at 12 minutes and work up from there) and challenge yourself to see how many rounds you can get before the timer goes off.

What we like to see with our density training at BOOM BodyShaping is to stay between 8-12 reps per exercise, keeping the repetitions controlled, really focusing on perfect form for every time. We can still be a little explosive on the concentric phase of the movement, but not as much as we like to be with the timed intervals from before. In this style of training you really have to stay aware of your pace because you'll fatigue very quickly if you try to go as quickly as with the timed intervals.

The key with either of these structures is to try to push harder each time you go to the gym. Whether that's pushing out a couple more reps, increasing the weight a little, or pushing through an additional round in your density training, it's important to always be pushing yourself to make progress in your workouts in order to get the best results possible in the most efficient way possible.

STEP 3: PROPER METABOLIC EXERCISE SELECTION

Exercise selection for your metabolic training is actually quite simple if you think in terms of movements. As long as you take care of each movement in the selection process, the muscles will balance out.

When I design the metabolic programs at BOOM BodyShaping I always make sure I have the following movements covered:

1. Squat
2. Bend
3. Single Leg Stance
4. Lunge
5. Horizontal Push
6. Horizontal Pull
7. Vertical Push
8. Vertical Pull
9. Rotational / Anti-Rotational
10. Core Stability / Dynamic Stability
11. Power

Let's take a closer look at each of these movements and give you some examples.

(Note: For videos of these exercises and more visit: www.BOOMBodyShapingStudio.com/YouTube)

1. Squat Movement

Examples:

- Bodyweight Squats
- Barbell Back Squats
- Barbell Front Squats
- Dumbbell Squats
- Stability Ball Squats
- Goblet Squats

2. Bend Movement

Examples:

- Straight Legged Deadlift

3. Single Leg Stance

Examples:

- Single Leg Squat
- Single Leg Straight Legged Deadlift

4. Lunge

Examples:

- Bodyweight Split Squat
- Rear Foot Elevated Split Squat
- Walking Lunges
- Reverse Lunges
- Lateral Lunges
- Rotational Lunges

5. Horizontal Push

Examples:

- Push ups
- Bench Press
- Dumbbell Bench Press
- Single Arm Dumbbell Bench Press

6. Horizontal Pull

Examples:

- Bent Over Dumbbell Row
- Bent Over Barbell Row
- One Arm Dumbbell Row
- Inverted Bodyweight Row

7. Vertical Push

Examples:

- Barbell Overhead Press
- Dumbbell Overhead Press
- One Arm Dumbbell Overhead Press
- Pike Push Ups

8. Vertical Pull

Examples:

- Chin Ups
- Pull Ups
- Wide Grip Lat Pull Downs
- One Arm Lat Pull Downs

9. Rotational/Anti-Rotational

Examples:

- Low – High Cable Chop (Rotational)
- High – Low Cable Chop (Rotational)
- Medicine Ball Chops (Rotational)
- Paloff Press (Anti-Rotational)

10. Core Stability/Dynamic Stability

Examples:

- Plank (Core Stability)
- Side Plank (Core Stability)
- Stability Ball Roll Out (Dynamic Stability)
- Side Plank with Reach Underneath (Dynamic Stability)

11. Power

Examples:

- Burpees
- Jump Squats
- Split Jumps
- Medicine Ball Throws
- Kettlebell Swings
- Kettlebell Snatches

Basically you're going to make sure you have equal selection from each of those movements throughout your metabolic program.

As you can see, all of the exercises in the examples of the movements use more than one muscle group. These are called multi-joint exercises because they move across more than one joint, utilizing many different muscles synergistically. The more muscles you use means more calories burned during and after the workout – which is very good for our fat burning efforts!

With the pushes and pulls, I also like to have to some single arm exercises as well because you'll get some awesome anti-rotational benefits throughout your core due to the off balance nature of the single arm exercises.

STEP 4: PUTTING THE PIECES TOGETHER

Now that you have the structure and the exercises in front of you, it's time to put it all together into a metabolic training program.

Here's how I would set this up for you on a weekly schedule if you only had three days to train per week with only metabolic workouts:

MONDAY	TUESDAY	WEDNESDAY	THURSDAY	FRIDAY	SATURDAY	SUNDAY
Timed Intervals A	Off/Light Activity	Timed Intervals B	Off/Light Activity	Timed Intervals C	Fun Activity	Fun Activity

Where "A", "B" and "C" would be different workouts using the same timed interval structure (i.e., Workout A, Workout B & Workout C). This is basically the schedule that most of our clients at BOOM BodyShaping are on, and they get fantastic fat loss results from it.

After 4-6 weeks on this schedule, I would then recommend changing to a density training model for the next 4-6 weeks to alternate the stresses on your body and avoid training plateaus.

Now, if you had 4 days for metabolic training per week, I would set it up a little differently for you:

MONDAY	TUESDAY	WEDNESDAY	THURSDAY	FRIDAY	SATURDAY	SUNDAY
Density Training A	Timed Intervals A	OFF	Density Training B	Timed Intervals B	Fun Activity	Fun Activity

Where "A" and "B" would be different workouts (i.e., Workout A & Workout B).

Again, we would do this for 4-6 weeks then change your program based on your progress. We would keep the schedule the same, but alter the rep ranges for your Density Training workouts and alter the interval times for your Timed Interval workouts.

Keep in mind the above schedules are just examples. You can modify those to fit your schedule quite easily by following a couple simple guidelines:

If you're using the 3 day per week schedule, try to have at least 1 day separating your workouts. It's OK to go back-to-back once in a while if needed, but try to avoid it if possible.

If you're using the 4 day per week schedule, always alternate between "Density Training" and "Timed Intervals" so you're not doing 2 Density Training workouts back to back or 2 Timed Interval workouts back to back.

On the 4 day per week schedule, alternate between the "A" and "B" workouts weekly so you're not doing the same workout twice in one week.

With the 4 day per week schedule, try to stick to the "2 Days ON - 1 Day OFF - 2 Days ON - 2 Days OFF" schedule laid out above to avoid overtraining.

All right, now that we have your schedule planned out, let's choose some exercises!

Obviously which exercises you choose will depend on what equipment you have available to you, if any. Remember, you can crush some solid metabolic workouts using just your bodyweight. This is typically what I'll do in my hotel room when traveling.

Here's some example Timed Interval workouts if you're limited to just one training tool:

Alternate between 30 seconds of WORK and 30 seconds of REST until you've completed all the exercises. Rest for 1 minute then repeat for 3-4 rounds.

BODYWEIGHT ONLY	KETTLEBELL ONLY	TRX SUSPENSION TRAINER ONLY
Burpees	1 Arm Snatch	TRX Jump Squats
Push Ups	Kettlebell Halo	Inverted Row
Hip Bridges	Push Press	TRX Push Ups
Mountain Climbers	Rolling Plank	Assisted Single Leg Squat
Prisoner Reverse Lunges	2 Hand Swing	TRX Knee Tucks

And then your Density Training would look something like this:

Complete 12 controlled reps of each exercise resting only as needed between exercises. Complete as many rounds as possible in 24 minutes.

KETTLEBELL ONLY	DUMBBELLS ONLY	CABLE MACHINE
Kettlebell Hang Clean	Incline Chest Press	Cable Chest Press
1 Leg, 1 Arm Straight Leg Deadlift	Straight Leg Deadlift	Wide Grip Lat Pull Down
Overhead Press	Dumbbell Chop	Low-High Cable Chop
Single Arm Row	Bent Over Row	Cable Straight Leg Deadlift

Now ideally you wouldn't be limited to just one training tool, but this should give you an idea of what your workouts would look like.

As I mentioned earlier, the most important part of metabolic training is pushing harder every time. If you're just going through the motions, it doesn't matter how perfectly designed your program is, you won't be getting the best results from it.

There you have it, your 4 Step Blueprint To Metabolic Training. All you have to do now is get started, crush your workouts and reap the amazing benefits of metabolic training!

About Cameron

Cameron Makarchuk is a bodyshaping specialist, metabolic training expert and founder of BOOM BodyShaping Studio in Winnipeg, Manitoba where he and his team are "changing people's lives, one pound at a time." He has worked with thousands of clients throughout his career and has helped them change their lives through sound nutrition, mindset techniques and scientifically-proven training strategies.

Acclaimed as "the most comprehensive fat loss solution in Winnipeg," BOOM BodyShaping Studio is just that, having all the bases covered and giving their driven, dedicated clients all the tools and coaching they need to reach their goals and beyond!

On a mission of helping 100,000 men and women transform their lives and bodies, Cameron is working on putting his entire system together into an easy to follow, comprehensive program called "BodyShaping BluePrint" that will be available for anyone, anywhere, extending his reach to helping people not just in Winnipeg, but all around the world.

To stay up to date on Cameron's mission, and learn how you can receive a free metabolic workout, visit: www.BodyShapingBluePrint.com

To learn more about how BOOM BodyShaping Studio is changing people's lives in Winnipeg visit: www.BOOMBodyShapingStudio.com

CHAPTER 29

Fat Loss For Dudes

By Craig Rasmussen

It may not be ingrained in our male DNA, but when most of us start lifting weights for the first time, it sure seemed like all of our workouts (no matter what the goal) were genetically predestined to be bench press, biceps curl, and triceps pushdown marathons 4-5 times per week, and not much else. I know that my own workouts sure looked like this when I first started weight training way back in the late 80s. I don't get to visit the typical commercial gym too often these days, but each time I do, I feel like I have time-warped back to the 80s as I see most guys doing the same stuff I did over 20+ years ago. For whatever reason, not much has changed and it's not their fault, they just don't know any better. So what's a dude to do? I am going to show you how to do better based on several things that we have learned over the years.

First, let's be honest dudes, you could probably stand to lose some "lbs" of body fat (I should note, back in the 80's and 90's, we referred to guys most often as "dudes" in our vernacular instead of the currently in vogue term of "bros"). A lot of guys, myself most definitely included, tend to find ourselves in a perpetual "bulking" or mass-gaining mode. Why is this? Interestingly, for a lot of us dudes, the mirror often lies and you will see a much leaner person staring back at you. If you were to take an honest self-evaluation such as a body composition test or take some simple photos with only your trunks on, you may be very surprised and/ or shocked with the results. It can be a real eye-opener when you learn that you are more than likely not nearly as lean as you think you are.

In other words, that 14-15% body fat that you think you are sitting at is probably much closer to 21-22%. If you have taken this evaluation and you have decided that it is time for you to get leaner, it is also high time that you overhaul your weight training program to make it more suited to the task at hand.

I write training programs at one of the leading fat loss gyms in the world and we have quite a few males who have come from the same place that you and I have come from. These guys are now typically middle-aged and looking to shed some fat, stay strong, and still feel a bit athletic while holding on to their inner "dude."

I am going to share with you what I feel are some of the biggest mistakes that I see most guys make – when left to their own devices as it pertains to their weight training programs – when seeking fat loss. Fixing these mistakes immediately will fast track your progress and get you to your fat loss goals. I am then going to share a snapshot of a training program that we have used with great success for dudes just like us.

1. DUDES ORGANIZE THEIR TRAINING LIKE A "BODYBUILDER."

I certainly mean no disrespect to the competitive bodybuilding community by the above statement, and I don't think there is anything wrong with bodybuilding as a competitive pursuit. There is certainly a lot to learn from bodybuilders. In fact, most dudes get our first exposure to weight training through bodybuilders via muscle magazines and the Internet. The problem is that most guys think that following the routines of competitive bodybuilders is the best way for the average person to train for fat loss without really giving it enough thought.

They will typically organize their training sessions in terms of the body parts or muscles trained. This is actually not very logical and not as productive as it could be since in reality your body works as an integrated unit, and not as individual parts or muscles. By the way, have you ever wondered how it was decided that certain muscles get their own day while others don't? It makes no real sense to base how we allocate our exercises to our training days by simply considering muscle groups as the main organizing factor. It makes much more sense to base the allocation in regards to what the body does as it relates to basic human movements. If you think more in terms of training basic movements and the body as a whole (the way it actually works), you will actually train muscles as a by-product and get the results you desire. I really like a quote that I originally heard from strength coach Nick Winkleman of Athletes' Performance who stated, "When we just train muscles, we forget movements, when we train movements, we never forget muscles."

The other big problem with this approach is that time is a major limiting factor for most typical dudes. We all have extremely busy lives with jobs and families. Do you really have the time to dedicate to training that a professional bodybuilder (whose job is usually his training) would have? I don't think so. In our experience at Results Fitness (currently working with well over 300 clients multiple times per week on individualized programs), full body weight training routines done three times a week based on a split of basic human movements will work far better for most dudes most of the time, in terms of fat loss training. This allows you to train with a higher frequency (you will actually hit muscle groups more often than typical body-part split routines) and get better results. At Results Fitness, instead of classifying our exercises by muscle group or body part, we classify them simply based on what they are – basic movements. The classification that we use is the following:

• Squat

• Bend

• Push

• Pull

• Single Leg Stance

• Lunge

• Core

We will then allocate these movements to training days, as you will see in the sample program at the end of the chapter.

2. DUDES THINK MORE IS BETTER.

More than likely, because of the heavy mainstream bodybuilding influence on general training that we mentioned above, most dudes usually think they <u>must</u> train on that good old 5-6 times per week body part split routine with extremely high volume to get any results. They also often think they must use multiple exercises for each body part with tons of sets. You must realize that you make gains while you are recovering from training, not during the actual training itself. There is also no need for exercises that are redundant. Think about it, what the heck is the leg extension going to do for you that the squat doesn't? The key is to focus on quality and not so much on quantity. As fitness expert Paul Chek has stated, "exercise is like a drug." With the correct dose and the correct drug, you will get the desired response and it all works. If you overdose or take the wrong drug, you can do more harm than good and not get the desired response. One of the reasons why a three times per week full body routine works so well is that you get a high frequency of training without over doing it in terms of volume.

3. DUDES DO TOO MANY SINGLE JOINT EXERCISES.

Is it a federal crime to do some biceps curls and triceps pushdowns? Nope, but when the volume/number of these types of exercises dominate your program, you will greatly diminish the effectiveness of your workouts, particularly when it comes to fat loss. If you focus your training on heavy, multi-joint (compound) exercises such as squats, deadlifts, various presses, push ups, rows, chins/pull-ups, etc., you will train much greater amounts of muscle overall, and this will lead to more calories burned during and after your workouts. As a general rule, the more muscle involved in an exercise the better.

But what if a dude's goal is to also get bigger guns? Realize that spending the majority of your time and effort on getting stronger on chin-ups/ pull-ups, various rows, and various types of presses will get your arms bigger faster than anything else. If you are unable to only do a single unassisted chin-up, what do you think will do more for your biceps size, those 25-30 lb curls or focusing all your time and energy on working on that chin-up and getting to the point where you are doing multiple reps with an extra 25-50lbs hooked up around your waist?

4. DUDES NEGLECT LOWER BODY TRAINING.

Squats aren't simply a leg exercise and deadlifts aren't simply a back exercise. They are full body exercises that involve just about every muscle in the entire body. If you have a 315 lb. bar on your shoulders or upper back and you are getting ready to bang out a set of squats for 8 reps, realize that not just your legs are involved in the exercise. Your shoulders, upper back, core, etc., are all very heavily involved. They need to be big enough and strong enough to support and move that load.

A lot of dudes think, "I get enough "leg" work from running and playing hoops, so I don't need to do squats, deadlifts, lunges, step ups, etc." Sorry, but that's just not the same thing! Understand that approximately 70% of your muscle mass is in your back, hips and legs. If you omit these exercises, you are severely limiting your results. Dare to be different and dare to get better results. At our gym you will see everyone doing deadlifts, squats, lunges, and various single leg exercises, thereby training "legs." It is part of our culture here and one of the reasons that we get the results that we do.

5. DUDES REST 'WAY TOO LONG' BETWEEN SETS.

You know the scene at the local gym - guys taking 5-10 minutes between sets of the same exercise shooting the breeze with their buddies while discussing any number of topics and paying no attention to time. This is not very effective at all if your goal is fat loss! Research and practical experience has shown us that shorter rest periods lead to maximal metabolic disturbance possibly due to the hormonal influence that is set off by these shorter rest periods. It also allows us to increase overall caloric burn and total work performed in the time allotted for the training session. The key is being able to combine shorter rests without compromising the use of heavier loads in our compound exercises. How do we do this? Quite simply, we pair non-competing exercises with short rests (30-60 seconds) between them. As an example we might use the following pairing in a program:

1A: Push Ups	2-3 sets	12 reps	60 sec. rest
1B: Reverse Lunges	2-3 sets	12 reps each	60 sec. rest

This allows us to increase the actual amount of work density done in a specified time period, as opposed to doing each exercise one at a time with longer rests, which leads again to better fat loss results.

6. DUDES THINK, "THE BENCH PRESS IS MORE THAN JUST AN EXERCISE, IT IS A WAY OF LIFE!"

I don't think that there is any doubt that the bench press is the most over-used exercise of all time. But, let me state this up front, there is nothing wrong with the bench press! I love the bench press (as most dudes do). The problem is when the bench press becomes your entire workout each time, rather than simply a part of your training program. In other words, most dudes simply bench press way too often and with way too much volume. This creates massive imbalances about the shoulder girdle. You need to strive for some sort of balance in the amount of pushing and pulling movements that you perform. Since most guys have been doing way more pushing for such a long time, it is a wise plan to purposely imbalance your training in the other direction in performing more pulls than pushes. You need to include lots of inverted rows, face pulls, dumbbell rows, and cable rows. Remember the fact that 70% of muscle mass is in the back and legs? This will do your shoulders a lot of good and help out with the fat loss process all at the same time. By the way, in looking at the push pattern from a fat loss standpoint, the good old-fashioned push up is probably a better choice than the bench press actually, as it involves a greater amount of muscle mass and integrates the core to a greater extent at the same time.

With all of that said, let's take a look at what a sample 4-6 week training program would look like.

THE DUDE WEIGHT TRAINING PLAN FOR FAT LOSS

Day A

Range of Motion, Activation, & Movement Preparation. (Dynamic Warm Up)

1A: Horizontal Cable Woodchops	2 sets	10 reps ea. way	0s Rest
1B: Ab Wheel Roll Outs	2 sets	8 reps	60s Rest
2A: Front Squat	2-3 sets	6 reps	60s Rest
2B: Single Leg Ankle Mobility	2-3 sets	8 reps each	0s Rest
OR			
2A: Deadlift	2-3 sets	6 reps	60s Rest
2B: Hip Flexor Stretch	2-3 sets	30s each side	0s Rest

(Alternate using the front squat pairing and the deadlift pairing each workout day)

3A: TRX Inverted Rows	2-3 sets	12 reps	60s Rest
3B: Reverse Lunges	2-3 sets	12 reps ea.	60s Rest
4A: Push Ups	2-3 sets	12 reps	60s Rest
4B: Neutral Grip Face Pulls	2-3 sets	12 reps	60s Rest

Day B

Range of Motion, Activation, & Movement Preparation. (Dynamic Warm Up)

1A: Kettlebell Windmill	2 sets	5-8 reps each side	0s Rest
1B: Prone Jackknife	2 sets	10 reps	60s Rest
2A: Bench Press	2-3 sets	6 reps	60s Rest
2B: Figure Four Hip Stretch	2-3 sets	20s each side	0s Rest

OR

2A: Chin-Ups	2-3 sets	4-6 reps	60s Rest
2B: Leg Lowering Drill	2-3 sets	6 reps each side	0s Rest

(Alternate using the bench press pairing and the chin-up pairing each workout day.)

3A: 3 Point DB Rows	2-3 sets	12 reps each side	60s Rest
3B: Single Arm Single Leg RDL	2-3 sets	12 reps each side	60s Rest
4A: DB Overhead Presses	2-3 sets	12 reps	60s Rest
4B: Swiss Ball Leg Curls	2-3 sets	12 reps	60s Rest

Notes:

- Use this program for 3 days per week on non-consecutive days, e.g., Mon/Wed/Fri or Tue/Thus/Sat etc.

- Alternate the A and the B program each training day. For example, weeks 1 through 3 will look like the following:

  - Week 1: Monday - Workout A / Wednesday – Workout B/ Friday - Workout A

  - Week 2: Monday - Workout B / Wednesday – Workout A/ Friday - Workout B

  - Week 3: Monday - Workout A / Wednesday – Workout B/ Friday - Workout A

About Craig

Craig Rasmussen is a program design specialist and performance coach at Results Fitness in Newhall, California. Results Fitness has been named as one of America's top ten gyms by Men's Health magazine multiple times.

Craig has been featured in several national publications including *Men's Health, Men's Fitness, Muscle and Fitness,* and *Runner's World.* He is a competitive powerlifter and Craig also coaches our powerlifting team at Result's Fitness.

Craig Rasmussen is a Certified Strength and Conditioning Specialist through the National Strength and Conditioning Association. For more information, please visit: www.resultsfitnessuniversity.com.

CHAPTER 30

Progress To Impress

By Seth Bobbitt

*If you do what you've always done, then you'll get
what you've always gotten.* ~ Tony Robbins

Growing up a skinny kid in Alabama, I had but one dream…to be a professional baseball pitcher. The cards were stacked against me though. As if that challenge wasn't daunting enough, it didn't help that as a kid I wasn't the biggest, strongest or threw the fastest. I had my work cut out for me for sure. I had heard the statistics that your chances of making it into professional baseball are less than 1% and get exponentially harder at each level you play. I was well aware that many people never thought I would succeed.

The road was tough and it was paved with a lot of blood, sweat and tears. I'm not sure at what point in my life it happened, but I came to realize that if I wanted to reach my goal, then I was responsible for getting it done. Nothing was going to be handed to me. There was an unquenchable fire inside that drove me to get better. I knew I had to improve and push myself to get better every single day. The process was physically and mentally grueling, but I forced myself to make progress every day towards my goal of becoming a professional baseball player. Eventually, the hard work paid off and I went on to be a pro-baseball pitcher with a fastball that topped 97 miles per hour. I challenged myself on a daily basis to break through those physical and mental limits. I fixed my eyes on my goal and forced my body and mind to change in order to achieve my dream.

Although my playing days are over, I still have to challenge myself to reach new goals. Everyone does and one thing is certain...you have to force your body and mind to change – if you want it to be what you want it to be and look like you want it to look like. It must be challenged to make progress. You must have a plan and you must know how to continually change that plan as your body changes.

The idea that you must steadily challenge your body with new demands to see results is certainly not a new one. Everyone knows that to get stronger you need a great plan and you have to make progress. Your intensity must match your goals. If you want to get leaner and more defined, then you have to lift more weight and get stronger. Period.

There's just one problem. Most people don't know how or when to progress. Too many people just aren't sure of the right way to increase their intensity in order to continue to see results. You can have a great plan, but if you don't really know how to use it to maximize your efforts then you're just spinning your wheels, or worse, you could get hurt.

Since my baseball career ended, I've trained people from one extreme to the other, from professional athletes to soccer moms to people who just want to move better and feel better. They all demand that I get them the results they are looking for. These are the same methods we use to help our clients to look and feel better than they ever dreamed, and we do it faster than anyone else.

I'll give you the plan and teach you how to feel comfortable – progressively increasing the intensity to see better results than you've ever seen, and quicker than you ever thought you could see them. The best part? You can continue using these methods to see great results for as long as you want.

THE PLAN

Science consistently shows that strength training is the most effective use of our time in the gym if fat loss is our ultimate goal. If we get stronger, then we should get leaner provided our nutrition is in line. Let's make the distinction between "fat loss" and "weight loss." We change the composition of our body by increasing our lean muscle mass while decreasing our body fat. In short, the more muscle mass we have then the higher our metabolism and the better our body is at burning fat. More muscle and less body fat will ultimately result in getting the "definition" in your arms and "toning or shaping" your legs. Conversely, "weight loss" doesn't necessarily indicate that we are changing our body composition at all. While weight loss may be a goal for some people, never lose site of the fact that fat loss should always be a goal.

You'll have two workouts that you'll alternate every other day. Each day will be a full body workout. The more muscles we can work, then the more calories we burn during the session and for a long time afterwards. It's the most efficient way to train for fat loss.

Week 1

Monday – workout A

Wednesday – workout B

Friday – workout A

Week 2

Monday – workout B

Wednesday – workout A

Friday – workout B

Repeat the workout in this fashion each week. You will complete each workout a total of 6 times each. If you plan on strength training 3 days per week, then you will complete each workout 6 times in 4 weeks. However, if you plan on strength training 2 days per week then you will complete each workout 6 times in 6 weeks. To get the best results as fast as possible, plan on working out 3 days per week, preferably on alternating days (i.e. Monday, Wednesday and Friday).

**Each strength workout will be preceded by a few minutes on the foam roller (or dense ball) then a dynamic warm-up session. Starting each session using a foam roller/dense ball will prepare our muscles to warm-up, getting the knots out, which will help us to move better and reduce the risk of injury.

The dynamic warm-up exercises will further prepare our muscles for the stresses of the workout by activating the muscles that need activating and increase our core temperature, getting us nice and warm before we hit it hard in the workout.

Dynamic Warm Up

Single Leg Glute Bridge – 8 each side

Birddog with rotation – 5 each side

Squat to Stand – 5 reps

Walking High Knee and Flick – 10 each side

Prisoner Pivoting Deep Squat – 10

Lateral Step and Reach – 5 each side

Workout A

1a. Suitcase Deadlift (using Kettlebells or Dumbbells) 2 x 15

1b. Alternating Overhead Shoulder Presses 2 x 12-15

1c. 90-90 Hip Stretch 30 seconds each side

2a. Standing Single Arm Cable Row (Feet Even) 2 x 12-15 ea

2b. Offset Loaded Lunge 2 x 15 each side

2c. Passive Leg Lowering 2 x 5 each side

Workout B

1a. Goblet Squat – 2 x 15

1b. TRX (or other suspension trainer) Pushups – 2 x 12-15

1c. Forearm Wall Slides 2 x 10

2a. Half Kneeling Neutral Grip Pulldowns – 2 x 12-15

2b. Single Leg Straight Leg Deadlift – 2 x 15 each side

2c. Half Kneeling Hip Flexor stretch 2 x 30 seconds each side

As you can see, the format of the two workouts is identical in that you have two circuits of 3 exercises with different numbers and letters. Always remember that exercises with the same number are exercises we will alternate for time-efficiency sake. For example, you will perform a set of Suitcase Deadlifts (1a) then go to Overhead Shoulder presses (1b) and so on. Then repeat the circuit. This alternating fashion helps keep us fresh before repeating an exercise a second time. If our muscles are fresh and fully recovered each time then we will progress faster and get better results faster.

THE PROGRESSION

Learning how to properly progress may seem confusing but it doesn't have to be. You just need a structured plan of how to move forward week by week.

There are some important things to keep in mind as we move forward:

1. Your lower body is probably much stronger than your upper body. You will increase the amount of weight faster with your legs than you will with upper body exercises. For this reason, we will focus on two different types of progressions.

2. Never ever attempt a repetition that you are not comfortable with or you're not sure you can finish.

3. Technique is paramount. **Never sacrifice technique for more weight**. If you cannot maintain with 100lbs the exact same sound technique you did with 40lbs, then the weight is too heavy for you. Stop as soon as you feel your technique start to fail you.

4. **Remember, if you are uncertain about lifting a weight you've never tried then make sure you have a spotter or fellow work-out buddy to supervise your exercise.** Teach them before hand what to do if you start to struggle and need assistance.

EASY WEEK-BY-WEEK PROGRESSION PLAN (WORKING OUT 3 DAYS PER WEEK)

A. Lower Body Movements - Suitcase Deadlift, Offset Loaded Lunges, Goblet Squats, Single Leg Straight Leg Deadlift

- The goal for the lower body progression is to be able to increase the total amount of weight in **one** lower body exercise each workout.

- The workout calls for 2 sets of 15 repetitions. What's important to note here is the repetition number as this number will ultimately determine how much load (or weight) we choose to use.

- The goal for the lower body progression is always 15 reps this phase. You'll shoot for 15 reps each workout while trying to increase the weight in **ONE** lower body exercise each workout.

Week 1 – Pick a weight that you can comfortably do fifteen times with outstanding technique. You'll stop at the 15 reps it calls for but you should've been able to move that weight 20 times if you wanted to. Ask yourself, on a scale of 1-10, "How difficult was this weight?" If it feels too easy then it probably is.

Week 2 – Pick a weight you can do fifteen times but still have the ability to do a couple more if you had to. The weight will be more challenging but you can still complete your 15 reps and maintain excellent form. You should increase the weight by about 10-15% from the week before.

Week 3 – Now it's time to start getting after it. Increase the weight by 5-10% this week. It should be a real challenge getting to 15 but you should be able to still get there with a little gas left in the tank. Pay attention to your rest periods and make sure that you're fully recovered before attempting your next set in order to maximize you performance.

Week 4 – This is Challenge Week. We are going to overload the body to make some serious changes. We're shooting to reach new personal bests in every exercise this week. Again, try to increase your weight by another 5-10% on each exercise if possible. It should be a real physical and mental challenge to set your new personal best in each exercise. It's going to take some serious focus and determination but you certainly CAN DO IT. Try to get to 15 reps at your new weight but don't beat yourself up if you only get within a couple reps like 12 or 13. Remember, it's called Challenge Week for a reason. It should be hard but think about the amazing changes you're forcing your body to make!

B. Upper Body Movements – Alternating Overhead Shoulder Presses, Standing Single Arm Cable Rows (feet even), TRX Pushups, Half-Kneeling Neutral Grip Pull downs

- The goal for the upper body progression is to be able to increase the intensity (or load) only after you reach the highest numbers in our repetition bracket, 12 -15 in this case.

- The intensity (or load) for the TRX (or other suspension trainer) Pushups will be dictated by our foot position as opposed to actual weight. Moving your feet back will increase the amount of your own body weight you're required to push up, thus increasing the intensity.

Week 1 – Pick a weight (or foot position for the TRX) that allows you to reach the lower end of the repetition bracket, in this case is 12. You'll stop at the 12 reps it calls for, but you should've been able to do several more if needed. Remember, the initial goal is to master the technique so that when it's time to increase the intensity you can be confident you'll do it correctly and safely. Ask yourself, on a scale of 1-10, "How difficult was this weight?" In week 1, it should be about 7 out of 10.

Weeks 2, 3 and 4 – Try to increase the number or repetitions in each workout until you're able to hit the top threshold of our repetition bracket of 15 repetitions for both sets. It should be a real challenge getting to 15 and you may not make it there in the 2nd or even 3rd weeks but keep pushing because you will get there. Pay attention to your rest periods and make sure that you're fully recovered before attempting your next set in order to maximize you performance. Once you can do 15 repetitions for both sets, then you should add 5-10% more weight or adjust your foot position and try to get 12 reps again. Then you'll work back up to the high end of 15 reps. and repeat as necessary.

The physical and mental demands here will be tough but have confidence and courage to reach your goals. *Remember that you have what it takes and you CAN DO IT.* To get the body you want, you have to tell your body what you want it to do because naturally your body will resist the changes you want to make to it. That's just the way the body works.

At Revolution Fitness, our clients are challenged on a daily basis to envision the person they want to be and to go after it. We motivate them to progress and get better at something every single day.

Take control of your fitness and your body by learning how to progress your workouts the right way, and you'll make changes to your body you never thought possible.

About Seth

Seth Bobbitt is the owner of Revolution Fitness in Peachtree City, Georgia. Seth has over ten years experience as a personal fitness coach and fat loss expert. He is known for the results-driven, scientifically-designed fitness programs he provides for his clients on a daily basis. He is a certified personal trainer through the American Council on Exercise and has an advanced certification with the well-known, progressive fitness company PTA Global.

Over the years, Seth has trained from professional athletes to people just wanting to improve their health and fitness. He is very passionate about meeting clients where they are at and crafting programs to get superior results in less time through the use of metabolically demanding strength and interval workouts. Seth understands that exercise is not just about looking better but rather feeling better and being able to move better, thus improving the quality of life in all three areas every day. Seth continues to learn from the brightest and most progressive minds in the fitness industry through intense mentorships and training. One of his main core values is to "Get Better at Something Every Single Day" and he lives it.

Seth developed his love for fitness as a professional baseball pitcher with the Atlanta Braves and Houston Astros organizations from 2001 – 2005, where he learned to manipulate his training to get the specific results you desire. His goal is to reach as many as possible in order to inspire and educate them on how to make the right choices to create lasting positive changes that can ultimately affect every area of their lives. If you like to know how you can connect with Seth and get involved in fitness and revolutionize your body and your life, you can contact him at:
Seth@myrevolutionfitness.com
www.myrevolutionfitness.com

CHAPTER 31

ABC's of Fitness For The Working Class

By Doug Schwaberow

JUST ANOTHER DAY IN THE WORKWEEK

You look up from your MacBook Pro and before you even realize, it's 11:00 pm, the wife and kids are tucked away in bed, and you're munching on a Snickers, drinking a Diet Coke, as if that "Diet" makes any real difference.

You just kept putting it off….When the alarm rang at 6 a.m.

"I'm just going to sleep another hour, I'll workout during lunch," you told yourself.

When your lunch break finally came around, it was 2 p.m.

"But everyone is going out to eat and I have so much work left *today. This will be my only chance to get some food.*" That pesky voice of procrastination again.

Right after the office at 7 p.m.

"I need to finish these reports quickly then I promise I'm going to do it, I'll even put on my gym shorts just so I'm committed."

Then, you give up at 11 p.m.

"I'm too tired and I don't want to wake anyone up. *I'll just work out tomorrow.*"

Sound familiar?

This is the all too pervasive story of the working class. Man or woman, this happens to us all. We keep putting off what is most important to our health and for what – getting that last report done out of hundreds?

It could be the new baby or that promotion you are aspiring to – that always gets in the way of your fitness and wellbeing. You are always thinking about everyone else, not yourself. Whether it's your boss or your spouse, you work so hard because you take care of the people in your life. But you need to take care of yourself, as well. Your loved ones want what is best for you too and want you around for years to come.

Your first question is probably, "What can I possibly do?"

You only have two, three days tops to get in some exercise, maybe an hour at most, and if you are like most people who work out off and on, you have tried the treadmill or elliptical twice a week for 45 minutes to an hour and have seen no results.

Then comes the inevitable - you quit! Or worse, you got injured first … then quit!

We won't see you back in the gym for years after a traumatic experience like that.

My associates and I came up with a program made just for this type of person, the person always dealing with business or family issues, maybe a new parent who just wants to see results after a few times a week exercising.

They want to work "smarter not harder" because the day is not getting any longer. There's only 24 hours in one day and you need to use it wisely!

THE ASSESSMENT

Everyone is different. Before you start any program, you should have some sort of movement assessment or postural evaluation, because not everyone can do everything and the last thing you want to do is get hurt.

"If you're not assessing, you're guessing" is something I have picked up from others over the years.

Everyone is going to have their own issues when they come into the gym. Even the most fit human being might have injured his knee playing sports when he or she was young, so that person must tailor a workout that WORKS for them. That goes for shoulder issues, hip issues and even ankle issues.

The last thing we want to do is put anyone behind an "8-ball," so to speak, because you are already intimidated and scared, I want to ease them into it.

No quitting! I never want to give someone an excuse (injury) to do just that.

THE PROGRAM

The way we program it, we may do between two and four exercises back-to-back to get that circuit pump, synergy and ultimate effectiveness.

We want to hit different areas at the same time. You could do a push and a pull at once, a split stance, a bend or a squat moving in all planes of motion. These will hit numerous muscles groups at once and get the results we crave.

We always throw a stretch in there to keep you limber and away from injury. It is also something that can be productive during your break time, so you're not completely at rest. Instead of just standing there, let's get a stretch going that is going to give us more range of motion.

CORE BEFORE EVERYTHING ELSE

If we do core at the beginning of our workouts, we are fresh and not fatigued as if you were to attempt it at the end, a time in which you're not going to get those true benefits of working the core. Some simple planks and stability ball work can really kick off your workout in a positive way.

A WEEK-BY-WEEK BREAKDOWN

So you got a lot going on but it's all for your benefit.

We might begin with movement preparation work, then mobility stretches, then a dynamic warm up, then core and/or power development training then you're ready for our resistance exercises and a little cardio. It's sounds like a lot but goes by quick and produces crazy results.

Week 1-4: We do two exercises (a pull and a squat) and a mobility stretch.

We would do 1 to 2 sets of 15 reps.

Then we do the opposing muscles (a push and a single-leg stance movement) with another mobility stretch.

Again, we would do 1 to 2 sets of 15 reps.

Week 5-8: We have a bend, a push, lunge and a mobility stretch.

Then, we change that to 2 to 3 sets of 10 reps.

Now, we have a squat, pull, single-leg stance and a mobility stretch.

Again, 2 to 3 sets for 10 reps.

Week 9-12: We have a bend, a push, a single-leg stance, a pull and a mobility stretch.

We do between 3 and 4 sets of 12.

Then we'll do a squat, a pull, lunge, a push and mobility stretch.

We do between 3 and 4 sets of 12.

First phase, we went high reps, then we lowered them a bit in phase 2 and finally in phase 3 went high reps again. So, we are always changing it up.

Adding in Cardio – This doesn't necessarily mean treadmill work but maybe using battling ropes for 30 seconds, where you move as fast as you can. Or you are doing burpees and sprints for 40 seconds.

Med ball throw and chases or speed squats are also fun and over before you know it.

With cardio, the time might be a **30/30 split** with 30 seconds of work and 30 seconds of rest for four to six rounds. You can also do a **40/20 split** with 40 seconds on, 20 seconds off.

Adding in Power Development – We use all our muscles at once here, creating that explosive atmosphere - Like a medicine ball slam, kettle bell swings or jump squats.

Now, a misconception is that moving on and adjusting your exercise is crucial to avoid your plateau, but you never want to move on if you haven't mastered the exercise.

If your squat is poor and you are not using good form, you don't want to move on to a split squat, a more advanced move, because that poor form will only carry over to the next move and gets little results or even results in injury.

The goal is to make sure you are doing things right during that period of time you perform these movements. Like with a video game, you can move on to the next level without conquering the current one.

SOME GREAT EXERCISES

Most of the exercises we do are supersets, so they are done one right after the other to get that aerobic feel and pump.

Stirring The Pot (Core) – This is a great core exercise we do at the beginning, where you are in a plank position with your forearms on the ball and you stir the pot in a circular motion, clockwise and counter clockwise.

Medicine Ball Slam (Power Development) - Just ready the ball above your head and slam it down as hard as you can, using your whole body. This gets the full extension and full contraction.

Split Stance Cable Row – This engages the core, engages the lats (latissimus muscle), engages the upper back and even your arms – you've created a plethora of movements by just doing one exercise.

<u>Deadlifts</u> – This works your backside more. You are going to work your back, you are going to work your glutes and your hamstrings.

<u>Incline Alternating Dumbbell Press</u> – This works multiple areas of your chest and your arms at the same time.

<u>Push Ups (As One Unit)</u> – As long as you do the push up as one unit, you are not only working your chest but your core as well. When you push up, your butt should come up also as one unit.

<u>Three-Point Push Up</u> – Keep doing as one unit but keep one leg in the air. This will work the side of your core a bit and really intensifies the workout.

<u>Step Ups</u> – More of a Quad dominant exercise, so you are working the quad and the hip flexor.

<u>Chin Up or inverted Row (Pull)</u> – This works your back and can hit your core as well.

<u>Squat, Goblet Squat</u> – We squat everyday, we are always sitting in our car or at our desk. This exercise uses key muscles that we need to function day to day. We want to train those muscles right.

During all this, you and your trainer need to make sure you get a proper break in between – not too long because you don't want your body to get cold but a break, nonetheless.

STANDARD GYMS ARE GREAT BUT NOT EFFICIENT

Machines in the gym are fantastic but usually only for one body part. So you can't do crunches and curls all day and expect a total body transformation. A bench press is great but just for your chest. A seated, supported row is excellent but just for your back. These are isolating exercises. Those are great if you're looking to improve one spot.

But if you are looking for the complete package and only have a day or two a week to get it done, you need combinations. If we can combine a pull with working your core at the same time, that is going to be beneficial and "kills two birds with one stone." It's called synergistic exercise because you are working multiple body parts at once.

If a customer of YOURS wanted a product but also wanted personal attention and to meet you, you wouldn't do these separately would you? You would just grab the essential product they are looking for and bring it to them yourself, taking care of multiple tasks at once. The same goes for your fitness!

THE BODY WON'T WORK IF THE MIND DOESN'T TELL IT TO

What I mean by this is that a positive mindset will influence your workouts in a positive way.

If you plan on succeeding, you are going to succeed, if you plan to fail, you WILL fail.

WRITE DOWN YOUR GOALS

This will keep you on track and focused on what it is you want. No backing down; and if you want to lose 10 pounds, don't adjust it to 8 pounds when it starts getting tough. Stay on track.

I always say, break it down. Break it down to where it's something that is attainable each day or each week. If someone says they want to lose 10 pounds and they have a bad few days and actually gain a pound, they are now at 11 pounds. That number is intimidating and forces you to quit. Instead, focus on a pound or two a week, or one exercise in a day.

Use milestones and benchmarks. Each benchmark is instant gratification and helps keep you motivated toward your goal. You need to add to your goals exactly how you plan on getting there. A detailed, step-by-step plan is always going to help you because it is incremental. Just do this one little thing today that is part of the plan and is easier than looking at the whole thing at once.

If you are not tracking your progress, how do you know you are making progress?

One final note on tracking your goals, the BIGGEST aspect of fitness is how you look or feel, SO DON'T LET THE NUMBERS TAKE OVER. It's not all about the weight, it is about how you look and feel. You could lose body fat and still weigh the same because you gained muscle. That's great, that's what we want.

Don't worry all about numbers.

NUTRITION IS JUST AS IMPORTANT AS THE WORK OUT

Remember that Snickers at 11 p.m.? That's a big No-No. We need to make sure you are eating cleaner, better foods that also double as fuel for your body and your workouts.

After the workouts we want to start that recovery process, so you need to make sure you are getting that post-workout shake to feed those muscles. Starting the recovery process today will help your workout for tomorrow, especially starting out. We not only want to have a good workout next time, but a better workout.

Also, make sure you have a protein, fruit and vegetable at every meal to keep your diet balanced. Make sure you are eating four to five times a day and the right things.

THIS WILL HELP YOU IN ALL ASPECTS OF LIFE

It can be sluggishness, moodiness, stress – If you don't feel well, you are not going to perform like you should at work, at home, in life.

Exercising is a good way to alleviate stress. Your body produces Cortisol when you are stressed, which adds to belly fat. What's the main thing guys and girls want to work on – their mid section! If we can eliminate stress, we are on the right track.

It is important to put yourself in a good situation to succeed.

A SUCCESS STORY

For the past few months, I have been working with a dentist, who is the mother of four boys and is near to my heart with all she does in life. She has her own practice and is very involved with the community, so she is always on the go. BUT, she always makes time for her training sessions at least twice a week.

She lost numerous inches and weight, and she just had her physical, which came back positive. She is 45 and the test came back that she has the body of a 31 year old. This woman does it all and so can you!

The 45 is the new 31 and she shows with the proper program and nutrition, anything is possible. Her boys are involved in all sorts of sports like football or baseball and now she can play catch with them outside.

These kids are from kindergarten to high school ages.

Bottom line is she can run a practice and participate in their daily lives. She is just being that all-around great person.

About Doug

Doug Schwaberow and Achieve Fitness, Mount Vernon, OH

Doug Schwaberow graduated from Walsh University with a degree in Corporate Communications and went on to be an Arena League professional football player.

He was always intrigued with exercise, with anatomy, so he worked as a trainer his junior and senior years of college. As a professional athlete, he got an inside look at what a physical therapist does, the training and rehab.

After getting his certification in ISSA Fitness, he combined this with his personal experience, what worked for him and what didn't. He didn't stop there; he got other certifications in CSCS, TRX, Kettlebell and USAW. The man was hooked.

Why keep learning? "If you are not getting better, you are getting worse," is a motto he lives his life and career by.

Three years ago, he took over personal training at Achieve Fitness in Mount Vernon, OH, when the club decided to go in a different direction. That new direction was Douglas, plain and simple. And he has yet to disappoint.

He jumped head first into taking business seminars coupled with continuing education on fitness and wellness. He put together a solid business plan to change the way fitness was done in Ohio. He created programs that would be effective for all his clients across the board.

For more information on any exercises or tips:
Contact Doug at: doug@af-training.com
or visit: www.af-training.com.

CHAPTER 32

WHY We Eat

By Jannette La Sota with John La Sota

Several years ago I found myself twenty pounds heavier than I wanted to be. A hectic schedule, poor food choices, and lack of exercise had finally caught up to me, and the time had come to make a change. Like thousands of other people who try to lose weight, I found myself struggling to achieve the results I wanted.

With so many choices available, I asked myself "where do I begin?" The numerous, so called easy-to-follow, weight loss plans left me confused and unsure of which one to choose. Did I want to count points, eat out of a cardboard box, juice my food, or try the newest diet gizmo? The list of diet fads, gimmicks, and "miracles" seemed endless.

Taking into consideration that we spend millions of dollars each year chasing after the newest and most popular weight loss methods, why is it that we often find ourselves frustrated and disappointed with the results? WHY?

Why was I and others around me experiencing such poor results from these diet plans, and what could be done about it? This is what the detective in me was determined to find out.

One thing I discovered is that many popular diet plans are promoted or perceived to be "quick" fixes. You simply purchase foods to eat or follow a sample menu plan and the results are supposed to follow. These plans do little to educate us on the science behind the plan, or how it works. Even when we are given this information, we tend to ignore it in hopes of not having to work so hard or to delay our anticipated results.

The problem with this is that "quick fix" plans do nothing to help us address why we need to be on a diet plan in the first place. Think about it, if you do not take the time to understand why or how you got to where you are, to begin with, how can you expect to find solutions to get you to where you want to go? Long term solutions to lose weight and to keep it off should start with understanding your current food habits, and what you can do to improve them in order to achieve the results you desire.

In order to successfully reach a goal, you need to have a plan. A well thought out plan should include the following 3 steps:

1. *Identification* of the problem

2. *Understanding* the problem

3. *Action* to correct the problem

Now that we have the steps needed to form a plan, let's start with step 1 and identify the problem. Poor food choices and over-eating are usually given as reasons why we don't lose weight, but behind these reasons is something much more important to look at, our habits. Our nutrition habits attribute to our food choices and eating patterns so therefore, let's identify the problem of losing weight to Poor Nutrition Habits.

Step 2 of our plan states that we need to understand our poor nutrition habits before we can change them, so let's understand how and why we have these habits.

When I ask clients why they eat, I am given many different answers. The obvious explanation is that we eat to survive. Our instincts dictate that in order to live we have to consume food. Our bodies need food to create the energy necessary for basic body functions and movement. While survival may be the primary reason why we eat, it is not the only reason why we do so.

Other answers that I am often given are "I like to eat," "food is my passion," "eating is my hobby," and so forth. As you can see, none of these answers are about survival. These answers relate eating to emotion. Emotion is related to a pattern of thinking and this leads to the formation of habits based on that pattern of thinking.

Emotional eating describes how we "feel" or how we associate food with our experience. Anyone who's ever been able to relate to the Hollywood cliché of the brokenhearted girl eating a tub of ice cream in order to "feel better" after a breakup, knows well the concept of emotional eating. The same could be said for other feelings such as guilt, "you had better eat everything on your plate, there are starving children in the world!" or, to cure the restlessness of boredom you simply eat to make yourself "feel" that you are doing something.

In truth, emotional eating is very closely tied to the social aspects of why we eat. The brain learns by connecting new information to events or concepts experienced in the past, forming what we call neuro-associations. Most occasions where we find ourselves eating ice cream, at birthday parties, celebrations, and fun times with our friends, are during events when we're having a good time. These experiences are when we're happy. The brain now associates the eating of the ice cream with being happy, so naturally during times when we feel the need to improve our mood, what do we reach for?

Social eating is influenced by our family traditions and values, religion, economics, and lifestyle. These influences are learned patterns of behavior, and many times are taught to us through those who we associate with on a regular basis: our family, friends, and co-workers.

Take for example, the traditional "Sunday" dinner. Many families gather every week for dinner together. This is one way of continuously bringing the family together and keeping it close while passing on family values and traditions to the next generation. From childhood to adulthood, we develop a lifetime of training gathered around food. Whether you grow up eating meat sauce with linguini and bread, rice dishes, or fatty meats with rich cream sauces, you typically find yourself subject to family pressure when you try to break away from the family norm. Walk through the door without a hearty appetite and you're met with calls of "what's the matter, why aren't you eating" or "don't you like the way I cook?" Despite the fact that a half a bowl or approximately one cup of pasta or rice, contains around three hours worth of carbohydrates, you dig in because after all you don't want to upset the host by not eating; that would be rude.

Religious beliefs are another influence on our eating habits. Depending on which faith you follow, you have been taught to eat fish on Friday's, to not eat pork, to refrain from eating dairy with meat, or to become a vegetarian.

Economics also play a huge part in influencing what we eat. If you come from a large family or if you are on a budget, food money may have to stretch out. Freshness and nutrients are sometimes sacrificed for foods that will last longer in the cabinets. Just as with family traditions, years and years of eating what is affordable push us towards the aisles with the poorer food choices. Having extra money to spend on food can also lead to poor habits. After all, it is just as easy to learn how to over indulge and eat too much as it is to learn to eat less nutritious food choices.

Many of our social activities also revolve around eating. What do we do after work or when we make plans with our friends? Where do we go? Usually we go to dinner or out for a few drinks. Other activities like our Monday night bowling league, our Wednesday night pool league, or our weekend movie matinee club all bring us to places where we are tempted to indulge in goodies from the active refreshment areas serving fried foods, snacks, sodas, and alcohol. Even attending concerts, sporting events, and going dancing largely entail the consumption of foods and beverages, many of which are terrible for our body.

Another influence affecting our food habits comes from the pressures and demands of work, school, and busy schedules. When we have deadlines to meet and are faced with time restrictions, it is very easy to reach for that quick and easy candy bar or that 90-calorie snack. Add to this the clever marketing of many products which fool us into thinking something is good for us when it is not, and we wind up not getting the results we want.

These are just some of the many "real" reasons why we eat. Taking the time to identify and understand these reasons give us the power to change our habits for new ones, allowing us to make progress and achieve better results.

Take a moment now to think about and identify the habits that YOU have which keep you from making the progress you desire. What food associations and learned behavior are specific to you? Once you identify and understand the answer to this question you can start to make a new association and stop yourself from eating out of habit or to fill an emotional need.

Now that we have worked through steps 1 and 2 of our plan, it is time for step 3, which is: to take ACTION. It is time to replace old habits for new ones. How do we do this? We do this by retraining our thinking and making new food associations.

Picture yourself twenty pounds heavier, a massive gut hanging so that you can't see your feet. Think of how it would feel to be so out of shape that you huff and puff, panting and wheezing just from walking down the block. Imagine the nauseous feeling in your stomach when you've eaten something that doesn't agree with you, really feel that feeling, have the sickness of it wash over you, feel yourself double over, struggling to catch a single breath. Really put yourself in that moment. Then conjure the image in your mind of the food you no longer want to eat. Picture that food in your mind while you feel bad, thinking "this is what got me here." Try this over and over again until the very idea of eating that food makes you ill.

This negativity is done to break the link in your mind between consuming things that are bad for you and feeling good about it, replacing it with feeling bad about eating bad. If it sounds terrible, it's because it is, you need to SHOCK your mind out of the old, bad behaviors.

Once you've done that, I want you to picture yourself in the best shape of your life. See yourself looking at the body you want in the mirror. Imagine people telling you how great you look now, the smile spreading across your face. How does that feel? Feel it. Imagine yourself being able perform in all the ways you've always wanted to, the confidence it gives you. Let that feeling completely come over you. Do you see it? Do you feel it? Now picture in your mind the healthy food choices that will bring you there. See those delicious healthy meals, smell them, and feel how confident you are, how great you feel, and say to yourself while picturing that food, "this is what got me here." Do that over and over again until it really takes hold.

This is how we form new, empowering neuro-associations that will help you feel the most pleasure out of reaching for those things that are best for you.

There are many practical ways to retrain our thinking in order to develop new habits. Take a class on healthy eating, learn to read food labels, and practice what you learn. Instead of walking to the freezer for that quart of ice cream why not walk to the park instead. If you find yourself bored, don't pick up the fork or spoon, pick up a hobby, go to the gym, or read a book.

The next time you are invited to dinner why not offer to bring a dish and show up with a healthy version of a family favorite? Be prepared and plan ahead. If you know you will be pressed for time why not cook some meals ahead of time or travel with some healthy snacks you made at home, and the next time you go to the bowling alley or pool hall, bring some healthy snacks to share with your team mates.

Think of how much fun it can be to start a new tradition by taking a healthy cooking class with your family or friends, and then invite them over to practice what you learned in class. When you make plans to eat out check the menu ahead of time and determine what the healthier choice is before you get to the restaurant. Ask the waiter to have your favorite dish cooked in a healthier manner steamed, poached, or broiled, and with sauce and dressing on the side.

Remember, it took time for your old habits to take hold, so forming new habits will also take some time and practice. Go ahead and use this three step plan to help you identify, understand, and take action – and you will be successful in achieving your goal.

About Jannette

Jannette La Sota is the founder of Enrichment Fitness in Forest Hills, New York. She holds a BBA from Baruch College and is a graduate of the American Academy of Personal Training. She uses her 26 years of investigative experience to research health information and uses the findings to design personalized and successful programs for clients.

Jannette believes that education is the cornerstone to any fitness program. As a fitness and nutrition coach she teaches clients the fundamentals of fitness and how to build upon these concepts to achieve long term success. She strives to coach and motivate others by being a positive role model and by promoting fitness as not just a lifestyle but also as a way of having fun.

To find out more about Jannette La Sota and how she can help you achieve your fitness goals, visit: www.enrichmentfitness.com

Co-author: John La Sota

CHAPTER 33

Let Your Desires Guide You to Your Goals

By Joseph Morstad

What is it about change that scares us? Why do we recoil at the thought of changing our normal routine when we know that change is the very essence of finding improvement? How come a new baby (a huge change) is a welcomed gift while a new exercise or diet program (relatively small change) prompts such strong resistance? Change sometimes comes without the option to well, *change*. A new baby is coming whether you are ready for it or not. However, a new exercise or diet program can always be pushed back until "next Monday" or "when the time is right." You are not reading this in preparation for a newborn child, so I am going to assume that you are looking to make another change and improvement in your life. You want to improve at least one area of your life, most likely something to do with your health or positive mindset, your physical fitness, and/or your nutritional habits. So why does something that you have actively decided you want to change become so difficult to actually realize? How come something you want so badly is so difficult to achieve? Could it be that you have been fighting a surprisingly difficult adversary that you thought was on your side? Does the notion that your brain is simultaneously craving and fearing your goal ring true to you? Have you ever felt that you were simply in your own way? I know I have been guilty of this before…and I want to help you conquer this internal battle right now.

For years I battled with my own internal struggles. For years I felt like I was always *"trying"* to do things. "I'll *try* to improve on that" or "I'll *try* to make it work" were phrases I used constantly. I felt as if I was always *trying* my way through life without ever actually **doing** anything! Multiple careers, various cities around the country, and failed relationships added up to frustration and pain. For me, this pain took a physical form in a chronic disease called ulcerative colitis – an inflammatory bowel disease (IBD) that causes inflammation and sores, called ulcers, in the inner lining of the large intestines. I was unable to properly absorb any food. I suffered from intense pain, rapid weight loss, and a compromised digestive tract and immune system. At 27 years old, I was *trying* to digest and absorb foods, ultimately becoming so sick and weak that I was admitted to the hospital. I had lost 50lbs in just a few short weeks. I was frail, weak, and scared. After I was finally released from the hospital I left with a new challenge to face, tons of questions to answer, and one main goal – to regain my health and recover from this disease.

After being released from the hospital, I woke in my bed the next morning with relief and confusion at the same time. I wanted to start rebuilding my body again. I needed to add muscle and weight to my frail frame, but I would need to eat and exercise properly to achieve this goal. I was still afraid of what food might do to my compromised digestive system. I lived in fear of every bite of food. Would this meal make me sick again? Could I manage to digest this food and absorb the nutrients or would it send me back to the hospital? My brain felt schizophrenic. I needed food but feared it. I knew that my body needed additional calories and nutrients, but my brain still thought of food as the enemy, something that would just cause more pain somehow. I believe that this conflicted love-hate relationship is at the heart of many self-chosen 'change' situations.

Of course, a rational person would want to lose those extra 30lbs of fat and fit back into the jeans she wore in high school, but it is that same person's emotional brain that fears the pain that change might cause. The fear and avoidance of current pain is stronger than the unseen pleasure that is only possible in the future. She knows what she would like her goal to be, but she is too afraid of the potential pain that this change might bring. She could work out for a few weeks then decide that it is too difficult and stop. She could start another New Year's resolution to get in shape again but give up before February. She may even join that new gym down the street, hire a personal trainer, and lose a few pounds here and there but never fully see her goal become a reality. Why does this situation repeat itself over and over again throughout the world of self-improvement so often?

I have created the following seven steps for you to elevate your wants above your fears. I had to fight this battle myself during my recovery and diagnosis with ulcerative colitis. I learned that my fears could only be as strong as I let them be, and that they grow only if I allow them to grow. I came to realize that my fears were not my true self. They were doubts and insecurities that I allowed to take up residence inside myself. However, I came to learn that I had full control over these fears. I saw that they were tiny and insignificant when compared to the vast power of a well-designed, well-thought-out goal.

Use the steps below to fully commit yourself to achieving your desires and finding happiness.

1. **Get fed-up with your current situation** – Finally coming to that moment when "enough is enough!" is incredibly powerful. Finally seeing a poor situation for what it is will help you to find the drive to push for and achieve change. When we live with the belief that "things aren't *that bad*," or that they "could be worse," we rationalize away any power we have to effectively improve. No one has ever gained 30lbs of fat overnight. Instead, those unwanted pounds came on with one rationalization after another. Saying to yourself, "just this *one* doughnut" or "another drink won't be *that bad*," lay the groundwork for the slow and steady creep towards those unwanted pounds. Stop making excuses! Find power in seeing things as they are. Once you understand, realize, and take an honest assessment of your current situation you have the opportunity to create major, positive changes in your life. See things as they are - understand this might be painful- but know that it is also *powerful* because you just took action to redirect the course of your life in a positive direction.

2. **Sync up your left and right brains** – There is no shortage of fitness and health information out in the world today. The vast majority of the population understands that eating vegetables are a healthier choice than eating a double-bacon cheeseburger. So with this vast amount of knowledge why are there so many overweight and unhealthy individuals in the world today? It is due to the fact that peo-

ple are trying to change their fitness and nutritional habits - but they do not really want to! Eating a cheeseburger with fries and a soda is usually more appealing than a plate of steamed broccoli and skinless chicken. But what about the people who consciously decide to still eat the broccoli and chicken, while refusing to eat the unhealthy meal? How do they do it? It is because they have synchronized their rational and emotional brains. They understand, and subsequently enjoy, eating the healthier meal because they know it is better for them. It will help them feel and look better. It will ultimately help them reach their goals faster. The people that are eating the greasy burger and fries still have not found a common ground between their rational and emotional brains. They emotionally think about the immediate taste and pleasure they feel from the meal (regardless of its quality) while dismissing and/or forgetting the rational brain's plea to avoid such foods. However, when both sides of the brain are in sync, positive and real change happen rapidly.

3. **Make a concrete and well-defined goal** – While our brains are incredibly intricate and amazing machines, they run best on very clear and simple instructions. And in the case of prompting change, simple is best. The modern computer is a classic analogy for our brains. But everyone knows that when too many programs are running at the same time even the most powerful computer begins to process information slower. This happens to our brains as well. Ever tried to drive while talking on your cell phone, while changing the radio, while looking for an exit to a new location? It's exhausting (and dangerous)! Imagine trying to achieve several different goals all at the same time? Not the best recipe for success. We are working to make change and improvement easier and more achievable. To better accomplish this find one simple goal that you want to achieve. One clear, measureable, and precise goal with a deadline. "Getting into better shape soon" may be great but it is too vague of a goal. "Starting today, I will exercise 30 minutes a day, 4 days each week" is much better. The more precise and specific you make it, the easier your brain can understand and accomplish that goal. It does not have to be complicated. Simple will help you achieve better results.

4. **Understand why you want this goal** – This may sound a little funny, but have you ever stopped and asked why you even want this goal in the first place? It is good to have a goal in life but it is

extremely powerful when you understand the **why** behind that goal. You want to earn a million dollars, awesome! But why? Because it would be cool to buy stuff…or because with that money you could create a charity for poor and homeless children. One is much more powerful and motivating than the other and a much stronger reason to stay on the path to achieving that goal when things get tough.

5. **Envision your outcome** – Where do you want to go? Our brains have an amazing ability to find a way to a destination when the destination is clear and precise. Get your goal, your destination, front and center in your mind. See it clearly; imagine what it will feel like when you achieve it. Act like you have already arrived there. Envision the joy and sense of achievement you will feel. If your destination is completing a marathon for the first time, then imagine how happy and proud you will feel the second your feet cross that finish line. If your destination is to lose 30 lbs before your next high school reunion, then imagine how great you will look in your new outfit that night. Envision the sense of accomplishment and joy that you will feel as you walk into the party and feel strong and confident in your body. Make sure you can vividly see where your destination is located. Hold on to that vision and make sure you can be as detailed as possible. Once you know where you want to go, the details almost take care of themselves.

6. **Appreciate the power of compounding** – Give me a penny that doubles in value every day for 30 days and I will have over a million dollars in a month! The value of that penny is $.02 on day two, $.04 on day three, but on day thirty it is $5,368,709.12! Every day we are able to find actions that will help us come closer to our goals– no matter how small. During my recovery from ulcerative colitis, I struggled to find foods that would be healthy, manageable, and easy on my digestive system. I was only able to handle scrambled eggs and soft bread in the beginning. From there, I began to slowly expand my menu and try different foods. Some foods worked and some did not. However, after using this strategy for a few weeks, I soon had built up a large and varied selection of healthy and nutritious foods that helped me rebuild my strength and add muscle during my recovery.

7. **Continually return to your goals along the way** – Make sure that you are checking and re-checking yourself as you journey towards

your destination. Continually monitoring your location and destination are not limited to airplane pilots and captains out at sea. Once you set your goal you embark to find it. But as anyone that has found their destination will tell you, things rarely seem to go as planned or without navigating around some obstacle. Pilots and captains are constantly monitoring the conditions, weather, and the status of their planes and boats. We must be as vigilant in our journey. Adjustments will have to be made along the way. This is inevitable and actually should be welcomed. By constantly overcoming obstacles and making adjustments along the way, you will become stronger. You will have found that whatever challenges you faced along the way will, in hindsight, have been small opportunities to prove yourself. And with each small, successful victory you will come that much closer to finding your ultimate destination. You will have found your success!

BONUS STEP: Remember to enjoy the journey – Legendary UCLA college basketball coach John Wooden was once asked what he missed the most about coaching and winning all those games and NCAA championships. "I miss the practices," he replied. He then quoted the famous line from Cervantes that, "the journey is better than the inn." Coach Wooden understood that we all find great pride and comfort in reaching a highly sought after destination – whether it be a national championship, a financial endeavor, or a weight loss goal. However, in his wisdom, he also knew that it was the journey – the act of striving for an admirable and difficult goal – that stirs such deep passion and desire in our hearts. And it is this deep passion, this enthusiasm that will propel you towards ultimate achievement of your goal and provide success and happiness.

You could have picked up this book for several different reasons. And whatever you strive to achieve, I wish you complete success and enduring happiness. Along your journey to that ultimate destination, please remember Coach Wooden's words. Make sure to take a few moments from time to time to take a step back, maybe kick your feet up, and simply enjoy the journey. Before long you'll arrive at your destination victorious and have plenty of time to celebrate. Until then, make sure to relish the journey and savor the amazing experiences along the way. They will only make your success that much more enjoyable.

About Joseph

Joseph Morstad is a passionate fitness coach driven to help his clients and those with IBD, feel, move, and perform better. He holds multiple fitness certifications and is constantly building upon his education to improve his client's results. Joseph also competed as a Division 1 collegiate golfer at St. Mary's College of California, where he was named team captain his senior year.

Joseph was diagnosed with ulcerative colitis in 2008 and lost 50 lbs in just six weeks due to this condition. After his release from the hospital, he used his knowledge as a fitness coach to help him recover and rebuild his body. Within a few months, he had regained all of his lost weight and became even stronger than before his diagnosis. He has been able to manage his ulcerative colitis and avoid any serious flares since then with the help of his doctors, proper medication, and adherence to principles that improve strength and sustain health.

In 2011, he completed his first sprint triathlon as a mentor/participant with Team Challenge, and plans to participate and improve his race time in 2012. Joseph wrote his first book, "The IBD Fitness Solution" as a resource for those battling with IBD to navigate through the uncertainty and confusion that IBD can cause. His goal is to help as many people as possible find their strength – inside and out – and hopes that this book has helped you accomplish that goal as well.

You may learn more about IBD, Joseph, and his fitness coaching at:
www.strengthandnutrition.com
Joseph can be reached at info@strengthandnutrition.com

CHAPTER 34

Top Tips to Get or Provide Results

By Philip Deer

SEEKING KNOWLEDGE

You know those moments when you think of a new thing you would like to accomplish, but then you realize, hmmm...I think I might need some help learning to do that? Those are the times you seek information or perhaps someone with the knowledge and expertise to help you achieve your goals.

We all choose new adventures in our lives and hit sticking points. You want to be successful but may need a little help to get "unstuck." The sticking point is often the same for most of us...education or rather a lack of education in the area we are stuck. There is some crucial thing that we haven't learned yet, so we have come to a halt in our progress. This means it's time to learn what you need to know to get going again. However, if it takes too long or too much effort to learn, you might start to procrastinate and your focus will fade. You would like to learn it quickly and get on with your journey.

This is where a great teacher, coach, or mentor comes in. They can lend a hand to help you learn quickly, simplify the topic, and help you seize and take control of the opportunities to change – better than if you were to go it alone.

Transforming your body and life through fitness and nutrition is no different. You will most likely seek a great trainer or coach to guide you and provide the expertise to fuel your journey and keep you from getting stuck for too long.

MY STORY

I grew up in the Midwest playing many sports, but that's not what got me into fitness. I was picked on in school and even through high school. That plus some personal problems had me feeling pretty down and I had low self-esteem and a general lack of confidence. I noticed that I felt best when I was active. Being active was a great stress relief, it gave me the confidence I needed to overcome daily challenges and being picked on, it was fun, and it boosted my self-esteem and I felt better overall. I wanted to feel this way more often, so I became much more involved in exercise – even during sports seasons. Next came college, I didn't play sports, but I went to the gym every chance I had. That is where I got my first opportunity to work in a gym. I loved it. It was amazing to me that I could work at the same place I enjoyed going to, and it didn't feel like work. Then, I decided to major in exercise science so that I could learn all that I needed to be a successful fitness trainer and help others feel great and overcome their challenges in life.

GETTING STUCK

I moved to Los Angeles in 2004 to learn more about fitness. It has often been referred to as the 'Mecca' of fitness, so I figured where better to go to learn the best information to use in my quest to help others. When I got there I thought everything would come together and hard work would make me successful. Then, I got burned out from my routine, stopped going to the gym, and I was tired and exhausted from trying to keep up my regimen, which had become boring. I gained some fat, but mostly lost a lot of muscle and strength. Even my family commented that I had changed a lot when I went back home for the holidays. I was stuck, and I needed help. I needed to get my focus and motivation back.

GETTING UNSTUCK

I eventually started exercising at a gym again, but was not very consistent and wasn't really pushing myself. Plus my diet was pretty crappy, and I was eating tons of ice cream. Friday nights I would eat an entire pizza and eat between one to two quarts of ice cream. Sure, I got some strength back, but I never really got to where I wanted to be.

I was in school studying too, but universities teach a lot of good theory and information about the components of fitness and nutrition. But they teach very little practical application or how to write programs tailored to peoples' goals designed to get results, and how to best help people achieve successful body transformations.

Everything was about to change. I was introduced to fitness seminars through my work. I started attending more of them and met some great people and some experts in the fitness industry. I was getting motivated again and learning how to put the pieces together to really help people change their lives. Then, in 2011, I hired mentors to help me learn how to design real programs for people to get great results, and the very best of how to help people change their lives.

Next, I decided...if I am to truly help people, I have to be the best I can and set an example for others. I gave it my all and aimed for my goals with intense focus. From November 21, 2011 to March 9, 2012 I lost 22 pounds. I went from 212 pounds of low energy and excess flab to 190 pounds of feeling great and being lean. Wow! I didn't know I had that much to lose. I wasn't trying to lose fat, and in fact thought I was okay with my weight. I was just trying to get stronger and feel good, but was shocked at the results I got. It was all from good nutrition and regular exercise. I am now strong, lean and feel better than ever!

Some Lessons

Knowledge is power, but you have to use it: I was learning at first, but only made a breakthrough once I applied what I had learned.

Positive attitude and positive environment is key: A great coach is positive and encouraging and never doubts that you will reach your potential. They see the best in you and know how to bring it out of you. A great coach also creates an environment for success by helping you connect with other people who are making their journey to change for the better.

Less is more: What was most surprising to me was that I didn't have to exercise as much as I thought. Playing sports most of my life had me thinking I had to exercise tons to change my body. With the right plan and a healthy, focused diet, it only took 2.5 to 3.5 hours per week of exercise to get the best results of my life! A great coach can simplify things to fit your lifestyle, help you get past sticking points, and amplify your focus to accelerate results.

So, based on what I learned, here are the **Five Things You Should Look For In A Trainer or Coach** to help you in your body transformation journey.

1. *All About You*: Find a trainer or coach who is about you and asks questions to get to know you and what it is you want to accomplish. He or she should be friendly, approachable, eager to know more about you, and excited to help you and not ego driven. Find someone who makes you feel good about your journey and believes in you.

2. *Goal Oriented*: Find a coach who designs an overall plan and workout program. If you are left to guessing or just given workouts, how do you know if you will get to your destination? You need a plan that lays out what to do and how to reach your destination, like a map that is based on your goals and fits your desired lifestyle or helps you get closer to it. Find a coach who teaches life-changing sustainable habits and not fads or gimmicks.

3. *Nutrition Coaching Component*: Nutrition is the number one most important component that needs to be addressed for transforming your body. If you desire serious change in your life and want to look and feel better, this is a MUST that cannot be ignored. Find a coach who incorporates a nutrition-coaching portion to your program.

4. *Accountability*: Find a coach who keeps you accountable by asking you about your progress on a regular basis and what struggles you are having. They should be able to help you find creative ways to overcome your obstacles and make forward positive progress. They should also incorporate teamwork into their model. People accomplish more together and feel more accountable when others are involved.

5. *Results Oriented:* Ask for proof that the coach can do what they say they can in the form of testimonials, and before-and-after pictures. However, they may be good at what they do and have not collected these, in which case a trial or test drive period can allow you to see if they offer what you need. This is a chance to see first-hand if you will be a good fit together before making the commitment. A good coach will understand if you ask for proof or a test drive, and will provide the opportunity to check out their services with no pressure, judgments or ego.

I've spent a lot of my career doing the wrong stuff, and it's only in these last few years that I've changed and started seeing better results and responses from clients. If you are a trainer or coach, make sure you are providing the best service you can to your clients by following the:

FIVE QUALITIES OF AN ELITE COACH.

1. *Lifelong Learner:* A smart coach can admit they do not know everything and always look to sharpen their skills. Learn from good books, experts who are still doing what they are the best at, like-minded colleagues, and mentors who inspire you. Stay current and ahead of the curve or you will not be helping your clients to your full potential, and you will be left in the dust by your competition.

2. *A Good Listener:* Ask a lot of open-ended questions and listen more than you talk, and you will always have your clients' best interests in mind. Until you can listen intently and fully, you cannot serve the client in their best interests. Do not judge or be quick to offer advice that isn't being asked for. Listening will help you discover the true concerns and obstacles that you should help your clients overcome. Avoid arguments, and try to see things as if you were in their shoes. Talk to your clients and find out more about them. Not all questions and concerns are verbalized to you, some are internalized, which is where smart questions and good listening come in. Clients appreciate when they feel they are being heard, don't you?

3. *Professional:* Nothing will undermine your efforts quicker than a lack of professionalism. Have great hygiene, a consistently-groomed uniform, and always be early and prepared for sessions

and client meetings. Be professional; do not bad mouth your competition, and always talk about people as if they were standing right behind you. Do not make the session about you or talk about your troubles. Be present and mindful and keep the focus on your clients.

4. *Have fun and be easy going*: Smile, laugh, and be yourself. Clients will appreciate you for being authentic and genuinely compassionate. Show your quirky side and be willing to offer up your life experiences as humor. People who are having fun are easier to get along with and laughter eases tensions. Be patient, supportive, helpful, encouraging, and educate clients at their pace. Be patient and easy going; not everyone starts at the same place or learns at the same pace.

5. *Solution Oriented*: A great coach solves problems. Your clients have hired you for your expertise and help in attaining their goals. You are their solution. Be their solution by knowing your worth and what you have to offer, but recognize when providing a solution requires that you pair up with allies. To fulfill the needs of clients you are not able to meet, you should have a trusted network of allies for cases such as when a client has pain, and needs a doctor or physical therapist. Building a network of allies will ensure your clients' problems are being resolved and they are getting the help they need. They will thank you for it.

SUMMARY

Success awaits you as a client or coach. Just be ready to recognize when you are stuck and that you can become unstuck at any moment you choose – by finding the right person to help you get or provide results.

Lives change by seeking knowledge and using it!

About Philip

Born in the Midwest, Philip Deer grew up playing sports and was introduced to fitness training while studying at the University of Southern Indiana – where he began studying exercise science. He went on to receive his Master of Science degree in Exercise Physiology and Nutrition from California State University, Long Beach.

Philip began his career as a fitness consultant at the University of Southern Indiana in the Recreation, Wellness, and Fitness Center in 2002. He has continued to learn from his various work experiences and mentors, and regularly attends seminars. Philip spends his time training clients at The Fit Life, and serves as adjunct faculty at Santa Ana College, helping fire fighters and police officers in Southern California maintain robust fitness for the demands of their professions.

Since 2010, Philip runs The Fit Life in Playa Del Rey, California. The Fit Life is an entirely outdoors fitness program which specializes in programs for busy people, and prides itself on transforming bodies and changing lives!

You can reach Philip at: www.jointhefitlife.com
www.jointhefitlifeblog.com

CHAPTER 35

The 168 Approach to Fitness and Life

By Chad Skrederstu, MS, CSCS

Our Great-Great Grandparents had it figured out:

When we really look at the whole world of health and fitness it's overwhelming how much information we have access to. There are literally thousands of diets and exercise programs that claim to get you lean and fit... FAST! The problem is almost all of them... DON'T WORK. So how do you determine if a diet or fitness program will work for you?

The answer is to ask, "Would my great-great parents do this?" No matter where your great-great grandparents were: in towns, farms, cities or islands, they stepped up/down, squatted, pushed, pulled, and carried heavy objects on a daily basis. In addition, they consumed food from their regions, and lived more simple lives.

However, years later we've found a way to make being healthy confusing! As a result, I went on a quest throughout the world for nearly a year to learn from the best minds on how to simplify fitness, nutrition, and how we live life.

Around the World and Back:

I was living in Hermosa Beach, California, running a large health club's personal training department. We were kicking butt! While sitting on the deck of Hennessey's Tavern overlooking the ocean with my roommate at the time, I was asked, "Could you just pick up and leave right now?" After a short panic attack, I said "No way, my life is planned out in Microsoft Outlook from 5am to 7pm everyday! "

After thinking about the idea for two weeks I made the decision on New Years Eve of 2009 to leave on a great adventure. I wasn't sure exactly where, with whom, or for how long. However, I decided to leave by the end of March and experience the world.

Subsequently I booked an around-the-world ticket. I would spend four months in Europe, three weeks in Japan, three weeks in Bali, three weeks in Thailand, two months in Australia, one month in New Zealand two weeks in Fiji, and finish up with a tour of the United States.

Initially the trip began to see the world with no particular agenda. However, my around the world adventure evolved into a life changing experience where I got to learn, live and train with over 70 of the best fitness professionals in 18 countries over a 305-day odyssey.

THE 168 APPROACH IS BORN

After traveling for six months and visiting 13 countries, I was on a small island in Koh Samet, Thailand, roughly three hours from Bangkok. The idea of a global fitness approach was suddenly thrust into my face along with a few fierce muy thai kicks. Immediately the 168 Approach was born. The 168 Approach was documented with over 25 pages of notes, hours upon hours of video, and thousands of photos of my world journey.

HOW THE 168 APPROACH WORKS

We have 168 hours in the week but only 2-6 hours in the gym with a trainer or coach. As a result, the 168 Approach was designed to get as many of the ideas and lessons from the gym incorporated into everyday life. With the 168 Approach, our slogan is: "It's More Than Fitness."

The 168 Approach is a lifestyle initiative developed from around the world to jump out of the gym's four walls into people's everyday lives. Our approach is broken down into 3 areas, which are: Move Smart, Eat Right, and Live Well. Below are 18 lessons (each one representing the 18 countries I visited) I brought back from my trip.

MOVE SMART

1. HAVE FUN

If exercise is fun you will do it! While I was in Liverpool, England I worked with Neil Parsley, the strength coach for Great Britain's Olympic Tae Kwon Do and wrestling teams. Neil would schedule basketball games on a weekly basis to break up the rigorous training schedule the athletes endured in preparation for the Olympics. The take home here is to program fun into your training sessions!

2. MASTER THE BASICS

When I was in Newcastle, England with world-class strength coach Nick Grantham, I learned that Grantham only uses 20 different exercises. This was a common theme with the best coaches and personal trainers I met around the world.

First you must master squatting, bending, lunging, pushing, twisting and pulling before progressing to more advanced exercises. An emphasis on deep squatting is key for preventing low back pain. In most Asian countries the majority of people do not have back pain because they have mobile hips and ankles, resulting from deep squatting as part of their everyday lives.

3. MOVE WITH A GROUP

World-class strength coach Michael Boyle said, "A great coach should ELEVATE the people they work with to improve every time they step into the gym." Working out with a group will help ELEVATE your level of motivation, accountability, results, and most importantly – its FUN!

4. DO WORK

As internationally-known strength coach Robert Dos Remedios says, "DO WORK!" In order to burn more fat, increase muscle mass or perform better you have to work hard and there's no substitute for hard work. A good workout might feel similar to a bad first date – awkward, uncomfortable, sweaty and over in under an hour.

5. TAKE RECOVERY SERIOUSLY

Ashley Jones, the strength coach of the New Zealand Christchurch Crusaders rugby team, expressed, "I don't believe in overtraining, I believe in under-recovering. To get faster results, you have to take your regeneration just as serious as training with foam rolling, stretching, post-workout nutrition and quality sleep."

6. DON'T STAND STILL

Don't waste time in between sets. Instead, complete 2-4 non-competing exercises. Add in mobility/stability or core exercises in between sets to get your training sessions done in less than an hour. This will keep the intensity high and increase the post-workout afterburn effect of your work out.

7. IT'S ALL GOOD

"Absorb what is useful, DISCARD what is not," is how the first mixed martial artist, Bruce Lee, approached martial arts. World-renowned fitness coach, Alwyn Cosgrove, used the Lee quote to describe what a well-balanced fitness program should look like.

Cardiovascular training, flexibility training and resistant training all have their benefits. As a result, they should be incorporated to make a well-balanced fitness program.

EAT SMART

8. EAT REAL (Organic) FOODS

In southern Europe, people eat fruits and veggies that are in season. The markets in Europe have a very small frozen food section because they eat fruits and veggies that are in season, which are rich in nutrients and not loaded with chemical preservatives.

9. EAT LIKE A SOUTHERN EUROPEAN

Italians pride themselves on using the best ingredients in their dishes. If you ask Italians what the key to great food is, they will most likely tell you the finest ingredients. If the ingredients are fresh, then no fancy sauces loaded with excess calories are needed.

10.BIGGER IS NOT BETTER

Most families in the southern parts of Europe carry their groceries in two hands and shop every few days. If the food is good quality it should go BAD! As a result, it's ideal to go shopping every 2-3 days because quality food will not stay good for long. Food loaded up with preservatives and other substances has a much longer shelf-life.

In Japan, everything is smaller from the people to the every day utensils. I never once found myself full because of inability to put large amounts of food onto my plate.

LIVE WELL

11. SPEND TIME WITH FAMILY AND FRIENDS

I experienced this first hand with my family in Norway. They had a second house about 30 minutes from their home in Vin-stra, a little handmade home with no electricity. Here we experienced the joy of each other's company visiting a nearby stream to enjoy the silence. There we were not distracted by phones, computers or televisions.

12. GET SOME YOU TIME

In Spain all of the shops shut down in the afternoon so people can get a siesta or just have some time to themselves. I've found this helps break up the day. If you had a miserable first half of your day, the second will be better.

In addition you will be more productive. I was always exhausted when I started work at 5am and finished at 7pm. The work I did was not effective after 2pm and I was just putting in long hours. Once I added a two-hour break, work became so much more focused.

Even just 20 minutes out in the sun by yourself works as a great way to break up the day, thus removing yourself from your work environment. Sometimes this is when you come up with the best ideas because you're not IN your work.

13. HAVE FUN!

In Spain bus boys and trash collectors have fun and take life lightly. In the movie Van Wilder he said, "If you take life too seriously you might not make it out alive."

We take life too seriously in the U.S. and in many ways, we have the wrong approach. Work really hard and thus sacrifice your health for wealth and as you age, you'll pay to get your health back. Now that's a crummy formula if you ask me. Just think Tranquillo...

14. THE 37-HOUR WORK WEEK

The Norwegians believe in a 37-hour work week and feel if you can't get done what needs to get done in that time, you're not working effectively. Sometimes we associate long hours with being better. Manage your time and work to keep your work week under 45-50 hours.

15. JUST CHILL

Take vacations that are at least two weeks long. The first big trip I took to Costa Rica years ago I thought I was so awesome because I was going for 3 weeks. I met people from Israel, Europe, Australia and Asia that had taken off for 3, 6 or 12 months. In order to really relax, a trip that is at least 2-3 weeks will allow more time to de-stress and get in vacation mode.

16. TECHNOLGY FRIEND OR FOE?

Technology is making us stupid. In other countries that we're "ahead of" people don't text. They spend time with each other and they don't use auto correct! When they're out to eat, they don't text but enjoy both the meal and the company. Next time you're at breakfast, lunch, or dinner, turn off your phone and focus on the people you're with.

17. DO IT RIGHT DO IT ONCE

We're in such a rush to get things done. In Italy, the biggest tourist attractions are the coliseum and other Roman ruins. Those monuments were built 100's of years ago and still stand today, drawing millions of people from around the world.

The Sagrada Familia has been under construction since the 1800's and won't be finished for years! The Spanish understand the importance of doing things correctly and not rushing. As a result, most quick fixes won't last long.

18. DO YOU FIRST

The best thing you can do for those close to you is to take care of yourself. If you move smart and eat right you will no doubt have a better quality of life. You will have more energy for your family and friends, be more productive, and you will have an overall better quality of life.

TYING IT ALL TOGETHER

To tie this all together, it goes back to your great-great grandparents! Step up/down, squat, push, pull and carry heavy objects on a daily basis. Stick to the basics and make things simple. Move often and intensely.

Once you start moving smart, some magical things are going to happen. You're going to have more energy. You're going to be much more aware of what you're eating, and most of all, you're going to start feeling great about yourself!

Now that you're moving smart, it's time to start eating right. This will probably have already started without you realizing it. Now you're moving smart you're going to think twice about making poor food choices, because you know how much work it takes to burn it off.

You're making better choices with the foods you eat now. As a result, you're losing weight by eating better foods throughout the day. With smaller meals throughout the day, your blood sugar levels are more stable and you're continually burning more fat.

Now you're moving smart and eating right, some thrilling stuff starts to happen. You feel better – which has changed your whole outlook on life. You'll find yourself dancing around your living room (this is what one client told me) and your dogs will think you're crazy because you have all this extra energy.

Ok.... this is the really the cool part. Now you're able to accomplish goals in life you didn't think were possible. You've completed half marathons, sprinted with your granddaughter in her stroller, wrapped presents for Christmas on the floor for 6 hours with no pain in your back, competed in a surf contest at pipeline in Hawaii, showed up as one of the fittest players on the team for the Mets spring training, got off all your medications, had 125 degrees of range of motion the day after a knee replacement surgery, lost 8 pounds in 3 weeks at 75 years old, dead lifted, front squatted, and bench pressed 200 pounds after losing 20 pounds and 9 percent body fat.) All of these are real stories from our members at The Training Center that are living well.

Move smart, eat right and live well, which will lead you to happiness. We're all looking for the same thing no matter if your goal is weight loss, muscle gain or increased performance. Once we achieve our goals, we're happy, and that's what everyone is looking for in the big scheme of things!

For more information about The 168 Approach, please visit: www.168approach.com

About Chad

Chad Skrederstu, MS, CSCS received his Bachelors and Masters Degrees in Kinesiology from Cal State University of Northridge (CSUN). He is also a Certified Strength and Conditioning Specialist (CSCS) with the National Strength and Conditioning Association (NSCA).

Skrederstu is a Southern California native who has been working as a fitness professional for ten years. As the Personal Training Manger at Equinox in Palos Verdes, Skrederstu was successful in compiling one of the finest teams of corrective exercise coaches in the United States.

In addition to coaching personal training clients, Skrederstu feels that as a fitness professional, it is his duty to give back to the community. Therefore, Skrederstu implemented the Students Optimizing Students Fitness (SOS FIT) to increase physical activity levels of unprivileged children for his Masters Thesis project. Skrederstu worked with the Los Angeles Unified School District (LAUSD) to help nearly 700 fifth grade students from the LAUSD to increase their physical activity levels.

More recently Skrederstu traveled to 18 countries on a yearlong trip to learn from more than 70 of the top fitness professionals from around the globe. Skrederstu traveled extensively through Europe, Asia and the Pacific Rim where he learned from some of the best minds and organizations in the field.

Skrederstu brought back information to the U.S. to share with others at his gym, "The Training Center" – which he co-owns with Mike Donaghy in La Canada, CA. The Training Center houses the 168 Approach, which was developed on his yearlong trip around the world. The 168 Approach mantra is "It's More Than Fitness" with the goal of educating others on: How to Move Smart, Eat Right and Live well. More recently, Skrederstu has had the privilege to speak locally and internationally to help educate other fitness professionals.

For more information about The 168 Approach, please visit: www.168approach.com

CHAPTER 36

Death to Excuses: The Guide To Sticking It Out

By Meika Louis-Pierre

It's 5:29 a.m. In exactly one minute your alarm will go off to the tune of Eye of the Tiger by Survivor. You will wake up refreshed, hop out of bed, amped for your 6:15 a.m. training session. After eating a light breakfast, you head to the gym where you proceed to smash your workout, creating a few awesome personal records. You are a fitness fanatic. Yeah!

(2 days later) It's 5:29 a.m. In exactly one minute your alarm will go off with an annoying repetitive buzz. You will hit snooze and contemplate every possible excuse for not going to the gym. You were up late helping your kid with a science fair project and your butt is still sore from the deadlifts you did two days ago. Five minutes later the alarm will buzz again and your pillow will start to whisper sweet nothings in your ear, begging you to stay. This time you will yourself to get up and drag into the bathroom to get ready for your 6:15 a.m. training session. Even though you know better, you only manage to throw back a glass of OJ and head to gym. You have a solid workout despite your fatigue and in the end you are happy that you made the decision to put the excuses to bed instead of yourself.

Sometimes you feel it. Sometimes you don't.

Whether you're a novice to exercise or a veteran, in the real world, the excuse fairy visits often, leaving perfectly legitimate reasons to ditch your workouts. The key is to develop strategies to overcome her powerful persuasion and stay focused. Developing a strong base and then learning how to keep the party going are the cornerstones to proclaiming death to excuses and sticking it out even when you don't feel like it.

BUILDING YOUR BASE

If you're a beginner to regular exercise, this is where you start. A strong foundation sets the tone for your relationship with fitness. Even advanced exercisers can benefit from reestablishing a foothold on their fitness routine instead of going about it haphazardly. These pointers will guide you in the right direction.

TREADING THE ROAD LESS TRAVELLED: ACCEPT THE JOURNEY

We live in a world of instant gratification. Microwaves, text messages and instant oatmeal permeate our existence and train our brains to demand that our desires be fulfilled NOW. The health and fitness industry is a prime example with everything from liposuction to shake weights. These temporary approaches to health and fitness are just that – short lived. Lasting change will only come from making fitness and healthy living a lifestyle and not an event. The first step to sticking it out is accepting that fitness is a journey over a lifetime.

Once your mindset shifts, it will be easier to see through all the infomercials that promise amazing results with little or no effort. The Ab Zapper and Butt Chiseler will lose their appeal and you will accept that breaking a sweat regularly really is the best way to flatten your stomach and lift your butt. Acceptance is the hardest, but the most important step!

THE CARROT IN FRONT OF THE HORSE: CREATE A GOAL

Now that you've gotten your mind wrapped around the idea that you're in it for the long haul, it's time to set a goal. Think of it as the carrot in front of the horse. Conventional goal-setting techniques will push you to write down a SMART goal: Specific, Measurable, Attainable, Realistic and Timely. Sure, you can write down that you want to lose 20 pounds by summer so that you can fit into a new bathing suit, but let's get real. The underlying fitness goals that everyone wants fall into one of four categories:

1. Look great naked

2. Feel like a million bucks

3. Stay away from the drug dealer (a.k.a. the pharmacist)

Or

4. Move like a bad 'mamma jamma'

These fitness goals supersede all others and should be your focal point when excuses creep in. Once this is established, you have the means to compare every action you partake in to its impact on your goal. For example, if your goal is to look great naked and you're contemplating eating a brownie sundae, your mental conversation should go something like this:

"Self, will this brownie sundae subtract inches from my waist or add love to my handles?" The answer is obvious and so is the corresponding action, or lack thereof. Over the long term, your goals can shift and reset depending on what's most important to you at the time.

TAKE THE ROCKY STEPS: DEVELOP OBJECTIVES

The Philadelphia Museum of Art offers the ultimate representation of how to make it to your goal. Those 72 stone steps commonly referred to as the "Rocky Steps" represent the step-by-step approach that will lead to your greatest success. Think of them as milestones on your journey. Choose one habit to tackle every week. Some may take more than a week to get a handle on, however. For example, if your goal is to feel like a million bucks, in addition to getting to the gym at least three times a week, one of your first objectives may be to start drinking at least 64 oz. of water everyday. Once you are achieving this objective consistently, your next objective might be to get at least seven hours of sleep at night. You will be much more successful if you tackle one objective at a time. The step-by-step approach ensures that you make manageable progress towards your ultimate goal - progress that will allow you to be successful over the long term!

KEEP THE PARTY GOING

Your base is set. Instead of taking the easy and temporary way out, you swallowed the red pill and entered the Matrix of long term fitness and wellness. You have selected a goal and developed some objectives to reach them. You are full of hope and optimism about your new commitment to self-improvement. Like a new relationship, you are eager and excited to get started. But also like a relationship, the initial magic starts to wear off. The spontaneity and the "newness" give way to routine. This is where the excuses tend to begin.

"I don't have time." Let's cut to the chase. This is the most overused excuse on the planet. The real question is how do you NOT have time? Exercise is the best health insurance plan you can invest in. Exercise improves cognition, develops discipline, shrinks waistlines, increases libido, raises confidence and acts as a preventative measure for a multitude of chronic diseases. You don't have time to live a better life? Really? Morning workouts are the best because you start your day with the ultimate wake up call. If you wait until the end of the day, life can catch up with you and other things can take priority. Morning workouts rock. Get 'er done.

COMPETITION IS FUEL FOR YOUR FIRE: JOIN A CHALLENGE

Competition is one of the best ways to stay motivated and focused. At Fit Neighborhood, we offer our clients various fitness and body transformation-based challenges throughout the year. The competitions take training to the next level and encourage commitment. Team challenges in particular, allow you to focus on a greater goal outside of yourself. Cool challenges include setting new personal records for weight training, running your first 5K or half marathon, or body fat loss competitions.

Don't think you're very competitive? Find a copy of Rocky and make yourself a playlist of songs that get you amped. Know that you are ultimately competing against yourself and when you win, celebrate! Treat yourself to something nice!

WITH A LITTLE HELP FROM MY FRIENDS: TWO IS BETTER THAN ONE AND FIVE IS A PARTY

They say misery loves company, but guess what? Fitness does too. One of the least effective ways to stay focused and motivated is to work out alone. Working out with a group of like-minded people acts as an awesome motivational tool. It turns out that while two people working out together is better than one, more is better. When two are joined, and one drops out, we all know what will likely happen to the other. Small groups work best to shield against the occasional defector.

Groups can also act as a resource for new ideas for your fitness journey. For example, staying on track with eating properly can be difficult. Your workout buddies can provide you with strategies that have worked for them. Recipe swaps are another great idea. If you create a circle of friends around your healthy fitness habits, you have not only created a support group, but you've also established an accountability team.

GET OVER YOURSELF!

Lay's brand potato chips has a famous line purporting that, "You can't eat just one". Many people take the Lay's approach when it comes to deviating from their fitness and healthy-eating goals. When things are going well and then temptation strikes and you give in, the sentiment is generally to go overboard. One cookie leads to a few chips and before you know it, junk food has crept its way back into your life. The same thing can happen with your workouts. One missed session turns into three and soon you find it hard to restart.

The truth of the matter is that you can, indeed, eat just one. You are human. Temptation exists. You will not stick with everything you are supposed to do 100% of the time. The trick is not to throw a pity party and give yourself permission to eat the whole bag. Fortunately, you don't have to be perfect to change your body. If you stick with your plan 90% of time, you'll still see what you want in the mirror. You can, indeed, eat just one. It's not a big deal. Have the chip and move on.

Staying fit and healthy through exercise is one of the easiest things you can do to improve the quality of your life. Creating a long term affair with working out is a function of creativity, group effort and a decision to stay the course, even if you get off track sometimes. Stand on your base and proclaim death to excuses and you'll be able to stick it out for the long haul, even when you're not feeling it. Turn on the Eye of the Tiger, get pumped and let's get it!

About Meika

Recognized as one of Atlanta's most effective personal trainers, Meika Louis-Pierre has helped hundreds of Atlanta's men, women and kids jump start their fitness regimen and make wellness a priority. Relying on more than a decade of experience in the sports and fitness industry, Meika has empowered her clients to lose weight, make healthier food choices and eliminate risk factors. Additionally, her nurturing, yet no-nonsense approach has helped her clients build the confidence they need to accomplish some of their most significant fitness and overall life goals.

Meika received a dual Bachelor of Science in Entrepreneurship and Marketing from Florida State University, where she was heavily involved with the university's sports program. Upon graduation she accepted a position with the National Basketball Association (NBA) before receiving her certification as a personal trainer and pursuing a career as a fitness trainer and life coach.

In 2007, Meika launched South Atlanta Adventure Boot Camp, the first boot camp program in the south Fulton County area. In 2010, she opened Fit Neighborhood, Southwest Atlanta's only Fitness and Lifestyle Coaching Center. Her rigorous programs challenge and transform a wide range of clients, including stay-at-home moms, student athletes and entire families seeking a dynamic program designed for optimum results.

Meika is an active member of the Atlanta community and a former assistant coach of the 2006 AAAA Georgia High School State Champion Girls' Basketball Team. Also considered an engaging local subject matter expert, Meika routinely speaks to groups and organizations about health and wellness. She has been featured in *Heart and Soul, Enliven Atlanta, Atlanta Home & You, Atlanta Tribune* and numerous other publications and websites.

Fit Neighborhood is part of a global network of top fitness training facilities.

CHAPTER 37

Better Interactions With Clients = Increased Results And Compliance

By Jennifer Parker

I was certainly graced with the gift of the gab, but my ability to effectively listen and empathize is what separates me from the pack. My own fitness journey is a bumpy road, but has certainly offered a great deal of "common" ground between my clients and me. It's not necessary to have walked in their shoes to understand how to communicate. It is, however, *imperative you identify with the emotional component* and recognize *that* is what you are really coaching and communicating with.

The assumption is that we are professionals and have the knowledge and ability to deliver our advertised services. At the same time, unless we have the ability to connect and effectively coach our clients – we fail. We have a short window of time to directly work with our clients (average of 1-4 hours per week). Therefore, a large focus of our practice must be to promote and facilitate healthful lifestyle habits so their effort is only supported during the rest of the week. How do we do this? I believe it begins with developing a strong rapport and relationship of trust with our clients. By developing our rapport-building skills, taking responsibility for their results, and really understanding it's all about them – we have the power to deliver a better service and better results.

During my career I've had, and continue to have, countless a-ha moments. I'm sure as you read this book you are collecting your own. I want to share how two a-ha moments in particular shaped my practice of relationship building and gaining trust with my circle of influence. My objective is to demonstrate the value and provide ideas for you to develop these skills. If you pay attention during conferences or courses you often hear the reminder from the speaker how important it is to practice the skills before you implement. These are no exception and I think you'll discover a lot about yourself along the way.

TO BE A GREAT COACH OR TRAINER YOU NEED TO NOT ONLY LEARN FROM OTHER GREAT COACHES, BUT YOU MUST *BE* A CLIENT AND *BE* COACHED.

During a *Reps to Revenue* seminar in New Jersey, Alwyn Cosgrove looked around the room and asked for a show of hands of the trainers/ coaches who had communicated to their clients and prospects the value of a trainer – the important role we play, how we facilitate the ability to reach fitness goals, create safe and effective programs, etc. Of course, every hand in the room was raised high and proud. Then a follow-up question was asked: "how many of you work with a coach or trainer?" As I looked around the room a majority of the hands went down. The poignant fact remained – not only do we not practice what we preach, but what were we so scared of?

Take a moment and think about all that could be gained from working with a coach or trainer. Think about the process:

- Deciding to hire a coach.
- Finding a coach that meets specific education, experience, personality traits, schedule, price range or any of the like.
- Having a new time, financial, and perhaps physical or mental commitment, which may actually include the development of more than one new habit (this will be expanded on later in chapter).

There is a great to deal to consider in hiring a coach, not to mention meeting and working with a coach. Review the following:

- Intake procedure – what differs in style or paperwork between your coach and what you do? What do you like/dislike or agree/ disagree?
- Development of a plan to achieve the desired goal – could you

see the thought process from intake to strategy? Is the plan SMART (specific, measurable, attainable, realistic, and timely)? Does it make sense and meet your ability and availability?

- Interaction client and coach – how was the tone? Did you feel connected and understood by your coach? Could you relate and feel comfortable? Are you looking forward to getting started?

Take the challenge and hire a coach. Maybe it isn't a trainer or someone that will help you with performance or fitness. Perhaps you work with a life coach, a financial coach, a stylist, or a business coach. It is such an incredible learning experience to have someone put you through an analysis and then provide a solution based on their observations – while considering your objectives, baselines, and commitment. I guarantee you will learn techniques or skills that help you better communicate with your clients. Or just as valuable, techniques you will stay away from or things to never say to a client or prospect because of how it made you feel.

The real objective in doing this is to better understand the client experience. You develop a deeper appreciation for being analyzed, learning what you thought was a good plan could be improved, and feeling vulnerable and/or uncomfortable because you are being held accountable to do things you either don't really want to do, never thought you would do, or didn't think you could do. I have used, I will even say flat-out stolen, techniques from mentors and coaches to better build rapport with my circle of influence. Remember getting results isn't just physical; it's emotional and about getting people on board with your vision and being part of your tribe.

COLLABORATE WITH YOUR CLIENTS AND VALIDATE THEIR OBSTACLES

Clients and prospects come to us to help them achieve a goal and for most it is weight loss/fat loss. Most trainers build their business helping to fight this prolific battle. At the same time, my hope is that these same trainers understand it's the clients overall lifestyle choices that create the foundation for long-lasting results. We know exercise is only part of the equation and I'm not downplaying the essential role that plays. However, wouldn't you agree that a positive mindset to change and a plan to make better lifestyle choices would have a larger impact?

As fat loss ambassadors, we have a lot to educate and help facilitate in regards to change in our client's behavior. We perform assessments or intake protocols so we are armed with the information to create a plan of attack to arrive at their goal. My assumption (I know, risky) is that these include questions about stress, sleep, nutrition, and other lifestyle factors related to fat loss. If you aren't doing this currently, start there and evaluate your procedure to increase your impact by increasing your knowledge. If you are, then let's review what you are doing with that information and some techniques to help break it down for your clients, based on motivation and compliance.

One of the best coaches, in my opinion, to seek out on this topic is Dr. John Berardi. I am so impressed with his coaching techniques and learned a great deal (and yes, I incorporate it as well) upon completion of his *Precision Nutrition* certification, as well as listening to him speak. Berardi's system is designed to increase compliance based on mastering one habit at a time. Further, as progress is made in mastering simple habits, more complex or challenging behaviors are assessed by collaborating with the client, to ensure habits and changes are realistic and achievable. Essentially, setting the client up for success by allowing them to <u>fully participate</u> in the decision and process to make change – not just do what I tell you to do or you will fail.

I fear we forget to empathize with our clients that this stuff comes easy to us. We are the freaks that want and even enjoy feeling pain and discomfort from a workout, we like eating 4-6 times a day, and don't even notice that our increased water intake has us spending more time in the bathroom – it's a moot point. For our clients, this can be inconvenient, difficult, uncomfortable, and for some, may seem downright impossible. We explain to them, it's easy – just change your eating habits, your sleep habits, and exercise. Yet, these *three* things could actually require thousands of changes on their side. They thought they were coming to you to get their butt kicked and now they have to "just":

- Make sure to get 7-8 hours of sleep every day
- Eat 1-2 hours before workout and sip on a recovery shake during or immediately after a workout
- Eat every 3-4 hours and within one hour of waking up
- Drink more water

- Eat more veggies

- Manage their professional and personal stress more effectively

All of this… and take care of yourself, family, social, and professional responsibilities. And we wonder why this is so difficult for our clients to comply or succeed?

Keep in mind, coming to see you in the first place is a really big step, recognize that and give them positive feedback. When reviewing their previous or current workout and lifestyle history, comment on any and everything that is positive and will help support their goal. They know they need to make change, but affirming they don't suck (even if you really are blown away by how far they are from "ideal") gives you the foundation, and to help them trust you – not feel judged.

EVALUATING YOURSELF AND YOUR PROCESS – WHERE CAN YOU IMPROVE?

I am a firm believer that most people learn better by doing and experiencing. Again, you don't have to have always had an injury, a food problem, a mobility issue, or any of the like to understand or speak about how they must feel or struggle. You do need to look them in the eyes and validate their feelings and communicate how *we* are going to develop and implement strategies to make *you* better. Begin to explore and evaluate your current systems and results. Perform the following challenges to see where you can simplify or even draw conclusions on where you can improve yours or your client interaction and compliance:

- Identify something that doesn't come easy to you and develop a strategy to work on that

  – For most trainers this may have nothing to do with fitness, I encourage you to think outside this arena (not to say you shouldn't continue to work on your flexibility). Or what is something you know you should be doing, but aren't – is it putting money in your savings? Spending more time with friends and family? Public speaking – do you work on things that make you feel uncomfortable if incremental small changes are to become better?

- Less talk, more listen – ask for feedback

  – I have been guilty and I have seen plenty of other trainers have such passion for what we do that we keep talking, and talking, and talking. But listening, acknowledging, repeating back and truly understanding – this makes your clients feel validated.

- Work with other trainers and coaches that you respect and get feedback on your methods – be it coaching cues, program design, handling client situations.

With the lack of standards and fitness being so broad, it's no wonder we become protective of what we do. But instead of putting ourselves on a pedestal or being scared that someone may tell us we could improve – embrace the feedback. Get better! I wish I had the secret formula to share but the truth is, there isn't one. Each of us has a special gift to offer and we work toward a common goal to help our clients look, feel, and move the best they can. The truth is, if we focused more on being a team rather than on competition, we would all be a lot more successful. Until then, I hope you have learned something about yourself and your business and I wish you success communicating more effectively, delivering better results, and growing your tribe.

About Jennifer

Jennifer Parker
San Mateo, CA
Fitness and Nutrition Coach
www.jenparker.com
Tel: 650-339-2880

Jennifer states: "My accomplishments are fairly humble, especially next to some of my co-authors, but I've always been a believer in quality not quantity. I began my career in 2001 in NYC, a young twenty-something with a Division I athletic background confident I had a great deal of knowledge and experience to share. I was certainly humbled to learn how much I didn't know, despite my passion and athletic experience. Luckily I am determined and excited about getting better and really helping people.

"More than a decade later I am still reveling in the great fortune of working alongside some great coaches, helping a diverse clientele be fit, and meeting and learning from the best in the industry. I have coached volleyball at both the high school and collegiate levels, trained privately and semi-privately, taught classes, and managed a multi-million dollar personal training department. My degree is in Communications but a majority of my time is spent pursuing continuing education. I currently maintain certifications with the following organizations: NSCA – CSCS, NASM – CPT, FMS, Precision Nutrition – Level One Nutrition Coach, and Combine 360.

"Like many of you, I'm still deciding what I want to be when I grow up. Until then I've made a career of challenging myself to be the best I can, helping others be the best they can, and learning a great deal along the way. I currently live and work as a fitness and nutrition coach in the Bay area. My goal is to provide better fitness solutions and a great experience, not just exercise programs. I spend a majority of my time troubleshooting on ways to help my clients when they aren't with me in the gym and developing strategies to make their fitness journey successful and fun."

CHAPTER 38

The Head Bone Connected To The Toe Bone

By Amy Wunsch, MSPT

"Your toe bone connected to your foot bone,
Your foot bone connected to your ankle bone,
Your ankle bone connected to your leg bone,
Your leg bone connected to your knee bone,
Your knee bone connected to your thigh bone,
Your thigh bone connected to your hip bone,
Your hip bone connected to your back bone,
Your back bone connected to your shoulder bone,
Your shoulder bone connected to your neck bone,
Your neck bone connected to your head bone..."

~ DEM DRY BONES
By James & Rosamund Johnson

Who would have thought that a song written to teach children basic anatomy in the early 1900s would be the basis for cutting edge injury prevention? It illustrates quite simply the fact that all the parts of our body are connected, that our "head bone" is connected to our "toe bone."

You see our bodies are made up of multiple systems or parts that work together as a whole. For example, everyone has fascial tissue in his or her body. Think of fascial tissue as an intricate spiderweb that runs throughout the body. It extends uninterrupted from the skull to the tips of our toes, connecting and surrounding our bones, muscles, organs, nerves and blood vessels. It forces all the "pieces" of our body to unite and function as one entity.

The **beauty** of this is: if one part of your body isn't working, the rest of your body will compensate.

The **downfall** of this is: if one part of your body isn't working, the rest of your body will compensate.

My first experience with this theory occurred during my second year as a physical therapist. A woman named Joan walked into my office, sat down and said, "You will never figure me out. You won't be able to fix me." I considered the gauntlet thrown. Joan had suffered for five years with pain in her back and neck and had frequent headaches. According to her, this pain "came out of nowhere," and got progressively worse over time.

Joan had gone to multiple doctors, chiropractors and physical therapists who told her either "nothing is wrong," or "I don't know how to help you." Doctors performed X-rays and MRI's on her neck and back but failed to see a viable reason for her pain. Some doctors even told her, "It's all in your head." It's easy to imagine the frustration she felt.

In hindsight, Joan gave me the best gift possible when she said, "You will never figure me out." It was a red flag. This obviously wasn't your "normal" back and neck pain brought on by the "usual" causes. This forced me to take a step back, forget everything I "thought I knew" about Joan's body, and get the microscope off of her neck and back.

Thus began the investigation. Starting from the ground and working up, I took notes on any asymmetries in Joan's body. The arch of her right foot collapsed, she had a bunion and the big toe was drifting to the right. Her pelvis was tilted forward on her right side. Her spine was twisted and resembled a wet towel being wrung out. Her right shoulder was elevated and moderate pressure on the neck muscles reproduced her reoccurring headache.

It seemed clear that the twist in Joan's spine caused her neck and back pain, but we had to go deeper, figuring out why her spine was twisted.

The reason was the collapse in Joan's arch. Why was this missed in her MRI? The answer was simple: Joan was lying down during the MRI. When she was lying down, her foot no longer affected the positioning of her spine. Her spine "untwisted" and looked "normal." The problem: Joan didn't live her life lying down.

The solution: tape Joan's arch, forefoot and big toe to "correct" the collapse. Joan thought I was nuts for treating an area that was not painful, but by lifting the arch of her foot, we were able to make her pelvis symmetrical. By leveling Joan's pelvis, her spine could align properly and the muscles that were being strained could let go. I also gave her simple stretches and exercises to address the muscle imbalances that occurred due to the compensation through the rest of her body. Most of these exercises were focused on her achieving an upright posture and not on her painful areas.

Two days later, Joan returned to my office. This day I was met not by a jaded woman with a furrowed brow, but a woman who smiled, hugged me and looked years younger. She reported 70% improvement and had been headache-free for the first time in five years. Can you imagine having a headache almost everyday for five years? I had the pleasure of working with Joan for one month. We got her new orthotics and focused on postural control, core stability and body mechanics. By the end of the month, Joan's symptoms completely resolved. Her whole body had compensated for the collapse in her arch. Who would have thought that a foot problem could cause headaches? The toe bone IS connected to the head bone!

There are 4 principles to grasp for successful injury prevention.

PRINCIPLE 1: The Toe Bone IS Connected To The Head Bone.

PRINCIPLE 2: Your Body is NOT a Jalopy.

Our bodies are just like our cars. If your wheel alignment is off, your tires will wear down and your car will pull to one side of the road. If we don't change the oil, our fuel economy will tank and our engine will wear out. In short, your whole car will suffer the effects, wearing down in seemingly "unrelated areas" resulting in decreased vehicle performance and life expectancy. Think about Joan. One wheel (Joan's right foot) was "out of alignment" wearing down her spine, decreasing her body's performance and resulting in pain in other areas of her body.

Smart folks know their cars will break down without "preventative maintenance," therefore we change our oil every 3000 miles, check our brakes, rotate our tires and top off our fluids BEFORE we have a problem. If Joan had come into my office for a regular check-up, we could have developed a "preventative maintenance plan" BEFORE she had a problem. The average American will own 8-12 cars in his lifetime but has only one body. It is crazy to treat your vehicle better than you treat your body! Repeat after me, "My body is not a jalopy. I will not treat it like one."

Building a Preventative Maintenance Plan from the Inside Out and the Outside In

Inside Out = the way our bodies function on the inside has a direct effect on how we perform our everyday activities on the outside.

Every person's build is unique and has a profound effect on how it functions and feels. A man with one arm will pick up a box or tie his shoes differently than a man with two arms. A man who is 7 feet tall has to duck under most doorframes and a man who is 3 feet tall has to stand on tiptoe to reach something on a kitchen counter. These types of "inside" factors are clear and it is easy to see how they play a role in our everyday lives.

Recognizing some of the subtler "inside" factors (like mobility deficits, spinal alignment and strength asymmetries) can be more of a challenge, but equally as detrimental to your health. If a construction worker is able to lift his right arm up higher than his left he may develop an overuse injury of the right arm or he may damage the left arm when forcing it into a position it has no business being in.

Outside In = the activities we participate in dictate the way our body functions.

Repetitive activities and postures (or "outside" factors) are a major cause of muscle imbalance and breakdown. Outside factors include work activities, recreational activities, household chores and leisure activities, and the environments in which we participate in these activities. A computer programmer will have different effects on his body than a manual laborer on his feet, lifting heavy or cumbersome objects. What activities do you participate in repeatedly? Are you a runner, weight lifter, reader, painter, cyclist, basketball player or couch potato?

Once you have identified your outside factors, we can:

(1) figure out how it affects your body

(2) change your environment to support your body and reduce strain

(3) establish a better way to perform your activities

(4) counteract the muscle imbalances these activities cause

A good preventative maintenance plan is like fixing the brakes on your car BEFORE they go out. Unfortunately, some of us will wait until we have a problem and our proverbial "Check Engine" light comes on before we act. The result: lengthy and more costly repairs.

PRINCIPLE 3: Don't Ignore the Check Engine Light

There is always a REASON for the "Check Engine" light to come on in your car – something is not right and needs to be addressed. If you ignore the light, the problem won't go away and your car WILL break down. Those of us who want our cars running well will act on the check engine light and bring our cars to the appropriate shops.

Pain has a purpose. It is the human body's "Check Engine" light, signaling to you that something is wrong and requires immediate attention. Ideally, preventative maintenance would have averted or slowed the onset of pain, but once the "Check Engine" light comes on, you need to DO SOMETHING ABOUT IT before you fully break down. The question is, "WHAT do you do?"

SEE YOUR BODY MECHANIC

The average person does not perform his or her own vehicle maintenance. Sure we can fill up our gas tank with ease, but this does not equip us with the knowledge to diagnose and fix a larger problem (i.e. electrical problems, strange noises or stalling). We must understand that there are limitations to what we know about our bodies and seek advice from the right people. For example, you wouldn't drill a cavity in your own tooth just because you know how to brush and floss. Even a dentist who has the proper education wouldn't do that!

You know where to take your car, but where do you take your body?

The answer = your Body Mechanic. A Body Mechanic, simply put, is a licensed professional or certified specialist dedicated to optimizing your health. This group is made up of medical professionals (i.e., doctors, physical therapists, dentists, chiropractors and dietitians), fitness professionals and massage therapists. They evaluate your body, identify your 'inside out' and 'outside in' factors, and devise a plan to meet your specific needs. Body Mechanics have different specialties like a NASCAR pit crew and work together to get your body operating properly.

Figuring out which professional to go to is dependent on your needs and goals. You wouldn't take your vehicle to the car wash if you needed an oil change. Deciding whom to go to may feel like a daunting task, but don't worry. If you are in the "wrong place" your Body Mechanic will tell you they cannot help and direct you to the person who can meet your needs. Joan started with Body Mechanic who understood his limitations, and referred her elsewhere. This occurred a few times until she received that care she needed. You can also be the judge if you are seeing the correct Body Mechanic. How? It's simple: if nothing changes or relief is only temporary, it is time to look elsewhere.

PRINCIPLE 4: CONSISTENCY IS KEY - Avoiding the "Danger Zone," and we are not talking Kenny Loggins!

Our bodies don't spontaneously change. We don't go to sleep one night weighing 150 lbs. and wake up the next day weighing 230 lbs. We don't spontaneously get cavities in our teeth. No, these things happen under consistent conditions over time. So when it comes to injuries, it is wise to apply the same reasoning. You didn't develop pain spontaneously, unless, of course, you were hit by a car and made into a human hood ornament!

The conditions causing your symptoms (inside-out and outside-in) have been present for quite some time. These conditions just became severe ENOUGH to wear your body down and cause pain. Pain is the LAST thing our bodies feel and the FIRST thing that goes away.

The **good news**: we control the conditions that either make us succeed or fail.

The **bad news**: we control the conditions that either make us succeed or fail.

In one way, we have the power to eliminate our pain, but once we feel better, our motivation to continue with the interventions that made us feel better plummets. This is the **Danger Zone.**

Danger Zone = when we stop doing the things that got us better and go back to the activities that caused our pain. The Danger Zone is where relapse is imminent. You see absence of pain does not mean we are fixed. As long as our inside-out and outside-in factors exist, we will need to perform some sort of regular maintenance. If Joan takes her orthotics out, her pain will return.

THE TAKE-HOME MESSAGE:
THE HYGIENE PHENOMENON

We don't brush our teeth once in our lives and expect to never have a cavity. We don't shower only once and call it "good." No, we need to continuously wash and care for our bodies to ensure our bodies are in good working order. The same holds true for injury prevention. It takes regular maintenance to keep your body pain-free and performing at its optimal level. Do not fear. Injury prevention is quicker and easier than injury rehabilitation. It is true that 'an ounce of prevention is worth a pound of cure.'

In short: injury prevention is EASY if you remember the 4 principles.

1. The head bone connected to the toe bone - the location of your pain may not be the CAUSE of your pain.
2. Your body is not a jalopy - treat it well and perform preventative maintenance to keep it running smoothly for a long time.
3. Don't ignore the "Check Engine" light - when something malfunctions, DO SOMETHING ABOUT IT!
4. Consistency is key - avoid relapse and stay out of the Danger Zone with quick and simple preventative strategies.

Don't wait until you have a problem to address it!

About Amy

Amy Wunsch, MSPT is part of the founding team of Results Physical Therapy, a division of Results Fitness. Amy received two Masters Degrees in Clinical Science and Physical Therapy from Ithaca College where she was a captain of the New York State Champion Women's Indoor and Outdoor Track and Field teams and a member of the NCAA Finalist Women's Soccer Team. She is licensed in the state of California and is a proud member of the American Physical Therapy Association with special interests in orthopedic rehabilitation and sport rehabilitation. Amy has experience working with recreational, professional and Olympic athletes, stunt-people, celebrities, Cirque du Soleil performers as well as patients with orthopedic, lymph edema, cardiac, post-surgical and neurologic conditions ranging from 7 weeks to 94 years of age.

Dedicated to excellence and continuing education, Amy has received her certification in Functional Movement Systems I and II, Selective Functional Movement Assessment and has participated in many conferences around the United States. Amy has been featured in Women's Health Magazine, Experience Life Magazine and has given many lectures to the medical and patient community.

Results Physical Therapy exists to make a difference in the local and global communities through supplying the highest quality of care and educational opportunities. Amy Wunsch, MSPT and the Results Team are focused reaching patient goals, exceeding expectations and realizing their patient's full potential.

Website: www.results-fitness.com
Tel: 661-799-7900